INTRODUCTION
TO
STRUCTURAL
PSYCHOLOGY

INTRODUCTION
TO
STRUCTURAL
PSYCHOLOGY

ROGER MUCCHIELLI

Translated by *Charles Lam Markmann*

Funk & Wagnalls

NEW YORK

TO THE MEMORY OF

Albert Burloud

FOREWORD

In writing this *Introduction to Structural Psychology,* I have sought to go back to reality and the observation of facts in order to describe the particular complex of phenomena that are of interest to psychologists and to all who search for information in this field.

In the modern history of psychology, classical (one should say "orthodox") psychoanalysis is characterized by two aspects that threaten to make it an obstacle to the advance of knowledge. On the one hand, it holds itself out today as a totalitarian theory of psychology, enveloping itself in esoterism and narcissistic self-improvement, making its concepts sacrosanct and attempting to assimilate new discoveries with its old arsenal; on the other hand, through an understandable defense mechanism, it convicts in advance those who challenge its concepts and its system, accusing them of *resisting* conversion as a result of the subterranean effect of their own personal emotional problems. The result is a tendency to classify among the "immature" all who do not agree, in anticipation of reclassifying them among the heretics to be reduced to dust if they turn stubborn.

Behind the parapet of this defensive, imperialistic aggressiveness, psychoanalysis "cultivates" its own conceptions among both laymen and psychologists, and, what is more, it fosters its interpretations among its patients, turning to its own advantage the powerful mechanism of suggestion that in the past always made it possible for Charcot to find in his observations confirmation for his theories:

Psychoanalysis is our sorcery. . . . With all the more reason when it becomes an institution, when it is applied to so-called

"normal" subjects, it utterly ceases to be a conception that can
be justified or discussed on the basis of cases; it no longer cures,
it persuades; it shapes for itself subjects who conform to its own
interpretation of man. It has its converts and perhaps its rebels;
it can no longer convince. Beyond the true and the false, it is a
myth, and Freudianism thus degraded is no longer an interpretation but a variant of the Oedipus myth. (Merleau-Ponty
quoting Lévi-Strauss in *Signes*, page 153.)

On the strictly epistemological level the mythification of
the theory is to be explained by the increasing distance
between its conceptualization and the data of experience.

It is easy to understand the process by which a theory
finally loses the reality that it professes to translate and
nevertheless continues to exist and to be produced: Every
theory is a system of concepts represented by words coined
in order to describe a complex of facts or data of experience,
which is relative to the point of view of its creator, to the
level of knowledge in general and of his knowledge, to the
ways and means that have been set in motion. These concepts, organized into a general theory by means of a conceptualization once removed, are not merely "representative"
of complexes of data, of "groups" of facts, of "categories" of
phenomena; they are *operative*. In other words, in the
luxuriant world of the real they actively establish separate
classes of realities; they create the wholes and the groupings
required by knowledge; thus they "take cognizance" of scattered phenomena by bringing them together into already
prepared categories. Naturally, these activities of scientific
knowledge—or what aspires to be such—are not carried out
at random; the investigator's target is to determine the
essence of the phenomenon, of its objective structure, and,
within the general theory, he hopes to grasp the structure
of the relationships among these objects of knowledge.

But there comes a point at which the scholar's personal
pleasure in the contemplation of the harmony of his output
of concepts makes him resist any new challenge to his thinking. If he does not permit controversy and if more than

anything he does not maintain his capacity for lifelong wonder at the upthrust of reality, he is in danger of sealing himself into the refinement of concepts that have become sacrosanct. In such a case the concept continues to be what it has always been—that is, an active categorization of reality, isolating reality in order to construct groups and classes of phenomena that can be identified, recognized, systematized. Thereafter the real is permanently diluted by the system of categories, distorted in order to be integrated into only those frames of reference that are available, "assimilated" to preconceived classes and recognized only on these terms, treated (and mistreated) in order to be brought into artificial patterns.

In the end the senescent theory is reduced to "supposing," "interpreting," "offering its explanation," instead of observing and emphasizing what is always accessible to observation without prejudices.

Knowledge advances when, without sacrificing the gains of useful concepts, one is willing to go back to the real, to that reality that may perhaps elude one forever, for in spite of ourselves we are always in danger, on all levels of existence, of ascribing to the lives and the objects that we observe meanings that come from within us and that offer us the reflection of ourselves rather than revealing to us what exists before us.

Notions that were once classic in psychology—impulse, instinct, tendency, motivation, or the unconscious conceived as the site of repressed "forces"—are outmoded today. They are no longer adequate to account for experience. On the other hand, the idea of *structure* comes forward with a new significance, entering the area of psychology after having made it possible to rejuvenate general linguistics and social anthropology.

In current speech this word *structure* means first of all organization, articulation of relationships among elements or parts; so one will say that a report is well structured in order to emphasize the methodical arrangement of its sections, the solidity of its skeleton, and the clarity of its movement toward its conclusion. An enterprise is also said to have a structure in the sense that its hierarchic and operational relationships are specified and that the responsible persons at its various levels understand their assignments and the significance of their jobs or their functions in relation to those of others in the general table of organization.

In a very closely related fashion we use the word *infrastructure* to identify the installations and services whose prior establishment and continuing operation are essential to a construction or a social organization the subsequent development or differentiation of which is envisaged. *Superstructure* is the name applied to those later constructions and developments that are closely linked to their "bases" and are dependent on them in one way or another.

In this first group of meanings, structure is "order" and *to structure* is to establish order among, or to coordinate, elements by means of a system of stable relationships that make them into an organized Whole.

This is the meaning from which the *Gestalt* school's interpretation of structure is derived. The psychologists who, with Wertheimer, Kohler, Koffka, and Guillaume, advanced the idea of form (or *Gestalt*) were attempting in this way to identify the natural configurations of the field of perception. A melody is a structure, a form, a *Gestalt* to the degree to which it is a system of stable correlations recognizable as a melody even if all the notes are changed (provided that the organization of the relationships is not changed), as occurs when the composer "changes his key." According to these psychologists, perceptive forms are *structures of correlation,* objective structures endowed with qualities (such as the "intensity" of the "good form," which impresses without difficulty and is resistant to change). The "elements" have no separate existence. Even a star solitary in the sky "stands out against the background" represented by the evening sky. When all the stars are shining, they are perceptively arranged into "constellations." Each "element" is a function of a whole in relation to which it has its place and thus assumes its significance.

A second meaning of the word structure appears in the concept of "principle of order and stability." Structure is no longer a ready-made order, a recognizable conformation; in a certain sense it becomes more dynamic. Any attempt to establish relationships and differentiations within a multiplicity of elements comes down to structuring it. From this point of view, classification as it is practiced in zoology or botany, like typology (which reduces differences to reference types), is an active structure in response to a principle of organization, a law established by the scientist. One can imagine how arbitrary or provisional such a law can be, and naturally one supposes that it is valid only to the degree to which it ceases to be a convenient or descriptive classification and penetrates to the *structure of things themselves,* or the law of observable phenomena.

In the chemical sciences, for example, structure is not the mere representation of the internal organization of the components; the structure of the atom, for instance, is the law of the disposition of electrons around the proton and of their respective movements.

In physics the structure of experience is its formula, its law, in terms of which the sequence of observable phenomena in a given postulated theoretical whole is arranged and understood.

This brings us closer to the modern meaning of the word structure. Applied to psychological (linguistic and ethnological) phenomena, structure ceases to pertain to systems of correlations and turns to meanings. A *structure of meaning* is that in relation to which an element in the world acquires a significance to a subject. More precisely, this is how one designates an operational reality in which there is nothing objective or conscious (it is not directly observable and it is not contained in consciousness) and whose influence makes the facts of the world meaningful to a subject.

The structure of meaning supposes and implies an essential and existential relation between the subject and his universe, and the structure is a constant dynamic form of that relation. Varying contents appear; from an external, descriptive point of view they seem to be different, but they all carry the same structure of meaning. Conversely, a given act or expression may seem identical in two subjects, but the meaning no longer remains the same if the act or the expression is related to the respective structures of each subject's life experience. Thus, in a given society, a given object acquires a meaning that it does not have in another society, although from a descriptive point of view it has not varied.

Structure alone has the capacity to impart meaning to what it structures. From this point of view structure is an empty but dynamic and definite form that "gives shape" and thus meaning to what is brought in to "fill" it.

Let us take a very superficial example. Jealousy is not a simple emotion (which it is also, undoubtedly, for the spontaneous consciousness in which the forms of feeling are reflected); in the person who is jealous it is a *structure that structures* vigilant perception and that gives meaning to everything that can be grasped by that perception in the facts of existence. A structure of this type "patterns"—that is, it actively models, fashions, shapes—the facts in its information (the evidences perceived) by "taking them in a certain way" that is characteristic of being jealous. Moreover, it becomes clear that a form of this type is capable not only of assimilating virtually any fact (in the extreme case, everything "feeds" jealousy) but also of structuring behavior, of "patterning" action and reactions, like a categorical constant with variable and indefinite content. We may say that we have here a *perceptive-affective-behavioral structure,* and I do not see how any other name could be given to this active, clearly defined form, "empty" though it be, that dynamically and unconsciously organizes the world of perception and the subject's conduct and to which all speech and describable reaction relate, even if, *to the victim,* it seems a "permanent distortion" of the real.

Similarly, in the comparative study of social institutions, Lévi-Strauss seeks—and finds—"relations that are likewise variable in content but whose distinct character is preserved through all vicissitudes"—in other words, structures whose active operation consists in imposing their forms on (and giving meaning to, since they are structures of meaning) unconnected elements that come from elsewhere. "And here, as in phonology, vocabulary is less important than structure. The lexicographical content must be screened in order to bring out the structural dynamic constants" that imprison the almost indefinite multiplicity of facts, acts, and words within a few simple patterns.

How are these structures constructed? How are they organized with respect to one another? Are there structures of structures? Can they be reduced to axioms, as is possible in other sciences? These are the problems that will have to be met by the structural psychology of tomorrow. This introduction to structural psychology has no aim other than to stimulate thought on these matters. The answers will be of prime importance in their repercussions on the techniques of approach to personality and on the method of psychotherapy.

CONTENTS

FOUR

Formulating the Laws of a Science

FIVE

Conclusion

ONE

What Does It Mean?

There is meaning when the facts of the world are subjected by us to a coherent distortion. —Merleau-Ponty, *Signes*

We are the prisoners of meanings

The most rudimentary attempt to understand someone, the simplest approach, the most immediate—and already this is the whole of psychology—consists in grasping, always in an approximate fashion, what things, persons, events *mean to him.*

If one considers the whole of the specific circumstances in relation to which a human subject acts or reacts, and if one considers this human subject's behavior, maintaining, with respect to these circumstances and this subject, an "externality" that one believes to be the guaranty of one's "objectivity," the inevitable result is the utmost incomprehension of his conduct. For one's so-called "objective" view of the given circumstances as a whole necessarily entails the meaning-of-this-whole-*for-oneself,* just as the so-called objective study of the subject's conduct is inescapably a characterization of that conduct (if only in order to describe it—and even to describe it as absurd or incomprehensible) in relation to what it means to oneself, in relation to that through which it would have had a meaning for oneself if oneself had behaved thus, and in the end in relation once more to what these circumstances mean to oneself.

Assume that I am with two Frenchmen, some twenty-five miles from Brazzaville in the Congo. The paved road ends here and the trail begins. Beside the road there is a tank of gasoline with a hand pump, and thus we are able to replenish our car's supply. In spite of the strangeness, we recognize these groups of meanings and we have a store of habitual cultural reactions with which to respond to them. We ask the Congolese who works the pump whether we can get something to drink, for it is quite hot. He takes us to his house, a few yards from the tank, and in the house we enter a large room that seems to be a jumble of isolated objects and assorted tins; in one corner there is a vast ultramodern refrigerator whose illuminated bowels amaze us with the spectacle of bottles of beer, Coca-Cola, fruit juices, and mineral water. So we are still moving through a universe of known meanings. The man's young daughter opens the bottles for us gracefully and skillfully. We pay in the local currency. But now one of us, with an abundance of gestures, mimicry, and verbal statement, asks the girl, who has been so hospitable, to step outside and allow him to take her photograph. The sight of the camera sets off panic behavior, but still he insists. This upsets the entire family. We beat a retreat in the face of general indignation.

Obviously "having her photograph taken" had some unanticipated significance for the girl. In this universe of things, beings, and behavior patterns that were recognizable to us thus far, there suddenly emerges an aspect of the Congolese universe of magic meanings as expressed by their conduct in the circumstances.

In spite of our effort to understand that, in a certain context of magic beliefs, the possession of someone's image by another enables that other to exercise an indirect influence over the existence of the person who has been imprisoned through his image, we cannot avoid the private conviction that such a reaction is absurd. And yet this reaction, in relation to the incident's significance to the Congolese, is completely *coherent*, to such an extent that it is this that makes it possible for us to infer these meanings, which are very incompletely "understood" insofar as we do not view them in the whole of their cultural context and even insofar as we do not share them in our own way of life.

In a certain sense this cultural example is a special one, for in the end we fall into the habit of telling ourselves that every people has its own beliefs, its own world of meanings, and hence its own specific conditions. Our "objectivity" is satisfied with the recognition that things, circumstances, events, human relations, etc., *may* have other meanings than those that they have for us.

We are visibly less "understanding" with our own circle. Consider the young mother who, finding that her seven-year-old daughter has not made sufficient progress in arithmetic, takes it upon herself to teach the child "the principle of subtraction."

"*Take away*—so you don't know what *take away* means," the mother cries in a rage. "This is incredible! You are a simpleton, you're going to make me furious." Fascinated by the changing movements of her mother's facial muscles as indignation gives way to despair, the child is absolutely frozen to her chair and it is plain that the meaning of the words is no longer the same for her as it is for her mother. She feels that she is being scolded, that she is guilty, that she is being rejected outright. She is apprehensive and as if paralyzed. Shifting now to what seems to be an active method of pedagogy, the mother orders the little girl to place her hands inside the pockets of her apron. After several repetitions of the order, the child obeys. At once the mother says imperiously: "Take them away!" When the child hesitates, the mother impulsively seizes her hands and jerks them out of her pockets, looks at her with an expression of the utmost concentration, and asks in a penetrating tone: "What did you do?" The child is mute and white. The mother's anger resurges. She goes back to the beginning and runs through the same episode again. When the third repetition results in the same behavior, she slaps the child's face.

It is easy for the psychologist to describe the two irreconcilable groups of meanings: the adult's, centered on a "pedagogical" intention and perceiving the reactions of the "pupil" as stupidity compounded by bad temper, and the child's, centered on a torturing and baffling accusation by a creature who holds unlimited power.

Let us remark once more that each of these two modes of conduct is completely "logical" in terms of its own collection of meanings. And again it is in our observation of the progression of behavior that we recognize the corresponding meanings that it expresses.

Here again, however, we might say that "modern ideas" tend to make us acknowledge that the child lives in a child's world in which things have neither the same meanings nor the same values as in the adult's world.

Let us take a third instance, quite as commonplace as the two others. A husband and wife are quarreling. Budget in his hand, he is telling his wife that there is no need for her to work, that he earns quite enough to support the household, and that "their mother's presence at home is essential to the four children and particularly the youngest, who is only four years old." His wife retorts that she "did not take a degree in order to spend her life washing dishes and doing laundry," that she refuses to "be looked on as a maid of all work," and that, even if every cent of her earnings must be spent to pay the wages of a housekeeper and a child's nurse, she would rather play some part in society and make use of her intellectual endowment and her training. Here two conceptions of family life, of respective functions, of the rights and duties of each spouse meet and clash. When the husband thinks that he is speaking to "the mother of his children," she hears him addressing "the gentleman's servant"; he thinks that he is assuring her that, by reason of his social position and his income, he can relieve her of the struggle for subsistence; she sees that he would like to sentence her to a degrading inferiority. He completely ignores his wife's diplomas and intellectual qualifications, and she flaunts her assets like a proof of superiority; he wants to be the authority figure in the marriage and in the organization of family life, and she refuses to submit to his authority and his point of view; behind this there is in her the upsurge of a masculine claim, a rejection of her state of wifehood and motherhood.

Even though they could be recorded, the same words are different and change their meanings when they enter the hearer's ear. And indeed are they "the same words," except in the sense of a materialistic illusion, inasmuch as they have one meaning for the person who speaks them and another for him who hears them? Communication between the two persons is an illusion; the reactions of each, the products of his closed universe, are defined and interpreted by the other in terms of his own closed universe; he in turn reacts to them, and so the battle goes on.

Hence we are all and always the prisoners of meanings. Under certain conditions and through the use of a certain method, one can alter the meanings of one's universe and at the same time alter that universe, but one cannot escape the fact that we are inevitably steeped in the meanings of the very moment through which we are living. And this means always the-meanings-for-that-subject-who-perceives-and-lives-them. There is no objective significance. There are shared meanings, exchanged meanings, but there are no meanings without a subject—or, more broadly, a living being—for whom they exist.

The psychological essential, then, is on the level of the meanings-experienced-by-a-subject, and it is irrelevant to raise the philosophical question of determining whether something objective corresponds to those meanings.

Such a question would be symptomatic of the very subject who raised it, because it would have a meaning-for-him expressing his questioning, anxious search for another-reality and another-self that would be more stable or less insecure, and indeed it is these even without the knowledge of his consciousness and his good faith.

We come into collision with a number of levels of meaning as soon as we open our eyes on our world, as soon as we speak, as soon as we listen, as soon as we act—in a word, as soon as we exist.

If you are reading this page, you are at grips with a meaning, and the question, "What does it mean?" echoes far indeed, for beyond the meaning of this sentence or this page there exists, as an open source of meanings, what I wish to say in this book.

But for you, the reader, this very act of reading, the area in which this reading is embraced (psychology), its relation with your existence or your purposes (leisure? work? criticism?), its place in your present situation, and so many other aspects of your current situation, all this is only a knot of personal meanings, regardless in what direction one explores. By appraising the subject as useless or important, you give it a meaning in the very act of ascribing a positive or a negative value to it.

Objects exist round you only with their multiple meanings. A certain vase has a meaning already because you have given it a name, and thus it has a cultural meaning (for-you-as-a-member-of-a-certain-type-of-civilization); it has or can have many other meanings (it adds beauty to a given part of the room, it forms a pair with another vase, it is a memento, etc.). If the object that you look at (but already *to look at* has a meaning-for-you) is an "exotic" one, it has among its other meanings at least that of being exotic, with all the personal reverberations that you feel in its presence, and it would constitute part of another complex of meanings for a person of the ethnic or cultural group that it represents.

Reading the daily newspapers affords us another wealth of evidence of the same phenomenon. Every news story conveys an immediate meaning, which is its content, and from this initial meaning a number of strata of significances radiate concentrically into the remote areas of perception.

One morning paper has a five-column headline on its front page about a demonstration in the Nantes area: CRS * FIRES ON CROWD AND KILLS FATHER OF FAMILY. Another paper, favorable to the government, headlines: WORKERS DEMONSTRATE IN CITY, and a subhead in much smaller type adds: "One Killed by Stray Bullet."

It is easy to understand from this instance (and you can find many more of the same kind every day) how the immediate, direct sense of the content ("a man was killed during the demonstration") implies, through the presentation of the facts, subordinate repercussions of more subtle significances, and readers' reactions are determined (intentionally, on the part of the editors) by these less obvious meanings. Let us briefly analyze these waves of meanings. Whether, as in the first instance, it is a matter of a five-column, front-page headline or, as in the second, a more modest subhead is already a determinant of significance: that of the "worth" of the news, its importance or its minimization. Every word in the first case projects a spray of meanings, and they are expressed in implicit images such as "premeditated, savage police repression," "a serious conflict foreshadowing rebellion," "a crime committed with impunity on the person of a defenseless man with whom the reader easily identifies himself," "mass indignation ex-

* French security police.—Translator.

pected," "legitimate intensification of the people's anger after this murder and provocation," etc. All this is *also* said in the mere manner of presenting the news.

The contrary is the case with the other newspaper; the order to "minimize" echoes in its references to the "accident that upset everyone," the "tragic mischance," in which there was "no offensive intent or premeditation," and "there was no real clash between the forces of order and the demonstrators." "Do not demonstrate in the streets, because a stupid accident has occurred and could happen to *you*."

The "state of mind" of the group to which the reader belongs is the impact of this report, and the report itself, even as it also assumes meaning in this psychosocial context, modifies this context in its turn, and this is the aim of the editor.

A state of mind of this character—whether in the one group or in the other—emerges as an active center for the diffusion of meaning and at the same time an active center for the selection of meaning in the report.

The same process is encountered, on a very different line of investigation, in the distorted consciousness of the mental patient. All the meanings of the world have altered for him and become incapable of verbalization or of communication. His behavior is organized in terms of these meanings that are "strange" to us and foreign to those of our intellectual and social universe, and this conduct becomes as impenetrable to us as his consciousness.

Furthermore, the "strange," the "absurd," and the "insignificant" are categories that seem devoid of meaning, but this is so only in relation to that "content" that *we* were expecting, in relation to *our* system of references, or, in a more general fashion, in relation to a system of references characterized by their exclusion or nonassimilation.

This is indeed the *meaning* of these words that seem to be negations of significance, and it is with this meaning that we use them in sentences or judgments by means of which we seek to signify something.

If you deny the sense of a statement, an object, or a form of behavior by calling it "absurd," you mean something by this. The absurd is a chasm from the point of view of your principles or of logic, empty, a possible source of meaning, perhaps, but no more than a possible source and experienced as such, neither assimilable nor integral in a known, recognized, or accepted whole. Unless suddenly, by virtue of some other context, this chasm of the absurd signifies nothingness, a "concept" that is intellectually empty but an affect charged with anguish, with distress, with blind questing for being and the meaning of existence. In this case the absurd is filled with an existential meaning and on this ground it assumes a place, often in a highly rationalizing fashion, in a philosophical system.

A meaning is added to the absurd in other cases too, such as the password, the secret or coded message, the dream, the esoteric phrase, or the enigma. Then the frightening void of the absurd conceals—one suspects—a complete but veiled meaning, known to the initiate and actively reconstituted by the decoder. A significance is then given to the absurd as to the enigma, as such, even before the discovery of the directly intelligible meaning.

The truly insignificant does not exist. For any given human subject, the very numerous aspects of the real that are truly insignificant (that is, that are not objects of judgment, of denial of value, for this is something else and means something else) *are not perceived*. In other words, they do not exist for him, they simply do not form part of his universe. To such a person they *are* only to the degree to which they suddenly assume meanings-for-him, leaping out of meaninglessness into existence.

Thus it comes to pass that we suddenly become aware of certain things that hitherto we had neither seen nor heard even though they were "right before our eyes": betrayal by a friend, someone's secret love, the hidden meaning of a statement. What was obvious to our neighbor or our partner had not even brushed our consciousness, and we *perceive* it once its meaning has emerged. When, on the other hand, we say that a given fact, or sign, or symptom, or proof is "not significant," we impart a strong meaning to our statement, and it is in relation to a given whole (itself assumed to be significant) that *we judge* these things in order to exclude them from it, without on that account denying that they may have meaning from another point of view—that is, in relation to another context.

Hence one must not fasten on "raw content" in order to grasp meaning or meanings; otherwise the first chance grouping of letters or any word in an unknown foreign language would show that something could exist-for-us without meaning. Meaning must be sought and grasped in all dimensions of the experienced and the perceived, in everything in relation to which the premise is placed.

A kind of postulate seems to enforce its reign at the entrance to the specific domain of knowledge that is the field of psychology, and that postulate might be stated thus: "In the beginning is meaning."

One cannot progress in the understanding of a human subject, of what he says and does, unless one has first mastered the meanings that he ascribes to what surrounds him, to what he intends or expresses by his words and his actions. If it can be said that every percept is a bearer of meaning and exists as such only through a network of meanings, it must be added that the general character of this statement ought not to conceal the particularity of each meaning, since this is always relative to the given human subject or, at the outside, to a human subject belonging to a given cultural or other group.

This permanent halo of systems of referent meanings makes every perception, every idea, every action emerge in a veritable superposition of multiple meanings for a given human subject, and all these meanings are organized and stabilized more or less by each of us in a world of perception and action that in a certain direction opens on meanings shared by others (there is, for example, agreement to read the same thing or to draw the same conclusion from the same premises), but that in another direction focuses on each of us alone and individually without any knowledge of its inception in our full consciousness—lived-not-thought.

This is why there is always a hovering uncertainty, like a threat of misunderstanding or incomprehension, as soon as there is communication between human beings. The disseminator of information wishes to denote something, but the meaning of what he says will be what is perceived by the recipient.[1] It is an everyday truism to remark that, the more we try to express what is in the area of personal impressions, the more we are not understood, betrayed, misunderstood, because what is in question is specific meanings that the words themselves express badly since words are made for collective meanings.

In extreme instances, the sensations that for us are most filled with meaning are for that very reason the most susceptible to misunderstanding and incomprehension. So Kafka, discovering the cold color of the square of winter sky framed by his attic window, experienced it as "a silver shield raised against whoever looks to heaven for help and protection," [2] and beyond the meaning that we guess there is something that signifies Kafka himself to the extent to which a world of meanings is summed up for him in that sensation, which is thereby made a symbol.

Every language is a way of focusing on the real and experiencing it

The study of languages as means of communication, for individual or social purposes, and most especially linguistic research, have directed attention to the dynamic aspect of man's presence in the world. Our presence-in-the-world is not the passive or photographic reception of a multitude of objective elements possessing similarly objective relationships or correlations among themselves. It is an ingenuous illusion that causes us to take as impersonal external reality what in essence depends on our personal way of perceiving and expressing.

Let us analyze what takes place at the level of language, since we "name" these so-called objective "elements" with *words* and, on the level of spoken expression, we have a store of pronounceable words by means of which we strive to convey some significance.

One of the first phenomena laid bare by the comparative study of languages is the fact that the stores of available words (made manifest by the dictionaries and lexicons of every written language, for example) are not precisely superposable one on another. Learning a language does not consist merely in knowing the connections between the words in one language and those in another, for in the first place such a connection is never word-by-word and in the second place the words do not appear in the same sentence structures. If you consider how a bilingual dictionary is arranged, you see that a given group of meanings offered for a specific word does not precisely embrace the whole represented by the word that is nevertheless offered as a translation.

If, for instance, you wish to translate the verb "to resolve" (an enigma or a problem) into Latin, you have the verb *solvere*, but this verb means also: to unknot, to untie, to unharness, to leave port (a ship), to ripen (a cheese), to separate or to be separated, to remove oneself, to detach or to be detached (the notion of a "gap" as it is found in the French expression, *une solution de continuité*—a break in continuity), etc.; and all these meanings can express the simple image of two hands joined to each other through interlaced fingers and slowly being parted while the fingers are extended. Whenever you wish to express in Latin some action that in concrete or figurative fashion can be assimilated to this symbolic gesture, you can use the verb *solvere*. In French, as in English, what is thus embraced in the Latin word is distributed among a number of concepts each of which embraces other meanings.

The French verb *faire* is generally translated into English as "to make" and into German as *machen*. One should say "generally" because in French *faire* appears in a number of expressions in which it cannot be translated by "to make" or *machen*, and the contrary is also true.

Without going into figurative expressions or Gallicisms (such as *"faire de l'oeil à quelqu'un,"* or *"lui faire son affaire,"* or *"faire le mort,"* or *"faire des provisions"*), *faire* properly used, translated by "to make," includes something of the French verbs *créer* ("to create") or *fabriquer* ("to confect"), but it is translated also as: to do, to work, to act, to form, while "to make" embraces groups of meanings as different to the French as: construct, cause ("he made me go"), manufacture, create, establish (a connection), lead to a conclusion, arrive at ("make port"), induce, head toward ("make for New York"), etc. (And this in the transitive form alone.) As for the German verb, *machen*, it is even more polyvalent and covers a "semantic domain" all its own.

The so-called figurative meanings, the idioms of each language, the so-called untranslatable expressions are not special abnormal cases; better than the others they demonstrate the peculiar genius of each language, which, in the last analysis, is a given way of isolating and perceiving the real.

Many recent words forged by technological civilization (radio, automobile, rifle, etc.) have more or less approximate cognates (to the extent to which certain words become internationalized), but the base of the spoken language reveals the specific universe of the people that speaks it. "Every language corresponds to a particular organization of the data of experience. Learning another language is not putting new labels on known objects but accustoming one-self to analyzing the objects differently." [3]

It might also be said that in the field of pronunciation (and here the written alphabets threaten to cloak the phenomenon), the articulatory separation is individual in each case; every language has its own sounds. The famous English *th* is not the French *z* or *v* or *s*, but an intermediate sound that cannot be spontaneously pronounced by a larynx accustomed to the articulatory models of French. It is true that the French *u* creates the same difficulties for Anglophones, and so it is with every language.

The catalogue is inexhaustible, the illustrations are abundant, and, the greater the cultural differences, the more numerous and conclusive the facts of this kind, so much the more comical to the native speaker are the articulatory contortions of the foreigner who tries to pronounce the significant sounds of his language.

But this linguistic aspect does not exhaust the phenomenon. In addition to the store of sounds and fonts of meaning, there is also the context—the system of relationships among words as a result of which the sentence is shaped and the meaning is sharpened. To this observation it must be added that every language, as a tool of communication, is a certain way of organizing the relationships among words, or, more precisely, a specific system of syntactical matrices.

Saussure pointed out that the Englishwoman who speaks of "the man I love" expresses herself as completely as the Frenchwoman who talks of "the man *whom* I love." This has afforded generations of English teachers the opportunity to explain to their students that *in the English phrase the relative is not expressed but implied.* This statement is based on the touching belief that the French language takes account of *real* relationships and that every other language ought at least tacitly to employ the same grammatical instruments. This is obviously ridiculous. French has a specific

word with which to express the relative in this phrase, and
the French phrase in its characteristic modulation would be
unintelligible without the relative pronoun. The English
phrase expresses the same meaning and in this case it dis-
penses with the pronoun. It is no more "implied" than
French implies the special word ending that in German,
Greek, or Latin designates the direct or the indirect object.
Will it be argued that French implies declension of nouns?

There are verbal forms that French "does not use"; among
them are the optative (found in Greek), the gerundive (in
Latin), the progressive form of the present participle (English), etc. But these forms are not objective means that are
used by one language and implied or replaced in another;
they are forms inherent in the spirit of the language, *organs
that modulate expression according to a peculiar inner logic
of which the subject who speaks is not conscious*. What are
called "turns of phrase" also represent examples of these
specific linguistic structures through which meaning is con-
veyed.

Thus, between the undertaking of communication (a specific intention that supposes the existence of some inter-sub-
jectivity, of a fundamental inter-human relation) and the intelligible phrase, every language employs linguistic "forms"
that are modes of the dynamic organization of the relationships among the signs utilized. Every language has its own
system for the structuration of communication, its game of
empty forms and of categorization of relationships. This is
the real domain of syntax, of sentence construction, in which
each language has its own play of characteristic models.
This problem is bound up with what has been said earlier
of language as a specific organization of the data of experience corresponding to each type of collective consciousness
and each culture (and even to each homogeneous group
within a given culture).

There is a primary effect peculiar to context, and that is
the determination of meaning through the intelligible rela-

tions established among words. Proof of this is to be found in the frustration of the effort to understand (which is a search for meaning) when one is confronted with a sentence out of sequence in which, however, the words as such are identified and, indeed, often well known, in which their spelling eliminates certain possible combinations, and from which, nevertheless, meaning is absent until one has discovered the proper order of the sentence and placed each word in relation to the others.

We shall consider an illustration. Here, out of order, are the words that express a thought by Guillaume Apollinaire: "memories sound wind hunting horns are dies of which amid the the." Its meaning is inaccessible in spite of the relative elimination of sources of error and solely as a result of the disarrangement.[4]

The correctness of the construction of a sentence, however, is not enough to determine its meaning definitively. A second effect, of context, becomes operative. "The fish is evaporating" and "the moon is triangular" are properly constructed sentences, but in each the context is abnormal in terms of its "elements." Context has a virtue of its own: It has the capacity to specify one among the many potential meanings of a word—the multiple meanings that constitute what has been called the word's semantic domain.

Here the famous "law" of the theoreticians of form is applied and verified: "A part in a Whole is different from the same part by itself or in another Whole." [5]

Context makes it possible first of all to assemble into words sounds that would otherwise be only ambiguous sources of significations. The sounds *a, d, or* are organized into different meanings depending on the context in which *adore* or *a door* appears, or even depending on the distribution of these sounds in other combinations, such as *ador*nment. Meanings, then, can vary in at least two directions, according to context, but context is never out of the picture, for most often a broader context becomes visible or remains possible and affords a permanent approximation of the meaning.

Most frequently one is content with an approximation that is considered satisfactory, one stops with an initial meaning sufficient for what one is seeking or for one's level of expectations. And this remains valid for what seemingly contradicts it, such as double meanings, implications, plays on words, allusions, comparisons, and the many "figures of speech" of written or spoken language. The meaning or meanings are always understood only through the combination of two series of operations: on the one hand, the mobilization of the entities represented by each word or each concept, and, on the other, the understanding of the context or possible contexts.

In fact there are two kinds of groupings: the groupings that constitute the semantic domains of words, of concepts, of expressions, of symbols, and the groupings created by relationships of context, in which each of the preceding groupings appears in the form of an element of the new entity, and this in the end brings out its meaning. Hence the meaning is a *function* of two references at the same time, one going back to the repertory (vocabulary, dictionary, organization of experience as it is represented by concepts or words), the other going back, by way of grammar (the models of concrete expression, the "forms" available to the subject for putting things into formal relationships—"putting them into shape"—the selected means in his store), to the context of meanings.

Both these structures go back to a kind of structuring operation that is the act of the subject who perceives or speaks. On the linguistic level this operation is not only individual but also in close relationship with a kind of collective relations, *a mode of perceiving, of organizing experience, and of expressing it,* peculiar to a sociocultural group and always unconscious on the part of the subject who is speaking.

But language overflows the banks of sociocultural meanings and introduces us to other levels of meaning that must be differentiated: for one, the level of intellectual and scientific understanding; for another, the level of total subjective experience of life for each human subject. We establish that a large number of meanings comes from a primary activity, which is that of our intelligence. Although to a large extent cultural meanings and intellectual meanings are interwoven, we ought to distinguish between what, on the one hand, expresses a sociocultural fashion of perceiving and experiencing the world and what, on the other, expresses an effort of intellectual understanding and a rational organization of our universe.

To take extreme instances, we do not confuse in the same category the meaning of a ritual or folk ceremonial with the meaning of a mathematical calculation.

Science is a continuing endeavor to define "the object" beyond its earlier meanings, to discover the necessary relations among "objects," and to formulate these definitions and relations in as unambiguous a fashion as possible. The ability to reckon the age of a tree by counting its rings or the age of a horse by looking at his teeth, the knowledge of the therapeutic properties of herbs and the ability to recognize the symptoms of a disease, these are all the products of efforts of understanding as definite as those that produced the discovery of Hertz' cycles or of vaccination, even if mankind did not arrive at all of them at the same points in its history.

It is true that, at the time when a scientific discovery is made or a theoretical intellectual formulation is stated, one never knows what magic or subjective meanings they still bear in themselves as nonconscious obstacles to accurate abstraction. Only subsequent corrections, further purification through the ascesis of reason, will demonstrate, in retrospect, the error of their inadequacies. "Objective knowledge is never complete." [6] Without going back to Aristotle's old thesis on the eels who were born of the mud of the marshes, the peak achievement of the science of his time, let us for the mere pleasure of it quote texts on fermentation exhumed by Bachelard and dating from the seventeenth and eighteenth centuries.[7] In the seventh edition of his *Course in*

Chemistry, published in Paris in 1680, Nicholas Lémery wrote:

Fermentation, which acts like fire, isolates the earthly and base parts in the production of metal. . . . Since metal is a product of fermentation, the sun or the heat of subterranean fires must necessarily cooperate in its production. . . . Fermentation often causes veins of lead ore to rise to the height of mountains.

Fermentation having been "discovered" as a factor in digestion in the eighteenth century, a medical scholar (MacBride, in 1766) proceeded to prescribe "causing exercise to be taken by nursing babies" in order that motion accelerate the process of fermentation-digestion.

Our modern chemistry courses and our texts on child-rearing contain enormities of the same caliber, but only our descendants will learn of them when they have established twenty-second-century science.

Intellectual and scientific knowledge, then, is not an acquired domain that broadens but, rather, an enduring endeavor aiming at total objectivation. The meanings it uncovers in this quality should be differentiated from the meanings experienced by a subject or a group on an unthinking level.

If the distinction is almost impossible in the domain of the history of science, in the epistemological domain one would be justified, as G. Granger suggests, in making a radical separation between, on the one hand, *a meaning* that refers to a *structure* (and these terms should be reserved for the results of scientific intellectual activity) and, on the other, *significations* that refer to *a system* (and these words should be reserved for individual or group subjectivity).[8] Thus the ultimate goal of knowledge would be "sense and structure," as the object's position, properly so-called, in the network of objective relations that defines it; "these would be the relations described by the mathematician, the physicist, the economist, the sociologist, etc." The significations that refer to the experience of an individual or a group are also related to a network of relationships, but this time it would be a question of a latent organization not yet thought through and constituting the affective-perceptive system of the individual or group subject under consideration.

This detour into linguistics has served first of all as a reminder of the way in which the idea of structure was effectively introduced into the social sciences, but, beyond this historical reference, it should accustom us to a certain manner of understanding psychological data. The words of a language express wholes (their respective semantic domains) that are the results of *a certain way of isolating reality*—in other words, of an active classification of what is perceived; moreover, each language has its own structures of construction, that is, its *specific models of structuration of contexts at the level of expression.* Active classification and structural models of relationships are *absolutely nonconscious* operations for the subject who expresses himself in his own language. Without this dual, nonconscious activity of structuration, no expression or even understanding would be possible. Knowledge, from subjective experience to the goals of the sciences, entails the activation of the same process, although in the former case it is a question of a structuration of the relation (egocentric or sociocentric) of the human subject to the real and in the second case it involves an attempt at structuration of "objective" relationships—that is, at a reactionalization of structure, or an objectivation of the structure of reason.

We perceive in consonance with our moods

If we come back to the universe experienced by each of us, we have to concede that meanings exist first of all in terms of our organisms. Above all, in fact, there is beyond any doubt a structure of the human organism as a specific reality that corresponds to a "world" of general meanings characteristic of man and as a result of which, for example, dimensions and distances, space, time, air, water, weight, foods, heat, daylight, night, other human beings of both sexes, etc., fall within a certain common "zone of meanings" in spite of cultural and individual differences. Thus there is an ecology of the species man, just as there is one for every other living species. We shall never be able to view the world with the faceted eye of the fly or the perceptive system of the blind fish that live in the lowest depths of the oceans. We shall never be able to perceive the fly as the spider perceives it, nor those fish as they are perceived by some other fish that live on them as parasites.

It is on this general human level that the "archetypes" of specific and basic human situations are found; they are by definition transcultural and they correspond to equally archetypical "behavior patterns" formerly called "instincts." The situations that mean "danger" to the species man are not those of some other species, and the range of behavior patterns corresponding to those situations is likewise specific.

On this general human "background" to which cultural characteristics are added, the "state of our organism" also creates meanings.

If I am thirsty, my thirst develops at the same time as meanings are reorganized for me; more and more numerous realities—in direct proportion to the growth of my thirst— finally divide themselves into two *categories:* what can be drunk, and everything else; the latter is the permanent, negatively significant backdrop (it cannot be drunk) against which whatever my perceptive search causes me to categorize under the head of "drinkable" tends at once to detach itself. If my thirst becomes torture, as in the case of those who are lost in the desert, it will become an atrocious obsession and all critical sense will vanish. We know that certain martyrs to thirst under these conditions, victims of the irresistible attraction of "liquid," which becomes hallucinatorily significant, have reached the point of drinking their own urine or the gasoline out of their cars.

Food for the hungry man, freedom for the prisoner, a sexual partner for the concupiscent, tobacco for the smoker, alcohol for the drinker, heroin for the addict—every *need,* whatever its level and whatever its value from the moral point of view, is to him who experiences it the onset and then the domination by an *active category* that selects the "elements" of his environment and, at the same time, by a pattern of behavior impelling to the act of achievement, and organizing his conduct toward this final objective, if necessary overcoming all detours.

For the focus of need is never an individualized object. Need focuses on a "genus," a category of realities. If yesterday afternoon I could hesitate, at cocktail time, when confronted with the multitude of possible drinks (all of which had already been classified as "apéritifs" in our cultural environment and were quite different from what might have been offered to me in mid-afternoon, or after dinner, or from what I wanted to drink this morning when I got up), it was because I was not very thirsty, and this allowed me to relax, to hesitate, to take time to think, to exercise "freedom of choice," and then to drink in leisurely, slow sips. And mentally I compared this persona with that other me who, when he was picked up from a battlefield during the war, wounded and having lost considerable blood, insistently demanded something to drink from his rescuers.

Need, in its experienced essence, focuses on the "satisfying object" in its corresponding general character, "anything at all" provided that it match the structure of the lack or the active, gaping void, exploring the environment or waiting for what will partly or wholly fill it.

The small child deprived of love attaches himself and clings to the first adult who shows "motherly behavior" toward him. The "real mother," the legal mother, is not a

mother if she does not fulfill this need, at once most definite
as to its "form" and most indefinite as to its possible contents, on which is imposed only the requirement of an
"essential" quality relative to the need, since it is only in
relation to the fulfillment of the child's need that one can
determine whether the satisfying response was "maternal."

Needs, then, vary with the "state of the organism." Age,
sex, circumstances affect it. The significant tonality of the
environment changes in the same manner and to the same
degree, modulated by our successive needs. Thus, in a certain sense, the organism is the source of meaning. *"Der
Organismus ist Reizgestalter* (the organism shapes the impulse)," as von Weizsäcker says.[9] The form of the stimulus—
its significance—is created by the very manner in which the
organism "offers itself to influences from without," [10] or intervenes actively in its own field of action. It is a matter not
only of the individual nature of its "receivers," of the sensitive thresholds of its nervous centers, but also of its needs
as dynamic forms contributing positive or negative meanings. "The environment stands out in terms of the organism's
essence," to quote Goldstein's excellent statement.[11]

The way-of-being-in-the-world, the active center that
gives meaning to what surrounds us, can be understood as
biological and physiological reality on all levels of experience, far beyond the archetypical or superficial needs of
our organism.

A subject's "mental state" corresponds to meanings that
he gives to his environment, to such a point that characterizing these meanings and characterizing his mental state
come down to the same thing.

"What the subject believes" is the most important and
the most determining thing in his organism's reaction. Let
us begin with an anything but dramatic "mental state," suggestibility. We know that in this area the most curious experiments have been made with placebos. Placebo is the
medical term for some innocuous product, chemically or
physiologically inert but endowed with apparent thera-

peutic efficacy as a result of the patient's mental state. Let us describe an experiment of this kind,[12] carried out in order to study the psychological component in asthma. Forty subjects of both sexes, ranging in age from fifteen to seventy-nine years and all sufferers from the disease, were subjected to forced-exhalation tests during which they were warned that they would be given injections of adrenalin (a medicine that effectively relieves respiratory difficulties by eliminating bronchial spasms). The subjects learned the breathing procedure (a deep inhalation followed by rapid, complete, forced exhalation) that was to be measured and compared.

After fifteen minutes' rest, they were asked to perform the breathing exercise with a subcutaneous injection of distilled water; then, fifteen minutes later, it was repeated with a subcutaneous injection of adrenalin. The results weré these: in twenty-four of the forty cases the effects after the injection with distilled water were almost the same as those after adrenalin—an increase in breathing capacity and improved exhalation. In sixteen cases the distilled water had no perceptible effect, whereas the adrenalin produced very definite results.

What is the meaning of this experiment, which is similar to hundreds of others in every field of organic pathology? It shows that a particular "mental state," that of subjects "susceptible to placebos," can produce effects as measurable as those of adrenalin in one of the therapeutic situations for which it is indicated. The signification, "distilled water as placebo," which, to use the excellent American expression, is the "experimenter event" [13]—in other words, which is "significance *for the experimenter*"—becomes "efficacious medication" *for the subjects* to such a point that the functional system disappears. Dropped into this mental state of *suggestibility* as if into an unconscious "context" that is active and informing (giving a "form" and therefore a meaning to what occurs next), a meaning appears for the subject at the level of unthought experience, and the reaction is physiologically measurable.

The "mental states" connected with endocrine disturbances are more dramatic and easier to detect. Mood changes in women in the premenstrual interval sometimes border on psychotic surges of melancholia; similarly, menopause has psychological manifestations in which the effects inherent in hormonal disruption are combined with personal reactions to what is experienced as a narcissistic humiliation, a loss of femininity-maternity. More generally, puberty, pregnancy, aging, etc., are periods of mood changes and thus of changes in experienced meanings.

Mood as an even more general phenomenon characterizes at the same time a certain overall "state" of our experience, which is matched, from the point of view of the "ego," by a "basic affective disposition," [14] and, from the point of view of the "world," by a tonality of all the representations, the specific values that are assumed by things, persons, and situations. "The sadness of things," Maldiney wrote, "no more arises out of the melancholy of men than the melancholy of men arises out of the sadness of things. It lies in the *at* of *presence at*. Sadness or joy, anxiety or trust, all are contemporary with the phenomenality of things before they have crystallized into objects." [15] In other words, the primal reality is that of a relation between the human being and the world, and this relation itself is made a theme. It is made explicit by the simultaneous emergence of a "state of mind" and, on the other side, a "kind of universe."

Without exploring here the controversy among psychologists on the meaning and place of the idea of "character," we must point out that in the broad sense a certain customary tonality of humor (mood) is implicit in the idea of character, and this in the most ancient sense to which the Hippocratic tradition invites us.

Our "temperament" represents a relatively stable mode of our relation to the world, a sort of fundamental humor or mood that is the permanent concomitant of our various behavior patterns, or, more precisely, a certain "register" of our affective reactions, a certain way of understanding situations and reacting to them. We know that, according to Hippocrates, *humor* construed in this sense corresponds to a style of character, a morphology of the body, the face, and the hands, a certain degree of "warmth" or "cold," of "moisture" or "dryness," [16] perceptible as much in inter-human "contact" (tonality of inter-subjective relation) as in the contact of the skin.

In effect our character, to the degree to which it expresses a constitution (or a certain structure of relationships among the cortical and subcortical nervous centers), is a kind of "regulator" of our behavior and at the same time an organizing principle for the meanings of our environment.

Robert Meili described in a paper [17] the typical reactions expressive of basic characterological disposition in babies a few weeks old:

In our studies in characterological development, we presented infants three to four months old with an object—say, a black ball two inches in diameter, suspended six inches above the baby's face. When the baby focuses on this object, his movements stop for a moment. Thus far these experiments have been made with almost one hundred infants, all of whom we have filmed. Now it is clear that it is possible to classify the infants according to their style of reaction in motor arrest. Some resumed their activities almost instantaneously, and their faces brightened, verging in extreme cases on the embryo of a smile. . . . At the other end of the scale there were the children who remained motionless, focusing on the object with obvious tension, and occasionally starting to weep. . . . We repeated the same experiment four times, at two-week intervals, and we observed a reasonably good individual consistency in the form of the reaction. It was subject to general development, but each child kept his relative position in the group. *So it was not the reaction in its outward form that remained constant, but something that determined it.* We can further broaden the field of observation. During their first year of life these children retain their way of reaction in similar situations: in confrontation with objects or situations that are relatively unfamiliar, or, toward the end of the first year, with strange persons. . . . We can classify these same children up to the age of eight years, which at the present time is the limit of our longitudinal study, . . . in reasonably close correspondence with the classifications arrived at when they were three to four months old.

It is clear that this "permanent form" of reactions expresses an affective or experienced "categorization" of the corresponding "object" as "attracting" or "upsetting," and the very consistency of this "attitude" goes back to the notion of "character." In one case we have "those who have a positive attitude toward new objects and new, unforeseen, or changing situations," and, in the other case, "those who in the face of the new, the unanticipated, or the altered have a negative attitude made up of fear, distrust, reticence, and inhibition."

Through its very structure, each character, in the field of the environment and *at a nonconscious level,* succeeds in isolating situations and regrouping them into positively or negatively evaluated complexes of meaning, and this takes place in permanent relationship with types of behavior—what we may call postural-behavioral patterns—that represent the character's resources in action and reaction.

Adult subjects of the first class described by Meili in children (the class in which one encounters characterological "types" out of various typologies: the sanguine of Hippocrates, the tonic-plastic of Allendy, the nervous-choleric-sanguine of Le Senne, etc.) "love" novelty, change, surprise, and therefore, in a nonthought fashion, they give positive, attracting meanings to such situations when they appear; they seek out and bring to fruition such situations, shunning their opposites (regularity, monotony, routine, stability of life). For subjects of the second class (which embraces the atrabilious and melancholy of Hippocrates, the atonic-plastic of Allendy, the sentimental-phlegmatic-apathetic of Le Senne, etc.), surprise, improvisation, change, urgency, quick decision are unpleasant situations, avoided as much as possible and therefore experienced with negative meanings, stripped of value, whereas their contraries (order, calm, reflection, familiarity and even routine stability of situation) are positive, satisfying, and sought after.

A whole series of levels of mood is already differentiated with respect to this reference. Character may be regarded as a basic mood discreetly accompanying the moments and movements of our lives in correlation with the shadings of value that we ascribe to the various groupings in our environment. But it is also with respect to this system that gives meanings and values that we are in this or that fleeting humor at the time of an event or a circumstance in which we feel that we are involved. If someone tries to compel me to go out when I prefer to stay at home in order to finish some interesting work, I become angry, and, in my character, the inception of anger reveals itself in various ways. A less demonstrative person would indeed regard my reactions as "excessive"; in him, given the same source of irritation, for example, the reaction would have been much less volatile but more lasting.

In relation to the limited frame of references represented by character, the expression of our reactions of transient mood is comprehensible also in terms of the cultural models of our allegiance to social groups.

But the phenomenon of mood goes beyond the frame of reference of character and culture. It has roots as well in the acquired structures of the emotions. Mental disorders show the extent to which the meanings experienced by a subject, his mood, and his general behavior are fundamentally correlated aspects.

In mental illness mood dominates the picture, and, intensifying as it becomes organized in a rigid fashion, it submerges all the rational means of apprehending reality, all the critical intellectual means of verification and control, and thus it destroys adaptation.

In a manic psychosis, the patient "clings" to everyone he

encounters and he abolishes any "distance" between self and not-self in a kind of incorporation or assimilation by fantasy as well as in an "extravasation" that is evidenced by the unbridled outpouring of his ideas and his speech. His mood is characterized by undisciplined exuberance, noisy and hearty, a demanding and fickle expansiveness capable of "devouring" every situation without distinction, regardless of its "significant differences" for a normal subject.

The pattern is analogous, although the universe assumes a wholly different tonality, in the depressive psychosis. It is expressed by the patient's behavior. He is silent, or niggardly with speech, he lies prostrate but cannot sleep, he moves not at all or very slowly, he is somber and remote, and his posture is one of profound discouragement, associated, furthermore, with a physical feeling of tremendous fatigue. His gloomy ideas center on morbid themes of guilt, despair, the necessity of suicide. His melancholy-depressive mood corresponds to a deterioration in all meanings. The world is reduced to the leitmotiv of the futility or the harm of living, and "everything proves it to him," everything is interpreted through this significant leitmotiv, and, as a result, it is the meaning of everything that he sees, hears, thinks, or imagines.

All mental illnesses, perhaps, are diseases of mood, and undoubtedly the most serious have to do with diencephalon-pituitary lesions or disturbances.[18] What is essential is to recognize that the mood is not only a certain way of being in the world but also an active thematization of the experienced universe that can go to the extreme of the disintegration of critical thought and reason in the illusion of utter lucidity about oneself and the world.

Every rigid thematization of existence seems to end in phenomena analogous or at the very least similar to the effects of the psychotic disturbances of mood. The world's meanings in their totality crystallize round key *Leitmotiven* and the whole tends to become systematized, almost as a hypothetical-deductive theory is constructed on a foundation of basic axioms.

In this aspect mood expresses an acquired structure of affectivity. Everything proceeds as if our personal history—our experiences as they have been lived in the past and as a function of everything that at that time constituted their contexts—were in the end to construct and solidify a certain number of *affective attitudes*.

The word *attitude,* unfortunately, is one of the vaguest and the most frequently used in psychology. Let us strike out its theatrical meaning—that of a part being played, a mask, as in the expression, "that's just an attitude, a pose" (which means that the person's posture, position, or speech does not match what he personally and actually feels)—and speak rather of mental and emotional attitudes. If we speak of an attitude taken during an event, an attitude toward a given person or ideological position or book or line of thinking, or a general attitude toward life, we mean by this to designate *a way of being or acting that is expressive and not fortuitous,* signifying, even by accident, a tendency of mind or of relatively *constant* feelings toward a certain *category* of objects, persons, or situations.

Analyzing the themes of a body of statements by a patient, Minkowski [19] endeavored to discern the structure of the complaints and ideas of a ruined life that the subject collected in the cloak of various phrasings. As he classified these ways of speaking, the investigator saw three themes emerge:

1. "A feeling of general impotence, expressing itself in special fashion in the statement that the patient could not go through the window or over the roofs of the neighboring houses, that she could not take people home with her, that she had nothing, etc." The constant theme that could be analyzed on the basis of the verbal expressions used was that of "I cannot," "I do not have the means," "I am lacking."

2. "An impression that the environment was receding,

becoming remote with respect to the self," expressed by another group of phrasings such as "People seem to be moving out," "Everyone is getting into the train," "They're going away," "They're saying good-bye," "Has this place been sold?"

3. "The impression that, even though she too was being invited to take part in the movement going on about her, she was incapable of doing so." The verbalizations were: "I don't know of any station, where do you want me to go, there's no railway," "I've never left my home," "What do you think I can do with a few cents?"

"It is hardly necessary," Minkowski added, "to stress the fact that these three factors are intimately bound together in our patient's utterances and, basically, they form an indivisible whole."

Let us try to arrive at a still more precise description of this "indivisible whole," which is not a sum but a kind of theme of themes: "Everyone is running away and running away from me, and I am left powerless, alone, disoriented, in ignorance of what is going on and what is going to become of me."

Here is an emotional attitude whose words are too little indicative of the vast charge of felt experience that they represent for the subject; it is this structure of affect that provides the basis from which one can integrate the whole of the subject's opinions, beliefs, and declarations, the body of what she has to say. Now *it is this same structure* that is expressed in the subject's perceptions of her universe, even though she is unaware of this latent structure.

The basic phenomenon of structuration-thematization of the perceptive universe by the affective attitude is obviously very definite in mental patients by reason of the morbid processes mentioned earlier in connection with mood and also because of the rigid singleness of the structure. The patient can no longer infer a new principle on the basis of his experience precisely because his reason has been reduced to impotence or absorbed by the development of an unhealthy theme that diverts the automatic vestiges of reason to its own service. On the contrary, every experience can only implement the structure that animates him.

"The ideas of coincidence, chance, and unintentional or unconscious acts no longer exist." [20] For the paranoiac suffering from persecution mania,

> . . . the slightest bit of thread in his path has been placed there deliberately; horses play the game by defecating beneath his bedroom windows; if a passer-by is smoking a cigarette, . . . it is a signal; if the electricity supply fails, there is a reason. . . . His thought does not stop with the concrete value of objects, it does not mark out the precise contours of each of them. . . . The object is only the representative of the general meaning. . . . So all objects are confounded with one another and resemble one another; the differences always connected with the apperception of the individual value of each of them are wiped out. Similarity is the only point of view from which they are envisaged. "Thinking," proceeding by analogy, discovers resemblances that ordinarily escape us, and the patient, in contrast, ascribes great importance to them. . . . Everything speaks the same unequivocal language for the sick man. . . . His attitude determines a precise picture of the universe that is subsequently reflected in his whole environment.

No doubt it will be objected that the example of paranoia, even more than that of mania or melancholia, tends to place primary emphasis on the ideas of *system* and systematization of the perceptive-interpretative universe. Yet everyone can verify in his own experience the point at which any affective attitude encountered in a partner or an interlocutor becomes an agent of "transformation of meanings" (this in relation to our point of view; in other words, to *our* body of meaning) and swiftly veers off into bias or opinion. Defend a man whom you find congenial to someone else who loathes him; argue with a Mormon if you are a Catholic—or with a Catholic if you are anticlerical. . . .

The most amusing aspect of the various discussion programs that appear on television is the radical impermeability of the respective opinions expressed; one senses how strong are their hidden bonds with experienced principles and affective attitudes in which there is nothing rational and which are never brought out into the open.

Bion attributes to Melanie Klein the thesis that psychosis constitutes the core of men's affectivity to the extent to which mystifying fantasies operate by being deeply involved in all the circumstances that human beings experience. All "private universes," more or less, seem to contain charged areas in which exotic certainties thematize existence.

In a sense one might say that every subject, to the degree to which he behaves in terms of the meanings that he ascribes affectively to his existential circumstances, is "duped." And this for the very reason that his affective system, the system that ascribes meanings, is rooted in fantasies or constructed on the basis of affective attitudes of which consciousness is the dupe because these are centers that organize beliefs that are never challenged, of certainties accepted as proofs as a result of long association with them and of the reflection of them that the subject always encounters *in what he thinks is the objectivity of his perception.*

An affective attitude is a structure that orients perception and action at the same time; it operates as an agent of thematization of perception, of selection of information, and of organization of behavior. The "sentiments" to which affectivity was for so long reduced (it is true that pleasure and pain, the emotions and the passions were also included in it) are only a kind of reflections-for-consciousness of our attitudes. The latter are in fact the enduring prefiguration of all our sentiments on an unthought level, as if consciousness, left to its own devices, could always "cogitate" varied and variable "contents" without being able to grasp the common mold that fashions them, the dynamic matrix that produces them.

One might, *mutatis mutandis,* apply to the structures of meaning the laws that the theoreticians of *Gestalt* have offered for the perception of spatial forms and sensory structures of correlation: "The effect of the repetition of Figure A (a reference to a particular shape that, removed from one context and placed in another, acquires an individual perceptual signification) is nonexistent or in any event completely incapable of overcoming the forces resulting from the solid organization of the B figures in a sense different from Figure A. . . . Each B figure puts up its own resistance to the perception of the Figure A that it con-

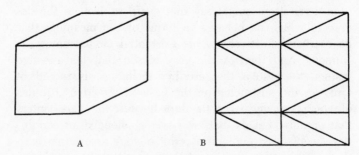

Fig. 1

Figure B contains Figure A, but the organization of B makes it impossible to see A in it.

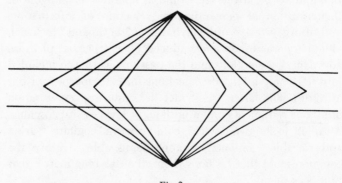

Fig. 2

The horizontal lines are parallel, but their curve resists this intellectual certitude of their construction.

tains." [21] Every *Gestalt* opposes a certain degree of resistance to its won transformation. In the domain of beliefs and affective meanings, similarly, every human subject proves incapable of perceiving a new structural organization of the situation when he has been impregnated with a given different organization.

Experienced meanings have a motor as well as an affective quality

Behavior has a necessary relation with perceived meanings. Traditional psychology individuated such fields as "affectivity," "will," "intelligence"; it distinguished between principles of knowledge and principles of action. Ribot, however, had envisaged the motor reality of "affective states," and Pierre Janet had shown in convincing fashion that the image is a summary of coordinated movements.

From this point of view Kurt Lewin's field theory [22] brought together these scattered ideas and defined behavior as a function of the situation experienced by the subject—in other words, of the whole of the *current* meanings making up his psychological field.

At first glance one is tempted to say that there is a "correspondence" between the organization of perception and that of action, and that perceived meanings entail, cause, or unsettle natural or reactional behavior patterns. This would be mistaking the logic of speech or argument for reality. Thus William James wondered whether one must not say: "I see the bear, I tremble, I am afraid," instead of: "I see the bear, I am afraid, I tremble," in order to respect the order of appearance of psychological phenomena. In fact, for a subject who has a very special fear of bears, the irruption of the situation of mortal danger (and therefore of meanings) and fear with its various manifestations and expressions characteristic of this subject in this kind of situation are *one and the same thing.* As the phenomenologists have pointed out, the occurrence of the emotive situation and the emotion (stirred consciousness) are one and the same thing. Let us add that *a form of conduct appears at the same time,* for an emotion as a pure phenomenon "of consciousness" does not exist as an emotion.

When Lewin says that a subject's behavior in a situation is the product of the situational forces acting on him, he makes a major observation with rare clumsiness, for there are no "forces" that act "on the subject" except in his didactic metaphor.

In the well-known sketch in which the object, O, is endowed with a "positive valency" (that is, "attractive to the subject"), and the subject, S, "receives" the impact of the force, O_1, which tends to bring him close to the object (Figure 3), one must say that the appearance of O_1 as "desirable" and the force O_1 are *one and the same fact.* S is not the subject, because the subject is also in the $+$ attached to the object, O_1, which by hypothesis is attractive to this subject. S is no more the subject than the force, O_1, or the positiveness of the valency of the object, O_1. This valency is a meaning of the object for the subject, and the so-called force, O_1, is a quality of that meaning.

What is S under these conditions? Nothing but the motor patterns available to the subject, arbitrarily represented separately. The subject's movement toward O_1 and the "desirable" significance of the object are the two faces of a single fact. One may, in a pinch, speak of "tension" in the field thus created, but only to the extent to which the emergence of the desirable object arouses the motor pattern

O_1

Fig. 3

corresponding to active appropriation. If the situation is reduced to this, active appropriation inevitably occurs and proceeds, the tension being only that of the need in the time taken for its satisfaction by the accomplishment. The impossibility of any other "solution," as Koffka would say, is of the same order as the impossibility for water to flow back up the hill instead of down.

Here Guillaume provides a more satisfactory formula than Lewin's:

There is always a direct relation between the intrinsic character-istics of the act and those of the situation as they show them-selves in perception; these two terms are not merely "linked" to each other, but the structure of the one depends directly on the structure of the other. . . . When reactions change it is because the situation has changed, whether as a result of the original reactions or subjectively through a reorganization that displays the object under a new aspect.[23]

You show a favorite cake to a hungry child who is not afraid of you (for here one must at least neutralize the other "elements" in the field in order to allow the desirable object to appear), and he "automatically makes a move-ment" toward the cake.

Conversely, you show the same cake to another child, who hesitates and remains motionless; you should be able necessarily to deduce from this that the situation for the second child is not the situation for the first. There are only two solutions to this problem. Either the cake does not possess a clear "positive valency" (the child is full, the cake is strange, or there has been an ambiguous prior ex-perience), or else your personal negative meaning "bal-ances" the attraction of the cake. Try offering sugar to a dog that you beat yesterday and you will note behavior that will show you how important fear of you is to that dog.

But let us not stop with lesser examples that might be open to suspicion.

Here is a student's description of his abrupt change of

affective-motor attitude in a situation that remained "objectively" the same to the observer. In the lobby of a university building two men sat behind a long table covered with displays of low-priced detective stories, used paperback books, and secondhand magazines. Two salesmen were "talking up" the merchandise to the passing students. Now comes the description of the reporting student's experimental introspection:

As soon as I arrived, I could not say why, I had a feeling of aversion, an inner rejection of this situation, a nonacceptance. I found myself studying the salesmen with annoyance, criticizing them, and I had absolutely no desire to go look at their display. . . . Then came an acquaintance to whom I wanted to express my growing anger. He forestalled me by telling me that these men were there on behalf of the Food & Agriculture Organization and that they were volunteers selling these books collected during the campaign against hunger with the purpose of using the proceeds for the purchase of food and clothing. Suddenly the earlier meanings changed although there had been no effort on my part. Unthinking antipathy became sympathy, aversion became attraction, criticism became approval. . . . I felt drawn by the salesmen and I quickly went up to the table.

Everyday situations are often more complex. A tension of a second kind can be created in the "psychological field," arising out of a blockage of movement whether through pure inhibition (vigilance, surprise, expectation) or as a result of counter-movements opposed to the first movements.

Lewin's formulation of *the reward-punishment situation* is familiar; it is called the traditional pedagogical situation. Let us apply it to a typical case:

Suppose a subject to whom an "authority figure" sets a task, T, which for the subject is negatively charged (and hence "to be avoided," unpleasant, repulsive). (See Figure 4.) The movement expressing this valency will be one of avoidance, the more rapid as the valency is more highly charged and the psychological field is more cleared of ob-

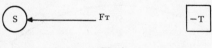

Fig. 4

stacles. An obvious acceleration in the flight may be produced if elsewhere, in a direction opposite to that of the task, a distraction with a positive charge appears or exists in the field.

But the authority is on its guard, naturally concerned to forge wills and hearts (*sic*). Normally it sets up a reward, R, the charge of which is by hypothesis positive, behind the task, T, and a menace, M, the charge of which is negative since it is a menace (having already, as a rule, proved its value as a menace and thus satisfied the authority figure). The subject thrust into this situation without any other element in the field will necessarily "flee" *laterally* in order to escape the menace *and* the task, or even, if the circumstances of the whole situation are favorable, try to win or take R or an equivalent while avoiding T and M.

For the subject there is an inner tension, a tension depicted and materialized by the conflict of the arrows in Figure 5, and lateral flight represents the psychological possibility that is available to him: the possibility of getting out of this field, of avoiding this situation and this tension.

Now this "solution" is itself an absolutely determined and predictable form of behavior only if lateral flight is made possible by the situation. The opposition of one or more obstacles to such a flight is enough to make it a new problem. What obstacle? This can be only the negative signification of flight itself to the subject.

Conversely, if flight as such becomes attractive (charged

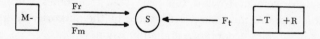

Fig. 5

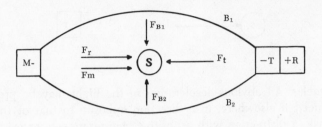

Fig. 6

with a positive valency, to return to Lewin's phraseology), it will be overdetermined and the subject will embrace it precipitately. Then it will turn into panic escape.

But let us suppose that the external compelling authority, observing the first hint of a movement of flight or a round-about attack on the reward, "closes" the lateral roads by raising what Lewin calls "barriers." (See Figure 6.) These can be physical barriers (e.g., locking the subject into a room until he has completed the task), physical-personal barriers (remaining with him and maintaining a threatening attitude while keeping watch over him), psychological barriers (escaping from the situation would be "dishonorable" or would "cause sorrow to those who love you" or would be "a sin" or would "incur the vengeance of God"), or social barriers (escaping from the situation would be to "detach oneself from the group" or "not be like the rest" or "compromise one's social prospects," etc.).

The situation having thus been sealed off, *behavior will express the product of its meanings* at the same time as the *resolution of the tension* created by their conflicts. The effect of this tension is that the situation as such cannot long be endured and action will be resorted to "in order to get out of it." Lewin envisaged five possible "solutions":

1. Movement toward the task, which becomes another situation; this movement is expected by the authority figure, for it signifies acceptance and submission.

2. Movement toward the threat in order to confront it.

This movement represents a kind of negative surcharge of the task, T, which the subject attempts to escape by paying the price required—that is, by accepting the punishment called for by M. This creates another panic situation for the authority figure, which usually resorts to exaggerating the menace in order to preserve its negative value and thus impel the subject toward T.

3. Assault on the barriers: appeal to the outside world, test of their real resistance, challenge to values, revolt against the authority that erects the barriers. The test of strength begins, and this too is another situation incorporating the confrontation of punishment and signifying non-submission.

4. Fixation on the spot, reactional apathy, indifference, immobility, or passivity, defense against internal tension by ceasing to be involved in the situation or experiencing it as an "impossible action."

5. Emotional explosion: attack of weeping, nerves, or rage, or, in the extreme case, the destruction of possibilities of adaptation, dissociation of the self. Discharge of tension, scapegoat aggression, an emotional release.

It is totally out of the question, of course, that these five solutions should be offered to the subject's "choice" or "free will." Since each individual case will express itself in definite meanings created by the situation as it is experienced by a given subject, his behavior will express the result of their conflict.

As for the affective-motor significations involved, they are and ought to be considered in their actuality-for-the-subject. The "weight of the past" or the "experience of the past" or the "reactivated Oedipal conflicts" beloved of the psychoanalysts exist only insofar as they are brought up to date in the situation, and, in this case, they are expressed through and in *current* meanings.

Conversely—and it is here that it is necessary to go farther than Lewin along the same road—the significances for-the-subject and their precise conflict will be inferable or deducible on the basis of observable behavior, because *this is not the effect of meanings but their motor reality itself.*

Let us look at other examples. A noncommissioned officer says to me, in connection with a colonel: "That man has incomprehensible conflicting attitudes; in many circumstances he shows real courage and takes major 'physical' risks. He makes delayed-opening parachute jumps, he competes in horse shows on animals that he does not know and takes them over difficult jumps, he is a champion fencer and pistol shot, and all this means a great deal of coolheadedness. Yet in battle circumstances I have seen him display unconquerable fear. The sound of battle plunges him into tremors that are painful for everyone near him. As soon as the noise and the shelling end, he regains all his pride."

If the principle of the necessary coherence between conduct and situation-as-structure-of-meanings is true, it may be concluded from this that *the incoherence is such only in the eyes of the observer.* It can exist too for the contemplation of the subject himself when he looks at himself as he is and if he accepts his successive states as facts. Then he will say: "That is how I am," without any awareness of the determining structure.

But, starting with observable behavior, we can suppose that the two types of situation that seem susceptible of assimilation to each other in the view of the noncommissioned officer who is making the judgment (and both of which, for him, fall into the category of "risking injury and death") are experienced *by the subject* in totally different ways and with diametrically opposed meanings, as opposed as the reaction of "cool-headedness" and that of "frightened trembling impossible of concealment from those round him."

Proceeding from this point, let us follow existential psychological analysis in its concrete endeavor to uncover the categories experienced by the subject. By comparatively classifying the situations corresponding to the two forms of behavior one should be able to uncover at the same time their respective themes—that is, their structures of meanings —and the differential characteristics that make the one the contradiction of the other. The differential emerges at once as a tonality contradictory to the danger experienced: In a first group of situations the danger is blind, not to be localized, compelling the subject to wait for it in uncertainty as to its impact; it hovers over him in a commotion that evidences its immediate and imminent presence (the noise of battle, of cannon, of machine guns, of rockets, etc.); in the second group of situations, the danger is known, specific, confronted in a voluntarily chosen action. In the first case the reaction is panic and anguish; in the second, it is self-control and clear thinking. The first type plunges the subject into a painful inferiority; the second affords him a feeling of superiority that he exploits to the limit (and no doubt by way of compensation), as is proved by his active seeking out of such situations and his competitive motivation.

The "pride" that the observer noticed after the shelling and the battle would be a reaction to the reaction, an attempt to cancel the early fear and the ridicule that it would arouse in others.

Another example. A student of science in a university is living under these conditions: he is twenty-five years old, mature, and recently married (his wife is pregnant), and he has begun his studies after a lapse of several years since his completion of secondary school; the interval was prolonged by his military service. In order to assist him with this resumption of studies in connection with a desire for social advancement that is considered praiseworthy, the parents of both spouses (the two families live in rural areas) are financing an apartment for the couple in the university town, all the furniture, and a car, as well as a comfortable monthly allowance to the couple for the duration of the husband's schooling.

Let us look at what goes on in the mind of a stranger

who is told of this way of life. When he learns of it he ascribes a certain meaning to it—"a remarkable opportunity being provided," or "a rare attempt by parents to give a young couple a good start in life," or "upper-middle-class advantages providing an outrageously pampered situation in relation to the average student's living conditions," etc. The entire system of opinions, principles, categories, and even prejudices can be shaken. The parents' point of view toward these conditions is that of a "willing sacrifice in order to make a good start possible and to assist the young man in his intentions." His student comrades' points of view must necessarily be colored by their own relative situations. One would expect infinite dedicated activity on the part of the young husband, particularly in the light of his imminent responsibility as a parent.

But in his laboratory courses he suffers from a kind of palsy that interferes with his performance of assignments in dissection and manipulation; he complains too of a kind of mental block that makes it impossible for him to pay attention to lectures or to learn from books. He takes refuge in silence and now speaks to his wife hardly at all "lest he burst into sobs before her," he explains, "because he is so thoroughly ashamed of himself." He considers suicide. Everything began with his admission to the university.

Here again let us apply the analysis of behavior in order to discern in it the experienced meanings that it expresses. This behavior is a coordinated complex of reactions of panic, anxiety, inhibition, and isolation, of feelings of guilt and frustration. These words are not "interpretations"; they designate what the subject says that he feels.

To the young man, then, the situation is this: anxiety and inhibition, paralyzing his talents as well as his mental and manual skills, making life unbearable, ruining communication with his wife; he feels completely alone in a situation that is perceived as unspeakable and productive of guilt.

Living conditions that, it was hoped, would inspire effort

are experienced on an oppressive level, and the prospect of study and examinations is charged with an anxiety of defeat bound up with an acute and dominant feeling of guilt.

Analyzed from this point of view (no doubt being cast on the young man's aptitudes or his voluntary orientation toward studies of this kind, since all this is part of the hypothesis), the situation is clearly determined by the way in which the subject experiences the exceptional conditions that have been created for him. In order to react to them in this way he must necessarily experience them as a feeling of suffocation—that is, as a favor that he does not deserve and, at the same time, as an overwhelming trust inspiring panic lest he disappoint others, and as a crushing obligation to be paid by passing his final examinations, which are thus charged with a terrifying value. In this context the ordinary difficulties of university study, even though aggravated by reason of the years away from school, assume gigantic proportions; defeat is at once construed as a punishment and dreaded as the nemesis of confidence and the future. He "knows" nothing of these meanings; he lives their fantasy-reality.

The overwhelming accumulation of responsibilities (marriage, imminent fatherhood, resumption of duties, moral obligation to parents) seems to have overtaxed the young man's capacities for adaptation.

Examples are as numerous as observable behavior patterns. If three persons are discussing the *absurd* and the first says, "The absurd makes me anxious," the second says, "The absurd revolts me," and the third says, "The absurd makes me throw up everything and run," one could say that in these three cases the absurd (defined intellectually by the three speakers as "nonsense," "unintelligibility," "contradiction of common sense and reason," "that of which the meaning, the suitability, and the purpose are invisible") is experienced as "unendurable." Let us remark at the same time that the significances experienced are expressed by

different affective-motor reactions (anxiety, revulsion, aban-
donment-flight), and this clearly identifies on the level of
direct expression the differences in behavior patterns; in
addition, it shows that the differences among these behavior patterns make it possible to define the exact tonality of
what is existentially unendurable for each of the three.

Thus we can say that the meaning of an element in the
psychological field or in life experience is a function of the
whole situation, which is itself organized by a structure of
meanings, and that the meanings are not "representations of
consciousness" but affective-motor realities—in other words,
determinants of movements, of behavior patterns, or, more
precisely, expressing themselves in and through actions and
reactions without the knowledge of the subject's waking
consciousness; it is quite likely that he can "understand
nothing" of what is happening to him.

It appears that there is no escape from that general law
according to which *behavior expresses the meanings experienced by the subject-in-situation,* and, consequently, no
type of behavior can be devoid of meaning, nor can any
be wholly artificial or enigmatic. I have often noticed this
in circumstances in which human subjects attempted to ar-
range their behavior artificially (and this occurs especially
in groups and in group meetings). What deceives the superficial observer is the fact that he does not relate the behavior types observed to the meaning that is possessed by
the group itself, in the overall situation then existing (general, historic, spatial, temporal conditions, composition,
alien observation, etc.) for each member (in the here and
now) at a level of experience excluding current clear consciousness.

The silence of one member, for instance, a silence under
the shelter of which he thinks that he "allows nothing of
his feelings and opinions to appear," expresses in full illumination and by its own tonality (in relation to the other
elements of the general attitude) how he experiences the
situation in question. If this silence is accompanied by a

touch of withdrawal (a slight physical distance from the table round which the group is sitting), the subject is showing in visible, observable, open fashion that *he wishes to assume the position of a critical observer and not of a participant.* That is his "immediate feeling." I do not know what opinions he seeks to hide, but this he is expressing irresistibly and displaying without knowing that he is doing so.* From this point of view one can catalogue observant silences out of a refusal to become involved, hostile silences of contained aggressiveness, silences intended to attract attention, silences of inhibiting anxiety, silences of discouragement, traumatic silences, silences of withdrawal into indifference, strategic silences that await the opportunity of intervention in order to be sure of success. All correspond to completely observable attitudes. The same thing is obviously true of all forms of participation.

Better still, if it were possible to define the structure of meaning of the situation "here and now" for the subject under consideration, the structure to which his silence of the moment is linked, then one could say without fear of error that the system of this structure of meanings and of this structure of behavior *was one of the constants of this subject's existence at all times and places.*

One can imagine the extent to which the subject who thinks he is concealing his feelings expresses, on the contrary, the permanent dynamics of his personality. *It is true that his "consciousness" is wholly occupied by "contents" and cannot reflect the structures,* at least when it is abandoned to its own devices.

So then our behavior is also the prisoner of meanings. "The meaning," Maldiney wrote,[24] "is that of the *how* of presence in the world and not the *what* of a representation."

---

* To state it in another way, he believes that he is concentrating his will power on the concealment of what he thinks, and he openly "says" what he feels, without having to speak, through this observable behavior. It is as if a card-player were carefully hiding cards in his sleeve without being aware that the cloth of which it was made was transparent.

That is because meaning is the presence of the subject's personality in his universe and in his perceptions, because it is not a mental representation *but a behavior pattern.* This point is important enough for strong emphasis, for meaning thus interpreted "depends on" behavior and is not "a thought" or even "a sensation" of a qualitative kind. Meaning—or, more accurately, the system that gives meaning (through which things have meaning)—is a certain style of being-in-the-world, an experience of relation with persons and with environment. It is time to make an end of the confusion between "perception" and "representation" if one wants to give meaning, a constituent of perception, its value as a determinant of behavior.

This explains why all the advice that you may lavish on all those who are close to you remains useless (except in those instances where they are concerned with pleasing you, and this creates another determining situation) when you are endeavoring to bring about *a change in their behavior directly.* "Don't do it this way any more, do it that way. . . . Make a radical change in your conduct. . . . React! . . . Change your attitude!"

As long as the meanings that the subject experiences from his particular situation persist for him, his behavior continues in its basic form and its existential orientations. He will reply: "It's beyond my strength."

Here too is the reason for the failure of "supportive" or "directive" psychotherapies that would attempt to alter the structure of behavior through direct intervention in it.

"You've never been able to approach a woman?" a psychiatrist says to his forty-year-old patient who has come to consult him about this unbearable problem. "Well, get yourself picked up by a prostitute tonight and make an experiment." This advice is accompanied by a friendly, "understanding" pat on the shoulder.

Seeking to be obedient, or to be "better understood," the subject comes back after the fiasco. "I did follow the girl for a bit, but I wound up running away," he says, or: "I

obeyed you, Doctor, but, once I was in the room with her,
I reacted like an idiot and buried my head in her lap and
wept."

This is because, in order to alter a subject's behavior, it
would be necessary inevitably *and singly* to change the experienced meanings that he feels in the situations of his
existence; this creates a very different problem and requires
a very different method because it would be necessary to
intervene at the level of the structures of affectivity, which
are outside thinking consciousness and centered on "states,"
feelings, opinions, beliefs, or ideas—in other words, on
"contents."

When a subject does not possess a certain category of
significations, he cannot assume the corresponding attitude.
This "appropriate attitude," which you regard as "adapted"
in accordance with your way of understanding the situation, cannot be "taken" by the subject in the same degree
in which the significant category is not part of his life
experience.

Hence there is indeed "reciprocity between the subject's
sentiments and the affective properties of objects in his field
of phenomena or field of behavior," [25] but one should add
that there is reciprocity between this behavior and the affective properties of these same objects in the field. This
"field of behavior" is our past; it is not a physical, objective,
external, or social reality, as the early theoreticians of form
said. It is charged with meaning, it carries in all directions
positive and negative values that orient efforts, and in it
actions are accomplished.

A subject's perceptive and behavioral field is his own.
For example, the significance of a situation experienced by
two or more persons together (as in a family) is not the
same for any two of them. A closely knit system of references gives each detail a meaning that it possesses only for
the subject equipped with this system; this same detail is
perceived by the others with other meanings because it is
incorporated into other systems. When such a system is

itself reflected in a subject's consciousness, it is experienced in the form of a sentiment enveloping a current content, but, basically, the system is precise, an empty, dynamically structuring structure linked to a way of action and reaction.

The meaning, then, is not an object of contemplation or a content of consciousness; it is the active outline of a posture, an attitude, or a behavior mode to the extent to which it produces a scheme or a category *of what has been experienced;* it incites or tends to incite *motion* as much as *emotion,* as the etymology suggests.

In their study on "the psychological significance of the types of conceptualization," Kagan, Moses, and Sigel[26] show that there is a certain individual stability of the type of conceptualization and that there is a correlation between this style and the dominant elements of behavior. Regardless what theory serves as one's foundation, they say, the fact seems proved that behavior is linked to the meaning of stimuli and that this meaning is immediately and consubstantially linked to perception. Analyzing what occurs simultaneously in perception, these authors find in it:

—the degree of vigilance;
—the emotional quality of the vigilance and the action of preperception;
—the mood or overall personal tonality (to which we shall relate the structures of the private universe);
—memory;
—conceptualizing activity;
—the style of perceptive-conceptualizing apprehension;
—the culture (and the patterns peculiar to it);
—the intellectual level and the affective-mental age;
—the nonconscious image of the subject's own body and its possibilities.

Thus everything is in perception, the basic activity, the primal effort of orientation and consciousness toward a world on which the subject must necessarily, vitally gain a grasp . . . a fundamental phenomenon of relation to the world . . . tension toward the world, inevitable projection into the environment . . . the bearer of the structuring structures of being, in active search of information already pre-formed in accordance with certain axes and certain categories . . . a correlative awakening of the motor or affective-motor systems that are governed by these same structures or these same categories.

TWO

In Search of
Information

*I should like to see the world with
the faceted eye of the fly or the
brain of the orangutang.* —Anatole
France, *Le Jardin d'Épicure*

The animal universe, a world of signals
and shapes

Every living creature, simply because it is living, not only
is in relation to its environment but also carries on an un-
ending conflict with its environment. Its immersion into the
environment of life is given to it at the same time as life
itself, and without exception. The permanence of the conflict is the basic constant of its activity and orients it. Every
activity of the living being, polarized by the obscure imperative of "survival," is an activity with successive short-
term ends, means of realizing these ends, and a metaphysical possibility of attaining to them in this sense that the
specific structure of the living organism corresponds to a
relative stability of the environment, or at the very least a
certain natural order that makes possible the essential ref-

erence-taking. In pure chaos adaptation and survival would
be impossible, radically impracticable. Survival and adaptation are achieved, on the other hand, to the degree to which
a balance is found between the organism and its environment.

The living being's "intentionality" toward its world seems
to me to be too neutral a concept to signify the *devouring
desire* to be in the world, a kind of impetuous, imperious
need to survive. In a certain number of cases the most
pathological reactional forms are an existence *a minima*,
economically organized for survival, and so again an adaptation to an unendurable universe. (Among other things
this might explain the neurotic subject's resistance to cure.)

*Now this will-to-live, this intentionality, is first of all and
necessarily a quest for information.* The "outer world" is
incessantly explored, analyzed, inventoried at greater or
lesser distance and interval, according to the means available to the living being for the discovery and manipulation
of this information.

Even in the vegetable kingdom phenomena can be observed that are linked to this general biological principle.
We know, for example, that plants possess a pigment that
is sensitive to light, a phytochrome rich in high concentrated proteins, which enables them to "measure" one of
the most basic factors in the rhythm of their lives: the
length of days and nights (photoperiodicity). In the beginning of September, the photo-sensitive analyzers of the
willow, noting the diminution in the length of the days,
cause the cessation of the formation of buds and the emergence of scales that protect the terminal meristem. If, under
certain conditions—and experiments of this type are fre-
quent in the Phytotron of Gif-sur-Yvette—illumination is
artificially established at ten hours per day, the willow
begins to lose its leaves, regardless of the actual month.
Florists know empirically that covering chrysanthemums
with a black cloth between six o'clock in the evening and

eight o'clock in the morning will make them bloom in summer even though "naturally" they flower only in autumn.

In 1909, in a work that has since become famous in animal psychology, *Umwelt and Inwelt* (*Surrounding World and Inner World*), J. von Uexküll destroyed the old theory according to which animals' reactions were the effects of physico-chemical causes; he opened the way to *ecology*, the study of the life-environments of living species, of their specific *Umwelt* as the correlative of a *Merkwelt* (perceptive universe) and a *Wirkungswelt* (the universe of their action).

The life-environment (*Umwelt*) of an organism is the universe of its vital values, the universe in relation to which its actions and reactions have *a meaning*. This specific universe is obviously related to the animal's morpho-structural type, which includes a type of nervous system, a structure of sensory organs, and organic means of action.

This was the elevation to the level of science, and hence of methodical research, of the uncountable empiric contributions to knowledge accumulated by fishermen, fowlers, hunters, poachers, animal trainers, observers of insects . . . and all the world's peasants.

Since 1935 the works of Konrad Lorenz, in turn, have advanced animal psychology, revolutionizing the conceptions of instinct and signal. By way of summary, let us say that Lorenz replaced the notions of instinct and signal elements with that of a repertory of systems of natural or reactional behavior patterns, intrinsically *incorporated into the animal organism* living in its ecological environment. For, Lorenz said, animal behavior is significant only in its natural frame of reference, where it can be understood in relation to the kinds of information that the animal selects in its qualitative, specific, and unrepresentable universe.

An animal's universe is a world of *signals*, Lorenz said—in other words, stimuli that arouse a mode of behavior composed of sequences possessing a biological meaning.

What is a signal? What must be examined first is what is

called *the specificity of the signal,* since each species has
sensitive organs of different structure; this is one of the
elements in the huge whole represented by the organism's
structure in relation to the ecological *Umwelt.* This aspect
of the problem is well known, it is apparent, and yet the
difficulties for experimenters are still great.

They do not know how the animal perceives what they
call the stimulus (the *experimenter event*), whether he
perceives it, or whether he does not perceive in the same
signal something different from what they perceive in it.

At the International Congress of Physiology in 1953,
Voronin (of the Pavlovian school) offered a few examples
of the "unpleasant" difficulties in the experiments, com-
plaining that "fish and turtles have a nervous system incapable of retaining any trace of the stimuli that succeed
so well with the dog and the monkey." Biryukov, in a paper
read to the same congress, recounted that the river beaver
reacts to ordinary light, the crackle of a branch, or the
odor of castoreum, but he does not react to that "powerful
stimulant," acetone. "Powerful stimulant?" for whom?

Following von Hess in the study of bees' capacity to distinguish colors, Tinbergen [1] observed that "a certain reaction can be set off by a light of a certain wave length,
while another reaction, in the same insect, will be determined by intensity independently of the wave length. Anyone seeing the first reaction would conclude that the animal
can perceive colors, while an observer who limited himself
to studying the second would consider it insensitive to
color."

The differences in receptor organs also affect sensory
quality; the bird's eye has a visual acuteness superior to
that of the mammal's eye. Certain animals are seemingly
"deaf" (snails, flies); others can hear sounds inaudible to
the human ear (dogs, grasshoppers, bats) or smell odors
not perceptible by us. It is known that owls of the *Strix
varia* species can see their prey at seven feet and pounce
on it when the light on the ground measures seven-ten-mil-

lionths of one candlepower per square decimeter—in other words, more than fifty times less than the threshold of visibility for man, or, to put it in different terms, when to us night is at its darkest and we would be completely unable to see something four inches in front of our eyes. "There are no two species that possess exactly the same capacities," von Uexküll said in 1921 when he introduced the notion of the *Merkwelt* (the specific perceptive universe).

Moreover, the signal is not necessarily perceived in the same fashion by two individual members of the same species. In fact, it varies in terms of at least four factors.

1. Sex. The "meanings" of stimuli vary according to sex. The most immediate example that comes to mind is the attack by the rival male and the "seductive" behavior of the female when the male is in rut and on his own territory.

2. The individual's inner state and his neuro-endocrine-humoral variations. The season, the moment, the state of this or that need make the animal sensitive, less sensitive, or insensitive to a given specific stimulus. "Hunger brings the wolf out of the woods," according to popular wisdom, and, during certain harsh winters, wild animals do venture into zones that are generally avoided, taking new "risks" under the impulsion of hunger (attacks on human beings, for example, by animals that ordinarily run away from man).

3. The nervous type. Here Pavlov's conclusions find their place.[2] He isolates three basic qualities that distinguish "types of nervous systems" by their combination: First, "the strength or weakness of the nervous processes" (greater or lesser capacity to integrate excitations and resist tensions); second, "the balance or imbalance of the processes of excitation and inhibition" (operative equality of excitation and inhibition, or imbalance according to the two kinds, predominance of excitation or of inhibition); and, third, "the mobility of the processes" (swiftness or inertia in adaptation to change).

4. Each individual's "past," contributing great differences

in accord with apprenticeships and acquisition in all its
forms (learning and traumatisms).

By virtue of all these "conditions of meaning" of the signal, it may be said that an animal's world depends not only
on what his sense organs can or cannot perceive but also
on inner and individual factors. Tinbergen has offered a
celebrated example. The male stickleback, whose belly turns
red in periods of sexual activity, reacts to the female, whose
abdomen is swollen with her eggs, by beginning his famous
zigzag dance, which is intended to induce her to follow
him to the nest that he has built. During the same period
the female stickleback reacts to the "red belly" stimulus
and to this behavior by the male. Another male stickleback
venturing into the first male's territory during this period,
in contrast, would incite combat behavior.

Thus, as Tinbergen emphasizes, "the animal's perceptual
world is constantly undergoing change and depends on the
instinctive activity that is brought into play." [2]

When the signal appears in the vital field in which all
the inner and outer conditions coexist, the postural or behavioral reaction is unalterably triggered.

Now it seems that everything follows as if the signal were
isolated from the whole of the perceptive field, as if the
animal, even though sensorily capable of perceiving other
elements of the ambient environment and therefore a sure
context, were neglecting these factors, although apparently
(to the human observer) equally perceptible, and reacting
solely and blindly to a specific stimulus, a detail of his
environment.

The beetle known as *Dytiscus,* for example, which has
perfectly developed composite eyes and which can be
trained to react to visual stimuli, does not react to them
at all when it captures its prey (a tadpole). The proof of
this lies in the fact that, if the tadpole is presented to it in
a glass tube filled with water in which the supposed prey
moves and swims, the *Dytiscus* never attacks. Its search for
food can be triggered only by the effect of chemical and

tactile stimuli; a liquid extract of the meat immediately
launches it into the activity of the hunt and capture of any
solid object to which the extract has been applied. Bruckner,
experimenting with hens, reports that the mother hen reacts
to the chick's cries of distress and not to its movements.
When he fastened a chick by its leg to a post and placed
it behind a screen that hid it from the mother's view, she
reacted intensely as soon as she heard the chick's cries (she
ran in search of it in great agitation). But if the chick were
placed beneath a glass bell in the same distressing situation,
close enough to the mother for her to see it trying to escape
but leaving her unable to hear its cries, the hen would remain utterly indifferent.

Duyn and van Oyem have verified this phenomenon of
the determining power (or suggestive significance) of a
perception-signal isolated in the potential perceptive field.
Let us take the curious and easy experiment on grasshoppers (of the species *Ephippiger*). The females, when it is
their season, are attracted by the males who sing and move
toward them. Observing this phenomenon in its natural
environment, one might wonder what its signal was—visual?
auditory? tactile? olfactory? The experiment makes it possible to answer. The females set out in quest of the invisible
males who are singing thirty feet and more away; they pay
absolutely no attention to silent males even if these are
quite close. In order to reduce the males to silence one has
only to immobilize their wings by sticking them together.
A male thus "prepared" is incapable of attracting a single
female. The signal-stimulus, then, is auditory in nature; it is
certainly not visual.

Tinbergen says that the crouching position of the female
interested in sexual activity is the signal-stimulus most important to the bird *Bonasa Umbellus*. The males are quite
capable of distinguishing between the sexes, but, in the
activity under discussion, they react to a peculiarity of behavior rather than to differences in forms or colors. Another
male in the same crouch, or a dead bird in this position,

would trigger the reaction of copulation solely because the male cannot resist a powerful signal-stimulus. It would be fallacious to deduce from this, with Allen, that the male in question makes no distinction between the sexes.

To this must be added the differentiation between trigger stimuli and directive stimuli. For example, water fleas swimming in a tank in which there is carbonic acid will make for the surface. It can be proved that it is the water's carbonic-gas content that sets them in motion and that it is the light that guides them, for, if at that moment one illuminates the tank from below, they will head for the bottom.

The culmination of these researches was the analysis of the influence of "decoys" and the discovery of "supranormal arousing stimuli." It was this new chapter in animal psychology that was opened by Niko Tinbergen on the basis of the theory of the "imprint" and of the models of Lorenz. From this, furthermore, it seems to me that we derive a highly structuralist conception of animal behavior, the full consequences of which we shall see in the study of human behavior.

For example, to the female wild duck the male is a bird with a green neck. If the male's green feathers are plucked, he will be rejected by all the females; on the other hand, the other male wild ducks will no longer attack him but rather, it would appear, they will take him for a female.

If there exist powerful isolated signal-stimuli the perception of which determines the animal's behavior in an irresistible manner, it becomes obvious that a signal of this kind fabricated by the experimenter and presented in the animal's perceptive field, provided that the conditions of season, moment, and inner organic state are suitable, will automatically trigger the matching behavior.

If this behavior is determined successively by a trigger signal and a directive signal, it will be necessary to plan for the emergence of the latter at the proper moment.

Here is a male robin that attacks another male robin venturing into his territory. To what is he reacting? In order to find the answer, the combative male was presented (Lack's experiments, 1943) with various "models" some of which included different elements drawn from reality. It was observed that a mere motionless tuft of red feathers at the end of a bit of wire triggered the behavior, whereas a perfect model of a robin except for a red breast aroused nothing (indifference).

Observe a little monkey that seeks out its mother and clings to her. The "mother" excites reactions in the monkey and should therefore be regarded as a stimulus. But what is "the mother" to the little monkey? What does this human word mean in the animal's universe? In order to find the answer, scientists sought to simplify the complex picture represented by "the mother" and they analyzed its stimulating elements. It was through the study of "phantoms" or "decoys" that this result was achieved, through the confection of complex stimuli from which one or another element was missing. It was then observed that certain "phantoms" were "effective" (triggers or guides) and others were not. (See Figure 7.)

The procedure was extended. Study of the behavior of fear-motivated escape in fowl showed that the birds reacted to a very precise model (form and direction) as shown in Figure 8.

Decoys are not merely experimental or practical artifices; they are natural realities, as one can recognize from the various "instincts" of animal camouflage. For example, the stereoscopic vision of animals organized for the hunt of swift prey (owls, falcons, lynxes, cats) is generally developed through the location of eyes side by side. This arrangement of the eyes becomes a *Gestalt*-signal and stimulates in the prey tendencies toward vigilance and defense that themselves differ from species to species. But other animals use this *Gestalt*-signal as protection and camouflage: "It has been established that small insect-eating birds abandon the chase and flee when the butterfly on which they are preparing to pounce opens its wings: these bear eye shapes

Fig. 7

Certain specific signals, presented by the decoy or "ghost" of the "mother," trigger appropriate behavior in the little monkey.

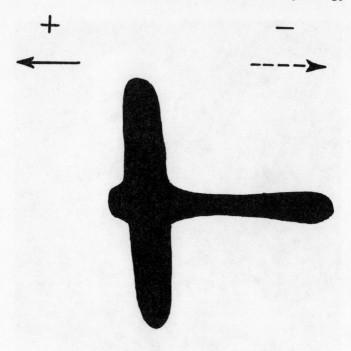

Fig. 8

Imitation of bird of prey (Tinbergen, 1948). This decoy set off no fear
reactions among gallinaceous fowl, ducks, and geese if it was made to
appear to be flying toward the right. If it appeared to be flying toward
the left, these reactions were automatically triggered. Hence it is not only
the profile that acts as a signal-stimulus but the significant whole of form
and movement.

that resemble the eyes of predators that hunt these birds."
(Cf. Figure 10*b*.)

Observation of the hunting, fishing, and trapping habits
of indigenous peoples of all regions of the earth, and particularly of the hunting rituals of certain primitive tribes,
reveals multiple illustrations of these modern scientific researches. In current practice decoys are used for specific
purposes. In artificial insemination, for instance, the male
is stimulated by a lure in order to produce ejaculation or,

if the female is not of the same species as he, to make him mount her.

Later studies in the simplification of complex real stimulation led to the discovery of "supranormal signal-stimuli." This is the term applied to those excitant signals whose power of stimulation is *greater than that of the natural signal*. Let us go back once more to one of Tinbergen's best-known experiments.[3] Having found that the young of the herring gull peck at their parents' beaks, which are yellow with a red spot, striking at the lower front (this pecking acts as a trigger on the parent, who then regurgitates food), Tinbergen sought to produce a model that would set off this specific behavior in the young bird. Various "models" or imitations were made, and their effectiveness was easy to measure because it required only counting the number of pecks by the little birds. Taking as his index figure the average number of pecks stimulated by an exact reproduction of the parent's head, with the red spot at a certain place on the yellow beak, Tinbergen obtained a figure of .25 with the same head in which only the red spot on the beak was lacking, .9 with the natural beak associated with a head of unaccustomed shape (thus "localizing" the trigger in contrast to the level of the beak), and 1.35 (in other words, 35 per cent greater effectiveness) with a decoy of obviously unreal shape: a cylindrical red pencil with three white circular stripes at the end. (See Figure 9.)

Tinbergen had discovered the supranormal stimulus. This kind of investigation was broadened, and here are some of its results: The ringed plover prefers white eggs with black spots to its own eggs, which are brown with darker brown spots (experiments by Kohler and Lazarus). The rock bird known as the oyster-catcher is more attracted by large eggs than by its own. It will be more drawn to a group of five eggs than to a group of three, although its species lays only three. The willow butterfly reacts more strongly to a black

(a) The young bird pecks (one hundred times) at a simple model representing a normal head of an adult gull.

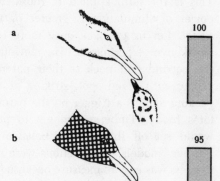

100

(b) The color and shape (c) of the head have only slight influence on the young bird's behavior.

95

91

(d) The red mark on the beak, on the contrary, is important. There were only twenty-five pecks when it was missing.

25

(e) A little red stick with white rings (here a pencil) is even more attractive to the bird than the model representing a normal head and inspires 131 pecks.

131

Fig. 9

lure than to a gray one, although gray is the color that triggers the natural reaction.

In the light of these experiments, two simultaneous hypotheses can now be formulated:

1. The signal is itself a certain *Gestalt*—that is, a structure, a certain configuration;
2. In the natural ecological order this *Gestalt*-signal has a symptomatic (and even a pathognomonic) value as an ecological situational structure determining a structured behavior. (See Figures 10a and 10b.)

Let us clarify these two points:

1. The signal is a *Gestalt;* this means that it is not a sensory quality isolated as such but a *form* the presence or the emergence of which in the ecological ambient environment evokes (in the strong sense of causing to appear) an automatic reaction on the part of the animal under certain conditions of time and need. It is not the red spot as such to which the young herring gull reacts, but a certain relationship of colors in a specific spatial configuration. It is not the color of its own eggs to which the great ringed plover reacts, but the relation between background color and spot color. When this relation is emphasized in the decoy, purged and detached from the unperceived "real" variables without significance, then the simulacrum's attractive potential is enhanced, and this gives us the supranormal stimuli.

In simple instances such as that of the robin the *Gestalt* is reduced to "tuft-of-red-feathers-at-a-certain-height-in-relation-to-its-support," but it is not on that account a mere sensory quality.

The configurational or structural character of the signal is so very clear in the experiments that prove its selective perception that Tinbergen was thereby persuaded to posit *the existence of a special neuro-sensory mechanism that would search out the form in question and trigger the re-*

Fig. 10A

Fig. 10B

Certain butterflies, such as this *Galligo Atreus*, show on the ventral side
these eye shapes that resemble an owl's face. This ornamentation represents an effective means of defense; when they suddenly open their
wings, these butterflies succeed in frightening off predatory birds and
even certain insectivorous monkeys. The observer will note the analogical
Gestalt between the two "signals," the real and the false used as defensive camouflage.

actional automatism. In certain especially clear cases this
hypothesis appears to be verified.

Take young thrushes, about ten days old. An optimal
"mother" decoy is fabricated, capable of provoking the
reaction of "opening-beak-neck-stretched-beak-in-the-air+

cries." The lure is any cylindrical object more than three millimeters in diameter—hence a twig, a pencil, a finger—that moves and that should be higher than the horizontal plane at the eye level of the young birds. Move your finger *below* this level and the young birds will follow it with their eyes but the behavior pattern will not be incited; raise your finger above their eye level and they will react behaviorally at once.

We know that Spitz [4] carried out experiments of the same kind with three-month-old children, in whom he was studying the conditions determining the emergence of the smile.

I established [he wrote] that what the three-month-old child perceives is not a partner, not a person, not an object, but merely a signal. It is true that this signal is the human face, but . . . it is not the whole of the human face that constitutes the signal: on the contrary, it is a special *Gestalt*. . . . This special *Gestalt* consists in the group composed of forehead-and-eyes and nose, the whole being in motion. . . . Anyone (and not only the mother) can produce the smile by fulfilling the conditions of the signal. . . .

A very simple experiment can be made to convince oneself that it is a matter of a *Gestalt*-signal: contact with the infant is established by showing him one's smiling face and making affirmative movements with one's head, and this provokes the *smile*-response in the child. If at the same time one turns one's face slowly into profile, while still nodding and smiling, the child's smile ends at once. He takes on a bewildered look. . . . Sensitive children seem to undergo a shock. . . . At this age the child smiles as easily at a mask as at a human face, and his smile will similarly stop if the mask is turned to profile.

Thus the signal is itself a form, a certain significant configuration. The proof of this is the fact that this form can be produced in and through a simulacrum, a decoy, or a phantom, which retains the power to determine the reaction when the necessary ancillary conditions are met.

Such an analysis, however, does not exhaust the problems raised by the signal insofar as the anti-structuralist argument can continue to emphasize the "isolation" of the signal structure in relation to the context.

2. Even if it is conceded that the signal is itself a *Gestalt,* there would remain the fact that its emergence triggers the behavior whatever the structure of the vital field at that instant. But it is proper to answer this by pointing out the artifice. The signal thus defined is a signal isolated artificially by the method of scientific experiment, and, in order better to understand it, it is sufficient to relocate it in fact in the natural life environment of the animal or other subject under study.

Let us not return to the internal conditions for the efficacy of the signal, conditions that represent the existence of a dynamic structure of the organism in relation to which the signal acquires its quality as a trigger or guide of behavior. Let us rather emphasize the other aspect, the relation between the signal and a clearly defined ecological situation. The central phenomenon that is to be examined is precisely the fact that the perception of the signal *is substituted for the perception of the situational whole.* This is the selective perception (to such a point that the subject becomes "blind" to the artificial elements of the situation) of the *Gestalt*-signal, which gives it its characteristics as a "signal." And this can be brought about only because, under natural conditions, the "signal" is a pathognomonic "symptom" of a significant situation, of an ecologically determined category of situation, in relation to which it appears as an index, economizing the implicit perception of the whole and summarizing or irresistibly conjuring up the situation. The reaction to the signal, then, makes possible the premature, essentially shortened triggering of the reactional behavior.

The male stickleback, in his own territory and at the nesting period, responds automatically with his zigzag dance to the "swollen-belly" *Gestalt* and with fighting behavior to the "red-belly" *Gestalt.* These signals, under the local and internal natural conditions in which they exist as such, necessarily sum up, represent, and signify—one might say, when speaking of the simulacrum, "symbolize"—in the one case the presence of the female to be seduced, in the other that of the rival to be battled. To deny this would be to deny that the decoy is an artifice.

In many cases the relationship is direct and obvious; so, for example, fleas and mosquitoes (insects that feed on the blood of warm-blooded animals) are drawn to their victims by the heat released by them; the insects' sensory apparatus is organized for the identification of radiant heat. The signal (perception of heat at a distance) is directly significant of the presence of a potential prey when the degree of the heat lies within certain limits.

The two heat-detecting lateral organs of the adder are of the same class. These organs enable it on the one hand, through their sensitivity, to detect the presence of small living animals and, on the other, through their lateral position, to take precisely and efficaciously the most direct course toward the source of this significant heat.

In contrast, social signals such as the circular or wriggling dance of the bees seem to us to be more indirect signals, but this no doubt is because *we* do not immediately perceive their ecological meaning. A typical situation, however, is in relation with these signals (selecting the course of the flight to be made, gauging the distance, identifying the kind of food discovered).

After the passage that I have quoted earlier, Spitz wrote: "Hence it is a question of a signal, but this signal belongs to and is derived from the mother's face; it is associated with the situations of food, protection, and security." [4]

So it may be said that things develop as if the signal, a lesser *Gestalt*, had acquired significance of its own (which is the test of its being a signal) only because of its essential and necessary relation with the situational form that is really vital to the animal. There is certainly a criterion of constancy in the association between the signal and the form, a criterion that is intelligible only in reference to a stability in the ecological universe. The signal enables the sensory analyzers to detect quickly and economically the presence of the required situational form, which might be described as "expected." In this way it is essential on the level of the organization of animal behavior patterns.

The animal's world is one of forms and signals. To the degree that the signals are also special forms, symptomatic of a more universal situational form, it may be concluded that *the animal's ecological world is only a world of forms.*

There is a major consequence, which has never yet been emphasized although all observations of animal psychology lead to it: No animal would ever perceive a situation in its particular and, so to speak, individualized content (this perception would be possible only to human consciousness); it could perceive only "classes," *Gestalten,* and, in a certain sense, abstractions. With this word that at first sight seems improper I want to emphasize a reality that cannot be represented in our universe of thought human perceptions.

How is this universe of forms to be understood? Let us refer to a few well-established experiments. Kohler [5] trained monkeys and chickens to react to a light gray and not to react to a dark gray. Obviously every experimental precaution was taken in order to make this difference *to us* in the colors the sole criterion employed. The training was regarded as successful when the animals made no error in ten consecutive choices. But of what did this training consist from the "psychological" point of view? Here Guillaume, following Kohler and making his own report on the experiment, says that "two hypotheses were possible: either the light gray color had acquired a positive value and dark gray had acquired a negative value, each of the animal's reactions responding to an *absolute quality* in the excitant, or else the animal was reacting to a certain relation between these two colors, to a relation of tones independently of absolute qualities"—in other words, independently of what is perceived by us.

The experiment succeeded in finding a decision as between these two hypotheses. In the critical tests the already employed light gray, G_1, was supplemented by an even lighter gray, G, which was a complete novelty to the experimental animals. If the first hypothesis was valid, they should have continued to react positively to G_1 as before. If the second was valid, they should have "chosen" G, which, though new, was as between the two colors "the lighter of the two," and deserted G_1, which they had hitherto preferred for the same reason.

The second hypothesis proved correct. In twenty instances against two and in nineteen against one during two parallel series of experiments, the animals "chose" G.

Another instance is even more instructive. Kohler trained monkeys to distinguish between two chests, the respective dimensions of which were $9 \times 9 \times 12$ and $12 \times 12 \times 16$, and consistently to choose the second. In what were considered the "critical" experiments he offered them the choice between two chests measuring $12 \times 12 \times 16$ and $15 \times 15 \times 20$. The problem was analogous to that of the difference in grays, but here it was a matter of geometrical volumes. Even when both chests were new to him, the animal chose "the larger," and not the one to which it might be thought that he had associated the previous choice.

It is true that Kohler, and Guillaume after him, concluded from this that *habit* therefore reacted to the identification of a *transposable form* independent of the absolute values of the colors that had been used for the training. It seems to me that one can go further and admit that *at the level of animal perception* it is never the "absolute quality" (in other words, the individualized sensory quality) that is perceived, but even here a relation—that is, a certain structure. If the same experiment fails with alert human subjects, it is because the human consciousness illuminated by *intelligence that characterizes in another manner* breaks the automatism of the immediate perception of forms and replaces it with the individuation of what is cur-

rently perceptible, what Guillaume calls "the absolute quality." It is known too that in certain experiments in human
psychology—the famous perceptive illusions—this operation
can be blocked and the significance of immediate forms can
be made to reappear at the neuro-sensory level.

As Guillaume very rightly emphasizes, the idea that the
"absolute quality" might possess a kind of psychological
and general seniority is an absurdity contradicted by experience. He declares with reason that "such structural
functions are very primitive, and later revisions can make
absolute qualities and their relationships appear in them."

But it may be added that, the lower one goes in the animal scale, the more perception is accomplished on the level
of shapes, and increasingly elementary shapes—in other
words, increasingly general. The process set in motion at
the biological level is comparable, in its own dynamic, to
the logical process of categorization, but the basic difference is that in categorization carried out by the human
intelligence there is an operation of conceptualization that
is an exploration of the essential structure peculiar to the
object (at least in the orientation of this intellectual activity), whereas, in the kind of *biological* "conceptualization-
categorization" at work in animal perception, it is in relation to the "need" and hence to the structure of the organism that the operation is carried out, determining *a
behavior* and not *an understanding*.

This would make it possible to reinterpret the pseudo-
phenomenon of generalization, on which so many studies
have been published. *Generalization of the signal* is the
term applied to a hypothetical performance by which the
subject of the experiment, after a number of operations,
demonstrates his ability to extend his sensitivity to stimuli
of the same category as the arousing stimulus.

So, if one teaches a dog to react to the beat of the
metronome at a specific rate (for instance, sixty beats per
minute), one then perceives that he reacts in the same way
to *any* beat. He is said to have "generalized." If one is then

determined to preserve the power of the signal at the rate of sixty beats to the second, the animal must then be forced into a new process of discrimination by a new conditioning, making use of the cerebral process known as inhibition (he is taught not to react to faster or slower rhythms, with due regard for his own limits of discrimination, and to react positively only to the rate of sixty beats a second).

In fact it seems that what takes place is at the same time more complex and simpler. In the mass of ambient relationships the animal learns to recognize a form. His discrimination generalizes from the start because he perceives only *categories*.

Through inhibition the experimenter may think that he is compelling the animal to isolate a specific kind of metronome beat, but in fact he is compelling him to vary the *Gestalt*. He then establishes the rate of sixty beats per second as a new category. The proof of this is the fact that, after this second conditioning, the animal very quickly and without special training will react to *a light* flashing at the rate of sixty times a second.

Experiments on the "second system of signaling" prove the same law transposed to the level of human language. A human subject is conditioned to two words (e.g., *tiger* and *nightingale*), of which one is regularly associated to an electric shock and the other is not. An apprenticeship of repetition having been served, the normal precautions are taken to measure the emotional reaction to the shock (using the apparatus for measuring psycho-galvanic reflex, which is sensitive to the reactional moisture of the palm of the hand), and various words are then presented to the subject. It will be observed that the subject reacts involuntarily to all words that belong to the same generic whole. If he has been conditioned to *tiger*, he will react positively and without further preparation to *lion, leopard, panther*, etc.

If suddenly he experiences new shocks accompanying words alien to the "wild-beast" category, such as "mouse" or "cow," the discrimination group will be reorganized on the basis of this new information and what will emerge will be the category of "animals with hair" as distinguished from "animals with feathers" and so on.

This takes us far indeed from the atomistic S-R system beloved of the behaviorists and Skinner, and even from the theory of Tolman, who, even though he discovered the importance of the situational significance, did not recognize structures and forms.

In passing, it might be said here and now that the generalization *of the response,* given full prominence by J. F. Richard,[6] derives from the same principle, contributing in addition a supplementary proof of the essentially postural-motor value of meanings, or, more precisely, the existence of a necessary relation between the structures of meanings and the structures of behavior.

But let us go back once more to the signal and let us, to the best of our ability, distinguish it from the *isolated* sensory quality. A stimulus that is imposed as "isolated," as Buytendijk has shown,[7] is, on the contrary, always a surprise and its unexpected character is a factor of disorganization of behavior. When, in contrast, the unaccustomed is avoided, the fundamental categories of life in the animal are preserved. For example, if, instead of the labyrinth with its marked doors, one employs a device that is reminiscent of ecological values and that takes into account the animal's sensory-motor structure (such as a pathway over slats, in which the obstacle is the insecurity of the support, which gives way under the exploring paw), one perceives that the rat becomes capable of learning artificial sensory discrimination such as the choice of colors, or right and left, or smooth and rough. Given a course of parallel slats cut into sections of alternating colors, in which one of the two slats yields under the exploring paw (and triggers passage over the other, which is stable), the animal "learns" always to choose the sections of slats painted in a given color rather than the others, *"after a small number of experiments and even after only one."*

This proves that, when experience makes it possible to descry a *Gestalt* clearly referable in certain aspects to the structures of the animal organism and its ways of living or of basic action, the animal is able very quickly to establish the new form and hence to "generalize," if one may use the term, from his first experience. "Behavior is immediately reorganized and readjusted, without shock and without conflict," Buytendijk says.

Many results take on meaning from this point of view. For example, the phenomenon of "resistance to extinction," so conscientiously studied on the basis of traditional hypotheses by Tolman, Miller, Withing and Child, Sears, Festinger, and Barclay Martin; [8] we deal here with observation of the delay in learning when the same behavior is sometimes punished, sometimes rewarded (within limits that preclude situations of experimental neurosis), a phenomenon comparable to infantile fixations on parents who are inconsistent in their discipline. It may indeed be wondered whether, in this case, there is not a pure and simple *prolonged alert to differentiation*—in other words, prolongation and intensification of the anxious quest for information until the form of the experiment is found (or appears), without which behavior cannot be organized. As a construct, indeed, the punishment stress is not adequate to determine negative behavior (automatic avoidance), and reward (food or security), an element of the same vital importance, also eludes its situational structural location. It follows necessarily that, in the framework of the "will-to-survive," the system of differentiation is placed on the alert; the subject or the animal attempts to differentiate or, if you prefer, to organize the adapted behavior. This, at a certain stress level, "excites" his vigilance. Whence that "dynamogenic" effect that has perplexed research observers.

It can also be understood how somewhat more coercive or brutal stress conditions lead to the complete disorganization of behavior—in other words, to experimental neurosis.[9] Two factors seem basic to the pathogenesis of these

situations: (1) either *trauma by surprise,* which can consist
in a sudden overthrow of meanings, as well as a sudden
emergence of new meanings that cannot be assimilated;
or (2) *conflict* among ambiguous meanings in a situation
that cannot be categorized.

The constant supervening condition, of course, must be
the character of "without-other-solution-than-to-endure-the-
situation," a condition of essential captivity in the situation.

It is clear then what creates the impossibility of organizing behavior as a result of the impossibility of discerning
form, as well as the phases, well known since Pavlov, of
the pathological disorganization of behavior: collapse of
differential values or of the capacity to differentiate (phase
of equalization), disorganization of excitation (paradoxical
and ultra-paradoxical phases), progressive paralysis through
blocking (narcotic phase and phase of total inhibition).

This road takes us to the study of the limits of integration
of structures—that is, from the point of view proposed here,
to the experimental conditions that block the perception
of situational form (and therefore of form as the organizer
of behavior), whether because the experiment is beyond
the capacities for renewal of the acquired, or discriminatory, categories of the central nervous system, or because
discrimination in structure has been made impossible by
the telescoping of highly structured situations (for instance,
the creation of an intermediate situation, or reversal of
well-known signals: what was positive becomes negative,
and the contrary), or by the initiation of contradictory reactional systems (e.g., making the hungry animal suffer
burning in order to get food).

Under "normal" conditions the exploration of the configuration of the experiment, recognition of the form of the
situation, makes it possible in other ways to measure the
limits of what is vulgarly called *animal intelligence* and to
compare possibilities according to species.

Technical illustrations: One attempts to teach the rat to
"recognize" the "right" box (the one that contains food

when he is hungry) in terms of its position in space, for instance, "always-the-one-in-the-middle" among five boxes, or "always-the-one-on-the-right," or "alternately-the-one-on-the-right-and-the-one-on-the-left." The "higher" animals manage this quite well. The "most intelligent" rat can achieve only fixation "always to the right" or "always to the left."

In a special labyrinth he cannot succeed in distinguishing "the second door going to the left," although he learns very well to go "always to the last door on the left." In the experiments of Atkinj and Dashiell the effort was made to teach the rat to go to "the-first-part-that-is-lighted-in-the-successive-illumination-of-the-doors," the succession for the rest of the doors being developed at random and only one door being illuminated first. The rat always failed; other animals (the monkey, for instance) learned the system.

Thus, through the experimental problems raised by learning one observes the capacity—or the limits of capacity—of animals to *discern the structure* of the more or less complex situations in which they are compelled to live in order to survive.

What is learned, what has to be discovered in its essence by the animal, is the situational structure. Now it is impossible to pretend that this discovery finally emerges full-armed after an accumulation of perceptions; it is carried out by trial and error, and this is what the nervous system, beginning with the initial experience, actively analyzes in the very perception of information, approaching this information with already formed active categories to be "assayed," categories born of the structure of the ecological organism-environment relationship (what have been called the instincts), or of the immediate state of tension of the organism with respect to this environment (what have been called its needs), or of its prior acquisitions (its apprenticeship or training).

"In investigations of apprenticeship," Jerome S. Bruner wrote,[10] "it is extremely important to understand systemati-

cally *what an organism has learned.* . . . It has learned a
certain *formal schema* that can be fleshed out by various
information and that can be utilized for the organization
of further information."

Thus a number of operations can be listed:

1. The organism seems to be capable of perceiving the possible structure or structures of an experienced situation.
2. It seems to be capable of learning the formal structure
   by probabilistic discrimination in the course of trials and
   errors and to be capable of fixing this within the limits
   of the discriminatory possibilities of its central nervous
   system.
3. It seems to be capable of manipulating these classes,
   categories, and *forms* as operational and dynamic structures that enable it to elaborate subsequent information.

Under these conditions the famous problem of the *transfer of learning* is easy to resolve, and within the perspective
already made available by the theoreticians of *Gestalt*.

By "transfer of learning" is meant the facilitation of the
learning of a given activity through the earlier learning of
a different activity. For example, rats that have "learned"
the strict right-left-right-left sequence in a maze easily
transfer this learning to the maze that requires the same
type of movement but "in a mirror"—that is, left-right-left-
right.

When children are learning to write, the performance of
the right hand can be improved through graphic exercises
learned by tracing letters in the dust with the toes.

Munn,[11] after having distinguished among three kinds of
transfers (bilateral or crossed; from one activity to another
that is similar, such as driving different kinds of automo-
biles; from one to another that is different in content but
similar in methods or principles), concluded that in the
third case the success of the transfer was complete. What is
this "principle" the identification of which *guarantees* the

transfer? It is once more the perception of form, its integration, its recognition in the new situation in which it is presented.

Even in the experiment cited by Bruner on the rats in the maze, the mirror transfer proved that what had been learned was not a series of successive particular turns, or even the right-left-right-left sequence, but, in even more "abstract" fashion, the *Gestalt* of "simple spatial alternation."

The form that represents this *operational pattern with variable contents* is the structure of the abstract relationships among the elements in the experiment. It is the integration of elements of information into a structure of this kind, serving as a grid or a dynamic category for its apprehension, that gives the "elements" a meaning. The pattern of active perception thus construed, of course, is matched consubstantially by the affective-motor schematic of the organism's reaction; and the formation of a new "pattern" affects at the same time the organization of already existing forms and the acquisition of subsequent patterns.

Robot animals

Life and survival plunge every living creature into an environment with which it is in an inevitable relationship, in which it must find its food, defend itself, act or react, and is necessarily constrained to analyze the "specific information" that it receives and seeks. *Information analysis* is the crucial, vital operation without which there is no possible utilization of information and, in other words, no information at all.

The concept of "information" comes to us from cybernetics. In cybernetics "information" is the term applied to every "physical influence" exerted on a recipient capable of retaining its significance. From this fact cybernetics proceeded to more specific definitions:

1. The "support" of the information (to which the cyberneticians have given the name of "form" in the sense of "modality," which has nothing to do with the *Gestalt* forms that are involved in this essay) is "what conveys" meaning. It can be language, mimicry, a group of light signals, etc.

2. The "semantic" of information—a term borrowed from linguistics—expresses the structure of meaning, or, if one prefers, the "meaningful content" of information—in other words, *its meaning.*

3. "Information" properly so called is the combination of support and semantic.

Obviously it is the "semantic" that constitutes the essence of any information. Indeed, if the same message is received through different channels, in different words, in different codes, it is exactly *the same* (in spite of the diversity in the supports that convey or "carry" it) only because the semantic is the same. Pieces of information that have the same semantic are called "equivalents." Conversely, "a sentence made up of words that individually have meanings, and, moreover, is structured in conformity with the laws of grammar, is nevertheless *devoid of meaning* if it cannot receive a semantic." [12] Thus it seems that the semantic alone gives a meaning to information and is its "expression."

But how is one further to define this semantic that is something other than the signs employed and yet is inaccessible without them? Couffignal, aligning himself here with Grey Walter, says that it is a matter of a "pattern producing a psychic effect." Let us go beyond this meager conceptualization of the process. Let us note that the semantic is a structure of meanings without which information has no informational *value* (and therefore does not exist as information). This semantic exists only for the recipient or the seeker of this information. The information, therefore, is necessarily "treated" by the "recipient" so that it may separate the semantic from its support. It is only through and after this *operation* that the meaning of the information is "received." Hence there is an operational (or operative) activity on the part of the recipient. This "reception" is in no way passive; otherwise the recipient could at best be only a potential transmission or relay agent, but never "informed." There is no information except for a recipient capable of analyzing information in order to be able to locate the semantic in it—that is, the pattern or structure-of-meaning-for-it. Now this can be done only if the analyzer possesses a range of possible *semantic models* and a kind of capacity of differentiation armed with criteria of differentiation.

The sense organs of every living creature are recipients and seekers of information. Properly, since Pavlov, they have been called *external analyzers,* and it seems clear today that these sensory analyzers are biological instruments for the reception of or the search for information that are capable of responding to needs or dictating behavior; these two expressions are superimposable.

The marine mollusk called *Buccinum undatum,* Tinbergen tells us, takes its samplings of the ambient environment by aiming its gills and taking in a thin stream of water. This stream is transmitted into its chemo-receptive cells and in this way, through the successive intake of samplings from various directions, the mollusk can *dissect* its chemical environment and perceive the distribution of these chemical elements in space.

We know that the bat's analyzer system consists in emitting ultrahigh frequency sounds and then listening for their possible "echoes" on the order of a radar apparatus in order to localize obstacles and estimate their distance. The same radar-related system has been observed in fish. Certain tropical species (Mormyrides and Gymarchides), which live in total darkness or turgid waters, have "electrical" organs that they use to project a kind of uniform electric field round themselves in a continuous fashion and with low voltage. Any object that enters this field or changes position within it alters it; specialized discriminatory analyzers detect these changes and "recognize" the prey in terms of the character of the disturbance in the field.

On the basis of meticulous experiments Bykov has shown that the sensory analyzers of the human tongue are capable of analyzing the chemical composition of food in the mouth and thus determine the various compositions *of the bile* in order to organize in advance the digestion of these foods.

Any device invented by man, no matter what, is constructed on the same basic principle. A thermometer, a barometer, a Geiger counter, litmus paper, and radar function like analyzers and thus convey coded information to the man who uses them.

As we see, this information is received or sought out by analyzers that obey specific commands of structure (the thermometer cannot provide the information that is given by the Geiger counter, etc.) and that supply a need for information in a certain field (information of a certain *class*) and in the bio-ecological frame of reference of no less specific relations between the organism and its environment.

A close relationship, well known since Pavlov, exists between these external analyzers and the state of the organism, analyzed at the same time by special sensitive organs: the internal analyzers, capable at any moment of "perceiving" the state of the constants in the internal environment. For example, the human body contains organs sensitive to pressure and capable of "perceiving" the level of arterial tension. Through the appropriate internal reflexes, organic reactions are brought into play in order to restore the tension to normal. The same thing is true for the carbonic-gas or sugar content of the blood and for body temperature.

The tension of disequilibrium on one of the factors necessary to humoral internal balance, detected by the internal analyzers, "orients" the external analyzers toward the search for "elements" in the ambient reality that might be able to correct the disequilibrium.

A rat suffering from artificially induced vitamin deficiency demonstrates his capacity to go after the food containing the vitamin in which he is desperately lacking; he will "choose" it from a whole array of edibles. If the experimental animal is surgically deprived of his suprarenal capsules, an operation the effect of which is to lower cell and blood sodium, the rat's "sensitivity" to salt is intensified; he goes in search of foods containing salt and eats more of them than do the rats in the control group, not subjected to surgery.

The external analyzer, according to the students of the Moscow school, is anatomically and physiologically (and structurally) in relation with the internal analyzer. The overall structure of the animal organism, like the ecological structure of its *Umwelt*, serves as an unchanging backdrop for relative variations according to stages of development and maturation and according to the successive correlative moments of the state of the organism evaluated by the internal analyzers. The old concept of need, desire, or impulse must be reinterpreted as the overall approximative label for an automatic process that has four phases:

1. detection of the imbalance or gap tension by the specialized internal analyzers and awakening of the behavioral postural scheme corresponding to what will relieve it;
2. increased or new excitation of the external analyzer in its sensory survey of the *Umwelt*, a survey "informed" by the category transmitted from the internal analyzers, which is part of the specific range;
3. gradual identification of the category in the *Umwelt* among all the coded information (detection of the corresponding signal);
4. stimulation of the appropriate postural and behavioral pattern and the corresponding movements or attitudes in relation to the satisfying category.

"Needs" are thus "ignited and extinguished" subjectively according to the periods of development or of the day, modifying the experienced universe in which signals are selected (while others go unperceived) that signify something through their reference to the system and trigger types of behavior.

Let us proceed somewhat farther into the hypotheses on the functioning of those analyzers known as the specialized sensory organs; or, in other words, let us try to penetrate the secrets of animal perception.

Everything seems to indicate that information is coded actively by the analyzers. Jerome S. Bruner wrote,

A system of coding can be defined as a game of non-specific categories, linked and connected in a contingent manner. It is the individual way of grouping and connecting information about the universe, and the system of coding is constantly subject to change and reorganization. The coding system described here is an operational hypothesis. It is inferred from the experiments. . . . For example, in the experiment on rats mentioned earlier, the animal learns to find his way through a maze (in which the road to food requires the comprehension of a sequence) by proceeding left-right-left-right. *I want to learn how the event* (the experienced situation) *is coded.* I move the animal into a right-left-right-left maze. He shifts his "learning" with a very marked economy of time. I conclude that he has coded the previous situation as a "simple alternation." But I have to continue the experiment in order *to verify the generalization of the coding system employed.* Is it alternation in general or positional-spatial alternation? In order to subject this idea to experiment, I confront the animal with a situation in which the maze contains a route marked off by alternating colors in pairs of black and white and the spatial directions are new and fortuitous (neutralization of the "movements in space" aspect of the earlier alternation). If the animal succeeds more quickly in this new maze, it may be concluded that the learning was coded as *alternation in general* and not as positional-spatial alternation.[13]

It seems indeed then that the analyzer, at work in perception and operating on the basis of available or alerted categories, codes information—in other words, "classifies" it according to kind, organizes it according to categories, sorts, selects, and discriminates against a screen of useful categories. Authors in the field of animal psychology currently talk of "discriminatory capacity," of "cognitive differentiation." So the analyzers would be "discriminating-cognitive analyzers." Theirs is an activity of exploration, always in terms of the organic-ecological structure, capable of perceiving significant abstract relationships in their reality and of analyzing the content of the real.

Let us, incidentally, repudiate any accusation of anthropomorphism. In spite of the vocabulary employed, which bears some traces of the requirements of human reason, it must be admitted that man is a creature of nature and also fated with his existing faculties, comparable *mutatis mutandis* to those of the other species, to a universe that is a permanent source of information and in which he recognizes meanings for him.

Seemingly greater justification would appear to exist for the line of argument according to which the analyzers, both internal and external, effect a *disintegration*. This conception presupposes an image of the universe in which elements are juxtaposed and the analyzing organ makes a choice. But in that case such an explanation would still have to be harmonized with the phenomena of recognition of *Gestalten*, with the notion of the implications of forms, and with sensitivity to modifications of forms when the elements remain constant.

"We have to suppose," to quote Bruner again, "that the organism is capable of sorting things into classes of equivalence, capable of learning the probabilist relation among events belonging to diverse classes, and as it were capable of manipulating these classes or categories by employing a certain formal system of coding."

This, furthermore, is also the technique that we use peda-
gogically. When we teach a six-year-old to add, we try to
make him fix, code, and memorize not the individual figures
that we are compelled to use but the "form" of the act of
adding, the operational structure of addition as intention
and act. This supposes that *by way of the informational
concrete employed he is capable of grasping the abstract
dynamic form of the operation.* The objective of instruction,
Wertheimer said in 1945, is that the child learn the usable
generic code. If we do not accomplish this, we say that the
child has learned in a "mechanical" fashion rather than
through (*insightful*) "understanding."

Cybernetic fabrications of robot animals are constructed
on this same model. Grey Walter wrote, on the subject of
his robots:

The system elaborated here comprises two main groups of operations: one selective, the other constructive. In the latter group
the change of condition brought on by a series of observed coincidences in no way resembles the coincidences themselves; it is
a formal, symbolic change, a signal of signals. When a number
of similar mechanisms operates together, in parallel or in series,
a new aspect of the constructive process appears: abstraction.
The multiple circuits of learning really *draw out of* a selection
of events the characteristics that are common to them in time
and space. In fact, *they recognize a pattern.* In an earlier chapter we had learned that the pattern is difficult of definition except as something susceptible of being memorized.[14]

Here I cannot help going back to the old passage from
Ribot: [15] "Assimilation is the consciousness of resemblances,
an elemental manifestation of the faculty of understanding
that is to be observed even in animals and little children,
the primal source of abstraction and generalization. This
spontaneous aptitude for grasping resemblances is an operation that has nothing to do with association." Again it must
be pointed out that this procedure of assimilation supposes
as well a process of differentiation and that the "work" itself

is in fact a kind of probabilist calculation: "the brain must quietly, carefully, instantly weigh the chances that are in favor of an event or a series of events entailing another," as Grey Walter wrote. Let us add that, through these gropings, the hazards, and the risks, the work of assimilation-differentiation consists in seeking the stable and significant form that makes it possible to construct understanding and action at the same time.

The structural analogy of events, of facts of successive experience, of life situations, is that to which living organisms are sensitive in and through their most primitive perception of their *Umwelt*. Perception, intelligence, and memory are "faculties" artificially separated from one another and artificially separated from the patterns that organize behavior. Just as "the generalization of the signal and the response" [16] is only the expression of the immediate perception of the general form of the event or the situation and of its organic bond with the innate or acquired forms of behavior, so the concept of the "transfer of learning" is an artificial one, for, properly speaking, *nothing is transferred*. The form, the *Gestalt*, the pattern, analyzed and fixed through the content of experience, is automatically set in motion to code and treat events or situations the analogy of which is detected as a function of the same operational system.

To learn is to construct and stabilize a general form. Once it has been constructed, it becomes operative by becoming part of the new system of information analysis and the new range of available behavior patterns. The same form is imposed on varied contents that, to the subject, represent an analogy of structure susceptible of recognition. It is on this principle that the new pedagogical experiments are based, as much at the level of primary education (with Dienes) as on that of reeducation. [17]

In animal psychology (as in human psychology) many facts that have hitherto been connected with the *transfer of learning* can be regarded as instances of application of the acquired system of coding to events or situations as they arise.

Consider the amoeba that withdraws its pseudopod at the chance contact with a drop of acid in its path—a primitive sensitivity, but indispensable to survival, has coded the event as a "mortal danger that must be fled."

Take a riding horse that suddenly shies tremendously, throwing his novice rider and running off at full speed because, in his vigilant exploration, he suddenly noticed a hat that had just been placed on a post a couple of feet from his accustomed path. What to him is the meaning of this perceptive complex that we simply cannot represent to ourselves? Something that determined fear and flight and therefore was coded under the category of "danger" by reason of its unknown and unaccustomed character.

Or imagine a child utterly baffled by his first adventure with a subtraction in which one of the figures in the lower line is larger than that above it. His memorized operational pattern does not recognize the accustomed structure and he has no pattern of treatment, no code, no category in which to place this "form of subtraction." Learning it means being able subsequently to put it to work when he is confronted with another subtraction perceived as belonging to this new category, the emergence of which improves and complicates (by extending its application) the simpler pattern previously drawn from the contents of school experience. The best teaching, then, would on the contrary consist in letting him first discover the more general pattern, the more basic whole from which differentiations will later have to be drawn.[18]

Modern studies on conceptualization as an operation of understanding encounter the same procedures, with this difference that, in the analysis of content achieved by the animal's perceptive analyzers (which are apperception of structures feeding a mechanism of probabilist elaboration), recognized, recognizable, or sought forms exist only in reference to the organism's structure at the given moment.

Man's structural analyzers

The study of human perception seems to confirm the hypotheses that animal psychology is impelled to propound with respect to the existence and functioning of "analyzers of forms." These analyzers are believed to be capable of coding information on the basis of a set of innate or acquired categories and, by reason of this coding, of "categorizing" information.

The conclusions of animal psychology accord with the principles on which the robots of cybernetics are constructed. Thus far, however, there has been a tendency to separate the phenomenon of *perception* into two levels. On the purely sensory level, according to this school, there is "reception" of external stimuli and at a "central" level there is an "elaboration" of the stimuli. In this one can see a kind of resurgence of the old theory (which phenomenology thought that it had finally destroyed) according to which meanings were the result of a higher elaboration that interpreted, memorized, understood, and objectivized sensory data.

Under the pressure of experience it must be admitted not only that "the organism plays an active part in the elaboration of stimuli" and that "excitation is never the passive recording of an outside action, because it is an elaboration of these influences by the norms of the organism," [19] but also that there is no elaboration *separate from perception*, which is the essential activity of the external and internal analyzers and categorizes information.

"Undoubtedly," Merleau-Ponty wrote, "the receptors—or their central projection—are competent to record *the properties of form* of the stimuli, which, far more than the place and the character of the excitant, determine the reaction."

It is this hypothesis that is confirmed, and it is not easy

to understand the difficulty experienced by students in pur-
suing the consequences of this idea to their conclusion. The
obstacle, as we shall see, arises out of the *strictly unconscious* character of this mechanism in *human* perception and
out of the fact that the psychologists give too exclusive
attention to the specific properties of human consciousness,
which are unique in evolution, namely, the perception of
the present and of the "qualitative content of the present"
as such, of the present "individualized" at once in the passage of time and in the subjectivity of an ego.

Let us go back to Merleau-Ponty's cautious hypothesis
and carry it to its conclusion. *The analyzers* (formerly called
sense organs or receptors) *are capable of detecting and recording the properties of form of received or sought information; it is these forms that will determine reactions.*

This would immediately explain the fact that the typical
reflexes are limited in number, for the "content" of excitations may vary without any variation in the response itself
when their "form," their structure (their category-in-rela-
tion-to-the-categories-of-the-organism) is the same. It has
been found that the cat's ear, for example, is sensitive to
only five kinds of excitation corresponding to five different
reflex responses. Every organism proceeds in an analogous
fashion on all levels of its adaptation (the level of "instincts
and reflexes" corresponds to the specific biological structuration of the relations between the organism and its environment). In its intentionality as a living thing—that is, in
its biological relation with its environment—every organism
has "analyzers of the structure of information" through
whose action stimuli have *a meaning* for the organism, however primitive it may be. This is what Sherrington verified
and called "the biological value of the stimulus." That is
why the *adequate stimulus* cannot be defined in itself independently of the organism. In fact it is not a physical reality but a reality of experience. "The excitation of the organism is already a response," as Merleau-Ponty put it,[20] because it is an active categorization and at the same time

an embryo of the kind of reaction. This should go beyond the purely physical hypothesis of the *Gestalt* theory in its first historic statement, which reduced the receivers to being passive recorders.

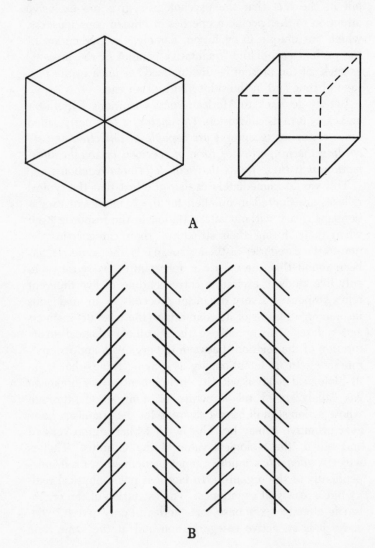

A

B

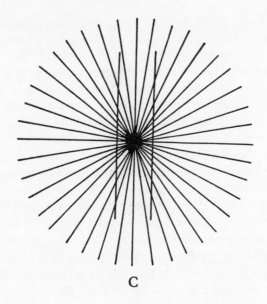

C

Fig. 11

EXAMPLES OF STRUCTURES OF CORRELATION

A. Two cubes. The regular hexagonal *Gestalt* dominates in the figure on
   the right.
B. Perceptory illusion. By construction the vertical lines are parallel.
C. Perceptory illusion. By construction the vertical lines are parallel.
The organization of the perceptive field is an active structuration starting from the level that is seemingly the most characterized by passive
reception.

In the second of his *Untersuchungen zur Lehre von der
Gestalt* (*Studies in the Lessons of Gestalt*), Wertheimer
offered a lucid description of the various factors facilitating
the structuration of perceptive data; for the greater part,
these factors (such as proximity, resemblance, continuity of
direction, isolation, symmetry, regularity, etc.) are furnished
by characteristics of a phenomenal nature—in other words,
by objective, physical qualities of configuration and structuration. (See Figure 11.)

Wertheimer falls back as well on another factor, the
Faktor der Erfahrung, the factor of experience. All other

things being equal, he says, structures that are *habitual* in our experience are organized "more easily and better than others in the perceptive field." Kohler spoke of "field," thus foreshadowing Lewin, but he mentioned only physical structuration, natural segmentation. Now it is clear, if one is willing to put aside the metaphysical *a priori*, that it is the subject himself that is the agent of structuration of the field, or, more precisely, of his experienced field.

"It is the activity of our perception that structures the field, in terms of tendencies, the first of which is the tendency to identity as a perceptive constant begetting the stability of forms," Musatti wrote.[21] It might be said that the active identification of forms and the categorical discrimination of types of information is a "primary tendency," or, more precisely, the fundamental operation of the analyzers, corresponding not only to the stability of the adaptation to the environment but also, for that and through that, to a *biological economy*. That there are real external forms seems undeniable, since without them the effort at adaptation would be impossible. The rhythm of night and day, the seasons, and to the same extent the differences in appearance among animals and in color and odor among vegetables are form that, insofar as they are stable, are not only of our human *Umwelt*. In this world of forms each inhabitant picks out his significant groups in terms of his specific or individual categories, and thus an economic organization of existence is brought into being and stabilized.

Reinstated in its realistic context of an exploratory scouting activity, perception expresses the continuing effort to learn the structure of experience, without which survival (adapted reaction) is not possible even for a moment. Through a process of permanent feedback, the probabilist categories employed are harmonized in the stabilization of a formal system of situations-behavior patterns.

The very numerous laws of perception thus far discovered reflect and codify the varied modalities of this effort at useful discrimination. Let us take a few samplings of it at random.

Gottschaldt's experiments demonstrated that the knowledge of a distinct object as a separate form cannot stand up when that object or that form is incorporated into a context such that a new segmentation of the perceptive image is produced. The animal and military art of camouflage is proof of this. Gottschaldt taught human subjects to recognize an isolated shape; then he "disguised" that shape by plunging it into a complex that was organized structurally in a different and individual fashion. If the "disguise" was effective, the old shape was never recognized (even though it was in front of the subject's eyes), and this was true regardless of the strength of the acquired habit. This shows that perception picks out its forms according to the implications of the perceptive field. But, if the subject is forewarned that a previously isolated form is present in the field, then a "specific expectation" is set up and it counterbalances the influence of the camouflage. This active, informed anticipation "rediscovers" the separable form in the real. Here is the principle of the "riddles in pictures" that diverted my childhood. When we thus bring to bear on the exploration of a riddle picture an attention informed by a previously alerted formal category, we should and we can isolate any whole capable of "answering" this directed search. Whence the experiences of "resistance to change" in the real when the anticipation or the search of a form is very active. (Cf. Figures 12, 13a, b.)

Similarly, in certain affective systems, we shall see that themes mobilized on a lasting basis as active categories of perception are capable of "recognizing" their structures in information deriving from the environment, however little the offered structure lends itself to this. In cases of extreme activation, these same forms can thematize any given reality and the subject thinks that he perceives (or, more precisely, perceives with a feeling of inherent certitude of objectivity) what he is expecting (hoping for or fearing).

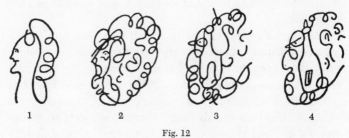

Fig. 12

Depending whether the subject views these four images successively
from 1 to 4 or from 4 to 1, the image of the face or that of the bottle will
persist longer in the second and third images.

It has also been established that the human experience
of pain and frustration produces a sharp change in the perceptive activity of the analyzers of the structures of the
situational data. This change itself seems organized by the
function of adaptative protection and exploration that is the
obscure, biological intentionality of all perception. It is ex-
perimentally demonstrable that relatively moderate pain
accelerates subsequent perception by alerting the analyzers
to a particular structure, especially when the conditions of
the experiment enable the subject to avoid or attenuate the
shock by perceiving quickly. The most severe pain, or the
shock that can be neither anticipated nor avoided, produces
a disturbance in perception as if the subject were curbed
by fear.

Going back to the experiments of Bruner and Postman,
Vernon [22] defined two types of subjects from this point of
view: the "perceptually sensitized," who perceive more
quickly, and the "perceptually defensive," who perceive
more slowly. The "objective" differences in the intensity of
the shock or the pain are augmented in fact by individual
differences in "threshold" as a result of which the subject
moves more or less quickly from accelerating discriminatory
alert to inhibiting defensive.

Frustration has equally curious effects. Postman and

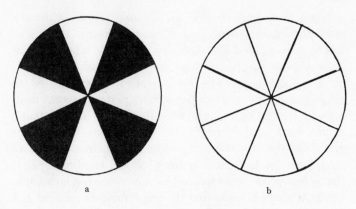

a   b

Fig. 13

The coloration in *a* creates a phenomenon of "background figure" that is
not perceived in *b*.

Fig. 13B

Classic illustration of background image: cup or two profiles?

Brown,[23] in an experiment that is already dated (1952),
showed that the very category of success or frustration was
mobilized on the basis of past successes or failures. The
experimenters placed their human subjects in a situation of
tension with respect to a value-laden task, asking them to

estimate their performance in advance. Then (after the tests) the subjects were divided into two groups: those who had underestimated the difficulty and those who had succeeded. Next the two groups were presented with *words* on a tachistoscope. The list included words related to achievement (success, excellence, win, perfect), words dealing with frustration (failure, difficulty, losing, incompetent), neuter words, and even words of competition. The subjects perceived the words corresponding to their estimates of their performances more quickly on the tachistoscope. If the tachistoscope was replaced by a memory test on various words, it could be seen that the same subjects recalled first of all the words that fell in the category of their performance.

In this experiment the tachistoscope was timed so that each word appeared only long enough for a rapid reader. The experiment deteriorated when the stimuli were produced at such a speed that attentive legibility was made impossible, as in the researches of Lazarus and McCleary: [24]

Human subjects were conditioned by electric shock to certain syllables *without meaning;* other syllables were learned without shock. Then the two lists were shown commingled on the tachistoscope at a speed *within the limits of legibility* while the subjects' hands were connected to the psychogalvanic machine in order to measure their emotional responses. It was shown that there was a psychogalvanic response when syllables that had been accompanied by the conditioning appeared on the tachistoscope.

It seems then that for human existence there is a possibility of differentiation among data *that precedes conscious perception* and that an activity of analysis of content takes place at this level and is adequate to distribute the data between two categories: "danger" and "not danger." The nonsense syllables (in terms of language) had thus acquired a significance in and through their membership in one or the other of these categories, in and through the coding performed by the analyzer.

We will come back later to these experiments on the pre-cognitive level of perception that for ten years have made vital contributions to the study of depth personality.

Going beyond pain and frustration, studies have been made in order to evaluate the influence of needs on human perception, and findings quite comparable to those in animal psychology have been published with respect to the operative dynamic of unconscious codes or categories.

In certain experiments [25] a variety of pictures of a number of familiar objects, including, among others, some connected with food, were shown at different intervals after the last previous meal. It was established that the number of objects related to eating increased when the interval was six or more hours since the previous meal, then decreased subsequently while the lack of response rose. If, among other words, words relating to food and drink [26] are shown to subjects prevented from eating and drinking for various lengths of time, a decrease in the time required for perception will be observed when the deprivation has lasted for more than ten hours, but this perception time will rise again if the deprivation has exceeded twenty-four hours; and, finally, there will be reactional apathy and silence.

The interaction between, on the one hand, the "need" or the anticipation and, on the other, active perception seems to be complex. Perception is all the more oriented as the satisfaction of the need becomes not only more urgent but also visibly more likely.

Experiments have also been made in conditioning to "themes" that have not been stated but that justify the choice of "contents," in this instance words that are at first glance various. It has been observed that the theme itself is identified at a nonconscious level, to such a point that, in subsequent tests of sentences to be completed or word gaps to be filled, the theme thus learned was mobilized and put to use.[27]

If the themes in question are affective leitmotivs of the

personality, the experiment succeeds even more. For in-stance,[28] subjects were asked to reply to a value question-naire in which they expressed their individual value hier-archies (aesthetic, religious, social, emotional) or their in-terests (scientific, philosophic, masculine-feminine, manual-intellectual, etc.). Next they were subjected to a tachisto-scope experiment with a series of words, some of which be-longed to the groups identified. This furnished proof that they more quickly perceived words related to their own values.

It has been objected (Solomon and Henry) that the great-est perceptual speed was to be noted with words that, through the very construction of the experiment, were the most familiar. But the *familiarity* of certain words, like the *frequency* of certain words in ordinary speech, is indicative, without the subject's knowing it, of the themes that are his, the categories that he uses in order to discriminate among and distribute information or expression.

Thus one progresses quite naturally toward the hypoth-esis that a subject's *attitudes* toward life or toward other persons are necessarily and closely linked not only with the corresponding classes of feelings, opinions, and beliefs—or, in other words, with the affective constants of the felt and lived relation—but also with the unconscious categories *of perception*, with the *a priori* system of coding set in motion by his information analyzers.

On the plane of social relations it appears that those whom we like and those whom we do not like are not perceived in the same way.* It has been possible experi-mentally to ascertain the hyper-accentuation of perception of stereotyped signal details (physiognomy, shape of the

* In his 1965 book Vernon [22] raised once more the old question whether this was not rather a "judgment" than perception itself. Unquestionably Taine's ideas are incisive, as much as the definition of perception as the passive reception of an external *datum*. In the traditional theory the action of the analyzers could be understood only under the aspect of the intervention of a judgment, the only classic concept capable of expressing an act and a categorizing operation.

nose, thickness of the lips, texture of skin, etc.) among the
antagonists of an ethnic group (haters of Jews, Blacks,
Arabs, Frenchmen, etc.). The inter-ethnic differences between the hater's group and the hated group are accentu-
ated at the perceptive level, whereas the inter-individual
differences within the hated group are minimized. Conversely, the perception of the persons in an accepted group
is more differentiated; that is, individual differences are
noticed spontaneously.

The influence of the group can also make itself felt in
the form of pure and simple suggestion, quite differently
from the influence of stereotypes and social attitudes. The
classic experiment of "auto-kinetic movement" is illustrative
of the phenomenon; it deals with the illusory perception of
the movement of a motionless point of light in a dark room.
If one asks a group placed in the dark room the size and
the direction of movement of the point of light visible at
a distance, the responses are positive (the point is perceived
as moving in a specific direction) and very similar from
one subject to another. The responses show considerable
difference when the subjects are questioned after they have
entered the dark room individually.

Differences in perception that arise from cultural differences have also been thoroughly investigated. To mention
only one example, it has been demonstrated that non-Euro-
pean and non-acculturated groups (Black, Bantu, and In-
dian populations) could not perceive designs constructed
on traditional European criteria and that they interpreted
the images on a single plane.[29] Conversely, our accustomed
categories that structure perception in perspective can be
brought into play by experiments in deception, veritable
decoys of our knowledge, as the American transactionalist
school proved in the work of Kilpatrick and his collaborators and as Jean Beuchet showed in France (Psychological Laboratory of Rennes). "Will power" is as impotent as
judgment in "rectifying" the perception. (Cf. Figures 14a
and 14b.)

Fig. 14

The picture represents Ames' "distorted room." The child on the right appears to be a giant a few steps away from the adult on the left. The reason is that perception is incapable of correcting the distortion of the context in which (and in relation to which) the figures are placed.

Fig. 14B

(a) Mock-up of Ames' trick room. A double distortion "explains" the illusions.

(b) Outline of the room's "floor."

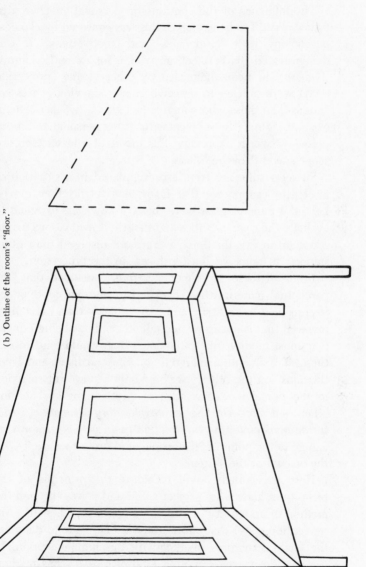

The influence of the constants in personal affective attitudes was still to be explored; this was confused by classical
psychology with "tendencies" and "motivations." It was
demonstrated that subjects in whom, for example, aggressiveness had been diagnosed by other means (projection
tests) were quicker to perceive images showing aggressive
actions than those whose aggressiveness was weaker or nonexistent.[30] Similarly, subjects with strong personal ambitions
perceived words expressing this theme at a lesser tachistoscope speed than the others.

Subjects suffering from anxiety, placed in a situation of
insecurity (supposing that faces seen full as they moved
behind a pane of glass were those of observers assigned to
evaluate their personalities and that these evaluations would
count in an examination), were more disposed than other
subjects to perceive "hostile faces" in the procession.

From all these experiments Vernon concluded that "the
perceptual material that is related to personal motivations
is perceived more easily and more quickly than perceptual
material that is not so related, all other things being equal."
One must modify this statement, which would tend to distinguish "perceptual material" on the one hand and "motivations" on the other, ascribing only a power of selection
to the perceiving consciousness. Motivations are nothing
other than *categories that arm exploratory perception, structuring or deciphering information in an active fashion* that
can go to the point of "distorting" it in order to code it with
the arsenal of the system.

Here psychologists will recognize the principle of the
techniques known as "projective," [31] and it was through the
method of ambiguity of stimuli (Rorschach, Thematic Apperception tests) that efforts were at first made to diagnose
the latent structures of affectivity through perception. In
the past dozen years another kind of research has made it
possible to go farther. In particular the American psychologists who constitute the "new look" group [32] have used the

tachistoscope with stimuli of reduced intensity. They have been able to arrive at important concepts on the "styles" of the personality, characterizing the individual through a variety of perceptive situations. Then one sees that *there exist perceptual stages that precede the final stage of correct recognition*—in other words, that there exist nonconscious precognitive levels that are approach routes enhanced by the dynamics of the personality. Once more experience has proved that "perception can no longer be regarded as a mere imprint of the object on a passive sensory organ" and that on the contrary the basic, constant affective attitudes, or style of the depth personality, are in close correlation with the preperceptive structures, to such a point that the attitudes lead to the structures.

The structures of affectivity, as *a priori* forms of perception at the precognitive level and as obstacles to the objectivity of knowledge, are as such *contributors of experienced meanings* and at the same time they are determinants of reactional or complementary forms of behavior.

Thus analyzers of structures of meaning function in perception and employ a system of coding that varies with individuals and that on the affective level expresses or signifies in its turn the profound dynamics of the personality.

From the purely perceptual point of view these matrix-like analyzers are essential to the recognition of forms and the categorization of information, and, if their functioning is disturbed, curious phenomena result. This perhaps is the explanation of the problems known under such names as *aphasia* and *apraxia* and generally classified in the broader class of the *agnosias*. In aphasia the patient no longer understands words, can no longer give the names of objects that he can describe in detail, cannot articulate speech, cannot set in motion the organization of the movements of pronunciation. In certain cases the structure of the sentence as a modulation and as a grammatical construction eludes him because he has lost his grip on the systems of relations among words. In still other forms it is "thought" itself that seems to flee. The patient cannot organize a reply to a question or summarize a story.

In the apraxias it is the regulating patterns of meaningful movements that elude control, and in the *agnosias* "the intelligence of meaning," the "significance of groups," of bodily postures, of attitudes, of relations of meanings, "symbolism" is lost.

All this seems to demonstrate that damage to the "analyzers" is not to be looked for on the sensory level properly so called but on the level of what their name really denotes —that is, the analysis of structures of meaning and the possession of discriminatory coding. Perception has in such cases lost its innate codes.

Earlier, referring to the ideas of Head and others, Goldstein and Gelb [33] were induced to think in terms of a loss of "categorizing activity," and they emphasized *the categorizing act in its relations with attitude*. As Merleau-Ponty has also said, it is not concepts that are lost but "the subject's establishment of positions in the world of his meanings." But everything seems to indicate that the loss of these points expresses the dysfunction or the destruction of the analyzers of structure, the influence of which we have shown.

Analysis of content and treatment of information

If the neuro-perceptive analyzers are thus adapted to coding the content of information, why not draw a parallel between the *analysis of content* as it is employed as a method of examination of information in social psychology and the biological processes that operate in an analogous manner on a preperceptive level? "Analysis of content," in social psychology, is the term applied to a combination of

methods systematically endeavoring to find and categorize
the meaning of any piece of information (external data, a
newspaper, a book, a speech, etc.).

The parallel appears chancy and runs the risk of anthropomorphism, but one is entitled too to think that the
psychosocial method is the intellectual and objective perfec-
tion of a natural process. From a comparison of this kind
it might even be possible to anticipate a clarification of the
two terms, the more precise comprehension of each contributing to the understanding of the other.

Furthermore, we shall have the opportunity to show that
psychotherapy and so-called comprehensive interviews, in
order to assure the penetration of the patient's subjective
universe and to identify its structures or its axioms, necessarily ought to proceed to a genuine analysis of content of
the subject's spontaneous expression in his attempt to ver-
balize what he feels.

It seems necessary to me, in order to bring a little order
into the many directions from which meaning springs, to
distinguish the levels of articulated meanings among one
another.

If one considers the classic method of analysis of content
in social psychology,[34] one sees that it entails the methodical
determination of *categories* with which and in which the
"elements" of information have to be classified. The determination of the categories is accomplished during a constant
oscillation between hypothetical categories that are part of
an *a priori* systematization, on the one hand, and the very
information that conveys a meaning to the degree to which
it has a semantic or "objective" structures of meanings.
Hence it is a *categorizing attitude* that is required in the
investigator in every way, and the techniques proposed consist in grasping the information from one angle of attack
or another. Since this is the case, it is easy to situate in
different techniques of approach what also represents different levels of depth (and difficulty). (Cf. Table B, The
Analysis of Content.)

TABLE A

Definition of Levels of Meaning

MEANINGS OF SIGNS THEMSELVES	Elements representing a group of objects, a conceptual whole, symbolic of a semantic domain in relation to which they have or may have meaning.	• Constitute the object of a possible catalogue. • Constitute the lexicon, the repertory of every operation.
MEANING IN RELATION TO A CONTEXT	Meaning properly so called, emerging from the current system of relationships introduced into (or, on the other hand, observed in) a sequence or a group of signs. Relative meaning in an organized whole.	• "Horizontal" meaning. • Direct object of probabilist exploration. • Structure of a correlative type giving meaning.
MEANING IN RELATION TO THE STRUCTURES OF SIGNIFICANCE OF THE SUBJECT	"Latent" meaning of the immediate content or immediate datum. Refers to latent structures. Goes back to knowledge of these structures. Expresses the subject himself.	• "Vertical" meaning; • Symbols; • Prior or constant structuration of consciousness in its previous operation. • Nonconscious as a result of spontaneous orientation of consciousness toward the outside or toward its own contents.
UNCONSCIOUS SIGNIFICANT STRUCTURES	Structuring structures that determine the previous meaning. Constituents of the subject himself or of the organism as an ecological and historical reality.	• Organizing patterns of the vertical meaning. • Discoveries of the forms of immediate content through the structural analysis of the latent meaning.

So we see that it is a matter of carrying out intellectually (and intelligently) an analysis of information that consists in neglecting certain aspects of the content in order to place emphasis on others as *significant,* in looking for the significant modes of the expression itself, or the ideas, or the

TABLE B

Comparison of Levels of Meaning According
to Different Sectors

	Psychophysical perceptive Gestalten	Intellection of the perceptive datum	Science	Depth personality	Analysis of content
SIGNS	Sensory objective elements.	Words with their respective semantic domains or signs or concepts.	Scientific symbols.	Objective events or events experienced as such.	Search for words. Statistics of vocabulary.
MEANING IN RELATION TO A CONTEXT	Perceptual *Gestalt* as totally perceived structure of correlation.	Context properly so called, as intelligible total datum.	Scientific formula indicative of a phenomenon or a theorem.	Experienced situation as a whole charged with immediate meaning and in relation to personal existence as history.	Search for expressed ideas.
MEANING IN RELATION TO STRUCTURES OF SIGNIFICANCE	Law of realization of this immediate *Gestalt* in relation to the level next below.	Latent modes of construction of the meaning of this content.	Implicit system of conceptualization.	Symbolic themes of the immediate situation in relation to the subject's affective-postural constants.	Search for affective themes and values.
UNCONSCIOUS SIGNIFICANT STRUCTURES	Neuro-physiopsychological structure of perception. Ecological structures of perception as activity.	Nonconscious principles governing organization of the signified universe.	Operations of objectifying reason.	Subject's postural structures. Nonthought experienced depth attitudes.	Search for unconscious postulates in their relations with the author's experience.

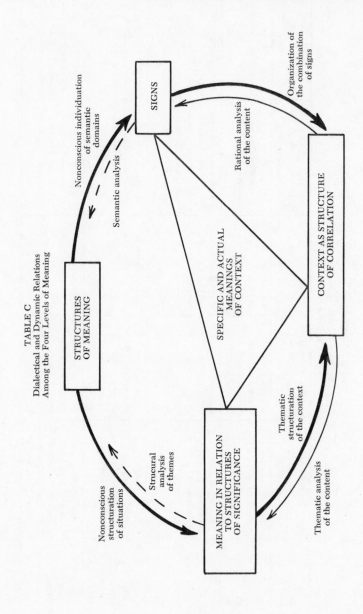

TABLE C
Dialectical and Dynamic Relations
Among the Four Levels of Meaning

themes and values, or the unconscious postulates through which the elements of information are distributed. These are *formal constants* * that are aimed for, retained, and classified.

With each unit of information the method consists in applying the categorical analysis that, in its first movement, leads to hypothetical meanings to the extent to which several systems of coding would be applicable. In proportion to the growth in information, the hypotheses are eliminated and stable categories appear; these are really (or as approximately as possible) the vehicles through which the information signifies something.

We have seen earlier (cf. page 7), in connection with the analysis of content of an ordinary newspaper headline, the system of meanings that was expressed and the "categories" the examination of which gave meaning to the news of a chance occurrence. The generalized character of these categories is striking. When successive information from the same source is accumulated or superimposed, it is as if each item became a variation on a common theme or on a certain number of determined themes, more or less hierarchically organized into a system that has its repetitive structure expressed in its dominating values, its principles, its axioms, its symbols.

We become involved with a lasting structure—here again let us say a "signifier"—the concrete expressions of which could be multiplied and from which in every way they draw their meanings.

Now, astonishing as it may seem, we encounter here, if on a much inferior level, the same operations performed by the analyzers of the living organism. Long ago biologists stressed what they called the organism's "function of assimilation." "Such organs as the digestive tract and its accessories, or the respiratory apparatus, have as their 'raw mate-

* It is obvious that *formal* here has nothing to do with the notion of literary "form" and means significant structure or structures isolated by filtering the content.

rial' the elements of energy that they extract from the air or from food. With these elements extracted from its environment the organism, through specific operations, carries out chemical syntheses the products of which are necessary to its life. But there is another raw material that the organism receives from the external environment in the same way as the elements of energy, and this is information" (see Couffignal, *op. cit.*), and with the same goal of survival, of growth of its being or stabilization of its way of living, the organism is capable of *processing information* by sorting it, seeking structures of biological meanings in it, combining its elements into syntheses, retaining what is thus acquired.

The analysis of information, the memorization of its products, the utilization of what is thus gained for the analysis of further information, even the making of decisions, as Grey Walter explains, are the operations of a "function of mentality" (the name given by him to a kind of reasoning, intelligence, and memory on a poorly differentiated archaic level) that exists as early as the biological level, as soon as a structured organism has any relation with a universe of significances and signals. Let us not forget that this combination of "mental" functions was realized by Grey Walter in his robots through cybernetic circuits. Nothing would be able to function (no living being would be able to survive) if in one manner or another it was not capable of "perceiving" not frequently fortuitous and always (at least potentially) new contents but *the formal and structural analogies* of various situations and various items of information.

Now no informational operation, no utilization of information, no learning, no construction of types of behavior would be possible without the prior operation of analysis of content. *The connection* between the processes of biological perception and intelligence has already been emphasized by many experimenters. As early as 1954 Starling Read showed that "the degree of mastery of the situation by experimental animals depends on the validity of the *generic coding*" [35] and from this J. S. Bruner derived the

following *law:* "When a system of information coding is
condensed into more generic codes, the problem of situation
mastery becomes that of mastery of the coding system rather
than that of mastery of the new combination of events."

The process of discovering what is generic in a given situation, in such a way that similar situations can be handled
later (in other words, so that their solutions may be known
without having to learn once more), consists essentially, to
quote Bruner again, in the capacity *to isolate the definite
characteristics of the class of events* to which the instant
case belongs. Beach too in 1954 had shown that this process
of abstraction can be assimilated to the process of intelligence in higher organisms.

Thus perceptive activity is above all a quest for information, an active quest, a genuine biological intentionality, a
groping exploration, an unceasing vital search like that of
those always moving antennae, those eyes that extrude like
tentacles in their thrust to encounter reality. This quest,
determined by the tension of disequilibrium between the
living organism and its environment, is already *informed* in
a certain fashion by innate structure and by what has been
learned. This search is selective; it can be excited by categories of situations or by forms of signals, themselves necessarily bound to an overall situation that they foreshadow
or designate. These *a priori* forms are matched by patterns
of postural or motor responses, and that is why *it is impossible to establish the "generalization of excitation" without
the "generalization of a response."* (Bachelard, *op. cit.*)

This architectural scheme of dynamic forms of perception
and reaction "digests" information in direct ratio to its reception. In this way *representative contents* become *significant.* What is represented of reality is augmented too by
what it represents for the animal or human subject.

So there is analysis of information (received, sought, or
found), and through the effect of analyzers operating by
means of a constant calculation of categorical probabilities.
This is *the* work of the nervous system, for exploration and

analysis go together, coding taking place in and through perception, in and through those "sense organs" that are extensions of the nervous system and at the same time selectors, captors, and analyzers of information.

Some activity of *generic coding* of everything that constitutes the *Umwelt* is found in the humblest of living organisms and in the highest activities of comprehension employing the superior faculties of the human brain. Generic coding—in other words, categorization by class, the identification and memorization of abstract forms, constellations of relationships, etc.—is an activity of conceptualization.

The most varied animals [Otto Koehler wrote] abstract sensorily in their perception as it is contended that we could do only with the help of words. From this it must be inferred that we have also inherited from the animals the faculty of sensory abstraction, a "faculty" that is as much part of their thinking capacity as of ours. And nothing prevents us from turning the coin and saying that it is our faculty of sensory abstraction that has enabled us to form sounds, for the concept has to be there before one feels the need to identify it.[36]

Bruner, analyzing the activity of the intelligence in the construction of theoretical hypotheses and formal laws in the sciences, wrote: "The activity of constructing formal models and general theories is the prototype of what we mean by *generic coding*, which makes it possible to go beyond facts to fruitful prediction." [37]

And Georges Bouligand, without the slightest allusion to the modern acquisitions in animal psychology or in cybernetics, analyzed the general processes of thought through the conceptualizing activity of the mathematician and concluded:

From its first glimmers thought has been able to govern itself, employing the constant support of memory, preserving in an "instinctive" fashion (just as it did for dawn and dusk) innumerable *recurrences of typical situations*. More or less conscious, this manner of mental exploration has contributed no less to the ascent of the mind. Side by side with *mnemonic aptitude,* a *predicting aptitude* has gradually developed, beginning with qualitative forecasts.[88]

Learning consists in abstracting and stabilizing a form, a pattern, through experiences, trial and error, successes and failures; and, as we have seen, the famous *transfer of learning* is nothing but the mastery of the generic code that makes it possible to deal with structurally analogous situations.

"Experience" in the broad sense—that of the old professional, for example—is the mastery of the system of categorization of corresponding situations and adapted schemes of action, and that is what is called know-how. The beginner's disorientation arises from the fact that he possesses no code by which to categorize new information and no pattern of response.

Modern methods of training that employ *simulation models* seek the accelerated construction of a generic code making it possible to cope with situations for which, according to certain rules,[39] the model reproduces the common analogous structure and thus to construct at the same time the adapted attitudes for effective response to them.

The concept is what is created during the struggle between the organism and its environment and it designates a category of phenomena or a complex of concrete data through the identification of what is thought to be the principle of their common characteristics. Hence it is the product of generic coding quite as much as, in the quest and processing of further information, it is an active category that forms part of the code and makes it possible to differentiate data. It develops naturally in its value for real knowledge when one goes from the correlative perceptive coding of the structure of an organism to the scientific activity that, though a deliberate decentration, endeavors to code the objective structures of phenomena with minimum reference to their subjective or personal meaning for the investigator himself, and, as a general rule, *against* this experienced meaning.[40]

Memory, abstraction-generalization, organization of behavior patterns-responses, all are operations that are consubstantially part of the operation of generic coding and that are encountered at all stages of evolution as at all levels of existence of a human subject. So there is a "conceptualization" of this kind at the level of the most physiological conditionings, where the categorization of stimuli and reactions can be observed; there is one at the affective level, in the coding of experienced situations, a coding that extracts and preserves their structure of meanings and that corresponds to the construction of *affective attitudes,* active centers of categorization and of behavior patterns or postures of response. And there is one, not to mention more, at the properly *abstract* level, according to Goldstein's terminology,[41] where the individual, having become *capable of suspending his affective categorization,* can reorganize his behavior in terms of an objective understanding of situations perceived in the present. "The individual is [then] capable," Goldstein says, "of regarding the situation from various points of view, of choosing the essential aspect, and of acting in a direction adapted to the total situation."

Here one anticipates the objective of psychotherapy, the methodical work of which will be aimed at the demythification of the *Umwelt* and, as a consequence, a change in behavior in the direction of a better adaptation to the present.

THREE

The Logic of the Emotions

Affective existence as a coherent structural whole

Leibnitz said that most of the dissension among men arose from the fact that they did not agree on the meanings of words. Stern, followed by Ribot, thought that dissension resulted from the fact that men ascribed different emotions to words. Undoubtedly he was saying the same thing. The illusory identity of the language used conceals varying systems of personal meanings in relation to which words acquire a meaning the more individual in that the expression of experience is in question.

It is possible to imagine, with Leibnitz, a kind of semantic Utopia in which, if language were rationalized in order to make it a logistics of expression, the result would be a universal inter-human harmony composed of understanding and clarity. But such a hope only negatively emphasizes the universality of the misunderstanding and the density of individual affective universes.

Contrasting the systematization and the unity of objective or scientific knowledge with what he called "the logic of the emotions," Ribot concluded that the affective life was an anarchic proliferation of "tendencies." "Left to itself," he wrote,[1] "the affective life adjusts very easily to the plurality of tendencies and even to their anarchy. Unity is not essential to its nature and penetrates into it only through the predominance of one passion or through an intellectual intrusion that imposes order."

This is a generally accepted point of view. As a rule the obscure life of the affective level is imagined as an underbrush of varied and contradictory "impulses," into which it is precisely reason and will that must introduce order and control. The image of reference for this ingenuous conception is that of a class of children in which multiple and irreconcilable egocentric desires are expressed in confusion and disorder unless the teacher's social authority is there to impose discipline and thus assure quiet, contemplation, and good behavior.

The terms employed can only reinforce this imagery; one speaks of "instincts," "tendencies," "impulses," "desires," "affective forces," "emotional or sentimental drives," "conflict of tendencies," while the very word *self-control* implies a kind of voluntary mastery of these obscure forces almost in the same sense as constant maintenance of firm control over a vicious horse through the use of the reins and the knees.

It is certain that, from the point of view of reason, of "objective" judgment—in other words, in this instance external and detached—the affectivity *of others* seems most often to us to be incoherent, but the truism is commonplace: It merely emphasizes the fact that affectivity is irrational— in other words, that it is not of the realm of reason. This is not altogether a surprise. A game is made out of separating and contrasting the two domains. "One is often astonished,"

Ribot wrote,[2] "to see a superior mind, disciplined in the austere methods of the sciences, accept in religion, politics, or morality an infantile view that he would not condescend to discuss for even a second if it were not his."

This curious *resistance* in opinions, beliefs, and other realities charged with affectivity should direct attention not only to the acknowledged fact that every human being "stands on" his emotions, however irrational they be, but also to the fact that these affect-charged realities "stand firm" among themselves like a peculiar concatenation the principle of which remains obscure even to the thinking of the subject involved.

Certain "affective" states, again from the unsophisticated point of view of common sense, are thought to escape the incoherent multiplicity of tendencies and impulses; such would be the pathological or prepathological states. Speaking of passionate love as well as any passion (the passion for gambling, voracious ambition, avarice, etc.), Ribot said: "This case is alien to logic, unless one means the organized, enduring, unconscious logic of *instinct*. A more accurate comparison would be that with abnormal cases of the monopolization of consciousness by a basic, fixed, immutable idea, the uncritical acceptance of everything favorable to it, and the exclusion of everything opposed to it."

Hence, according to Ribot, there would be systematization and unity at the level of affective life only in the case of the conquest of consciousness or of all the so-called higher functions by a dominating, exclusive desire that annihilates critical thought and freedom of behavior and that takes over for its benefit alone the whole of the "tendential energies." Apart from the pathological (or almost pathological) cases, affective existence is a swarming mass of obscure forces.

Let us point out that it was not psychoanalysis that was to educate the common view on this point through a better description of reality. "It is quite justifiable," Freud wrote,[3] "to say that the psychoanalyst's medical activity can be compared to the chemist's work, and this analogy stimulates us to open new roads to our therapeutic. We have *analyzed* the patient—that is, we have broken down his psychic activity into its component parts in order subsequently to isolate *each of its driving elements.*" This conception (which completely ignores structures) is elementarist and associationist; it is regarded as "dynamist" because it treats the "psychic elements" as elementary *forces* or as "energies." In consequence the deep affective life, the life of what Freud called the "unconscious," is supposedly a nest of "drives" striving to become action by taking possession of the ego—in other words, of behavior. In a brilliant summary of the Freudian conception, Collette [4] interpreted "the four basic characteristics of the unconscious" in this way:

1. The unconscious contains * only irrational forces obedient to no conscious control and immune to all inner and outer logic. These forces are subject neither to time nor to reality; they exist through themselves.
2. The forces in the unconscious form an undifferentiated whole, at least in their initial state. As potential, as unrealized energy, not linked to a specific final end, they afford infinite possibilities of differentiation that can lead to very different paths of action.
3. All unconscious processes are subject to the *pleasure principle*,† and this excludes moral problems and implies flight from lack of satisfaction.
4. The various forces in the unconscious have no direct relation with one another and exist independently of one another. But these forces do not come into conflict with one another even if their final goals are conflicting.

There could be no finer description of that zoo, the Freudian unconscious, outside consciousness, separated,

* Note the phraseology, "The unconscious *contains* . . ."—a formulation that makes the unconscious a container, a receptacle, a place, a storehouse.

† It should be remembered that in Freudian coding the "pleasure principle" means "demand for immediate satisfaction."

censured, fragmented into a myriad of blind, exigent forces thrusting with all their dynamism against the barriers that the conscious ego attempts to erect (even though it has no energy of its own available to it). Thus there is the danger of the perpetuation of an image of the "affective depths," a picture of a polymorphous-perverse world of incoherent impulses.

If one really wants to come back to the real and observe it methodically, one recognizes on the contrary that in a certain manner opinions, beliefs, emotions, and, we might add, a human subject's expressive utterances and acts—in a more general sense, all the expressions of his "affectivity"— are neither anonymous nor incoherent to the degree that one attempts to understand them "from within." It seems that everyone "stands on" what the situations of his life mean-to-him, and these situations are *thematized* by a certain number of *Leitmotiven* that also maintain specific relationships among themselves.

From this point of view let us go back to the famous analysis of the *shy man* [5] made by Dugas in Ribot's time:

> Excess of sensitivity develops a keen insight in the shy man. . . . Moreover his perspicacity is very special. It is based on indications, not on proofs; it is composed of impressions, not of judgments; it is sure of itself but engages in no discussion and no self-justification. . . . It is intuition, or, rather, the swift interpretation of spontaneous movements, words, vocal tones, physiognomy, gestures . . . impression formed by details caught on the wing and subtly analyzed; it is in contrast to the reflective judgment that we would make on persons in accordance with their characters or their actions observed with detachment. Many minds place more trust in their impressions than in their judgments, but in fact the shy man's insight is not infallible; passion guides it but also misleads it. His lucidity has all the assets but also all the flaws of instinct.

If in reading this document we put aside the author's personal opinions ("shyness is a passion, it is comparable to an instinct . . . we can trust our impressions under certain conditions," etc.) and restrict ourselves to his observations related to "shyness," we have to remark that everything is organized "logically" for the shy man, beginning with a certain way of experiencing relations with others. This relation with others, as well as corresponding situations, is experienced as *a danger of unfavorable judgment handed down by others*, whoever they may be, this judgment therefore being dreaded as an existential risk (injury, collapse, diminution of self, bound up with the fear of rejection or of scorn).

From this starting point it is clear (and here is the trace of that "logic" of which we spoke) that this way of experiencing the relation determines an *attitude of anxious vigilance* in confrontation with others. This shows itself in two correlated phenomena: (1) concentration of attention on the other person's words and acts with a diminution in the threshold of attention; (2) thematization of what is perceived—in other words, perception (not "objectively" justified) of indications significant-to-the-subject.

Situational "contents" can vary indefinitely, just like the persons with whom the shy man comes into contact; emotions and reactions, no doubt, will be equally variable according to the circumstances of these situations, but something constant gives the whole an inner coherence, in relation to which the observations of Dugas and others as well could find their place. From a certain point of view it might be said that the passage quoted lets the essential get away and enumerates only the superficial *indicia*. (Cf. Table I.)

In illustrating the systematization of the timid subject's experience, I did not want to go beyond the level of observations made by Dugas, and it is probable that this manner of living relations with others in a given shy individual must in turn be part of another whole. The roots of his shyness would certainly be found in these other dimensions of the picture. I do not say "the causes," for the genesis of this way-of-being is again something different that must be traced as an evolution of forms or a deploy-

TABLE I

Orderly arrangement of observations by Dugas (in italics here) on the "shy man" and elaboration of the structural organization that determines them without the knowledge of waking consciousness.

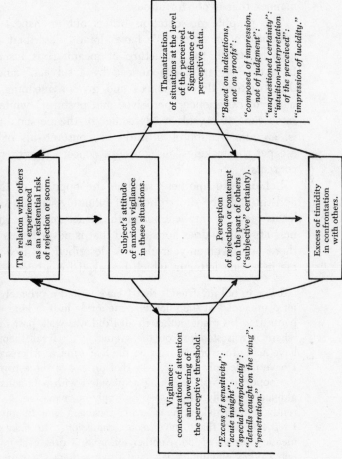

Thematization of situations at the level of the perceived. Significance of perceptive data.

"Based on indications, not on proofs";
"composed of impression, not of judgment";
"unquestioned certainty";
"intuition-interpretation of the perceived";
"impression of lucidity."

The relation with others is experienced as an existential risk of rejection or scorn.

Subject's attitude of anxious vigilance in these situations.

Perception of rejection or contempt on the part of others ("subjective" certainty).

Excess of timidity in confrontation with others.

Vigilance: concentration of attention and lowering of the perceptive threshold.

"Excess of sensitivity";
"acute insight";
"special perspicacity";
"details caught on the wing";
"penetration".

ment of forms fed or incited by significant events incorporated as such into the system itself and yet altering it in a manner that is not fortuitous.

The graphic presentation brings out an aspect of the *structure of meaning*. We have already described the degree to which the "structure of meaning" is inseparable from the "situation experienced by a subject," since it is the structure that organizes and gives a meaning to the whole of experience (perceived and postural) while at the same time it reveals a "dynamic" of the personality—that is, an affective-motor attitude or constant—all of which escapes the waking consciousness, concerned with *variable contents*.

Let us take another example, the opposite of the first, and through the descriptions of infinitely varying contents let us read the implications of the structure that consciousness absolutely does not see and that is nevertheless always there. A seventeen-year-old boy described his behavior to me in a long letter in which he asked for advice:

I like to tell my friends that I have visited a privately owned jet plane and that the pilot gave me a ride in it, a kind of aerial baptism in his plane, although all I did was walk past the plane where it was standing on the ground. . . . I tell them that I have made four or five trips on the S.S. *France*, whereas in fact I have made only one . . . or that on one of these trips I had the opportunity of becoming acquainted with a famous singer, although actually I have seen him only on television. . . . Currently I am "making films" with a camera lent by my uncle; I tell everyone that I have been commissioned to make a documentary for television. Another example: I dream of getting to know pilots of military jets, and driving them about in my car in front of the boys and girls I know so that they would see me with these pilots in full uniform. . . . I dream of myself being a jet pilot in full uniform. . . . I dream that I am driving with a pretty girl in an American car and that many people I know see me going by . . . ; when I talk with my friends I always have a lot to say about the subject of the conversation even if I know nothing about it. And in addition I should like

to have a dry sarcastic humor and make subtle witticisms. . . .
Generally I associate with persons older than myself and in fact
I prefer to be with adults. . . . I feel that I "have big balls."
. . . Nothing stops me. . . . When I come out of a theater
after having seen an adventure film, I feel haunted by shame,
shame because I lead such a run-of-the-mill life amid dull routine
in which nothing ever happens. I think others can see this
shame in my face and I try very hard to look natural. . . .

Here then is a reasonably broad sampling of behavior
forms and perceptions, inasmuch as the boy gives examples
of lies, personal fantasies, behavior in company, value-
charged behavior, subjective sensations, perceptions, and
reactional conduct.

And yet all these phrases, these acts, these dreams, these
impressions, although each individually signifies something
(every phrase in my transcription has a meaning), are organized as varied, different contents of the one unique
structure through which they become *significant of the
subject's experience* although they are perceived by that
subject's alert consciousness only as lies. This common structure, the significant potency—or, more accurately, the potential significance—of which outruns in every direction the
individual, incomplete, and random expressions that are or
might be observable, is the formal constant of all the postulates: namely, "attracting attention, producing consideration or respect, being noticed and admired." In this specific
case the attitude is dominant, voracious and imperious
enough to shatter the meaning of reality (whence the
mythomaniac tendency) and to be blind to the fact that
the result achieved threatens to run counter to the result
desired (he will be looked on as an anything but admirable liar).

An identical structure of meaning is revealed again by
way of the many formulations and the seemingly varying
situations. At the same time it is what causes the situations
(relations to others) to assume this meaning and no other
for the subject, and what stamps and organizes ("patterns")

his spontaneous behavior or his reactions. As for the subject himself, it might be noted by the way, he lives on the level of the successive contents without becoming aware of their formal constant, which makes of all these contents analogues, infinite variations of the same "model." And yet, if these situations (those of possible boasting) have a real meaning to him (and they do have one), it is because their structure of meaning is one of the components of his relation to the world and to others.

These two examples already enable us to understand the structuration of experience that makes it possible for us to "circulate," without regard for the traditional separation of domains in classical psychology, from the universe of the subject's "perceptions" to his apparently varied modes of "behavior," from his "states of consciousness" to his "values," from his "personality" to his type of "relations with others," from his "feelings" to his "decisions," and from each of these areas to all the others. Everything is connected and organized by the formal constant acting not only as an active categorization of "information" but also as a "regulator" of behavior modes on a nonthinking (or nonconscious) level.

Dugas thought that he was describing a "state of conscience"; the seventeen-year-old boy was describing his day-to-day existence in its manifold aspects in the current of his life. But something pierces through that organizes the various expressions and makes them the variants of a single form.

It seems to me to be useful, in order better to explain this peculiar coherence of the universe of experience, to detail a complete case in order at the same time to show the diachronic sequence and the synchronic coherence of the expressions of a personality. Let us take as our illustration a psychoanalytic case, that of Ida, described by Helena Deutsch.[6] In my report of it I will eliminate all the author's interpretative observations, so that all that will be left will be known or observable facts. Then we will attempt to penetrate into the subject's affective system:

Ida was a clergyman's only daughter. Her mother, herself the daughter of a reactionary pastor, was a fanatical bigot. Very early (at the age of thirteen or fourteen), Ida had demonstrated an atheism that had driven her parents to frenzy and created a painful family situation. At the age of fifteen and a half, when she was at a vacation resort, Ida met a young man four years older than herself. They fell in love and planned to continue their relation after the vacation. Ida wanted to learn to be a kindergarten teacher. George, the young man, intended to get into some business or other as quickly as possible. They would be engaged and then married.

But, before these plans could be realized, George was drafted. The young couple decided to marry before his induction. Ida's parents dogmatically opposed the project because they were conservative Protestants and George was a Jew. Ida battled her parents vigorously and finally prevailed on her friend, who was rather passive, to run away with her. They went to the village where they had spent the previous summer and, in the belief that they would soon be married, began to live together. Ida, who had been extremely amorous, soon became colder to George; now her emotions intermingled passion with sudden attacks of indifference, and one day, without offering any explanation to her lover, she left and went to stay with a girl friend. She told this friend that she wanted to have nothing more to do with George and that her only desire now was to realize her old ambition to become a kindergarten teacher, but without any financial help from her parents. In order to earn the money that would enable her to carry out her plans, Ida accepted a job with Mrs. D., an aunt of her friend, who was looking for a governess for her three children. Mrs. D. was quickly captivated by Ida's kindness and the excellent care that she gave to the children. Mrs. D. was ready to do anything to help Ida. Two months after Ida had started this job, she began to have attacks of dizziness and nausea.

Thinking that these symptoms were neurotic, Mrs. D. took Ida to a psychoanalyst; Mrs. D.'s belief was reinforced by the fact that Ida refused to see her parents or accept any help from them.

The nature of her symptoms gave rise to the suspicion that she was pregnant. Ida admitted that, since her departure from her parents' home, she had not menstruated. Although this had never happened to her before and she was quite well informed on sexual matters, it never occurred to her to consider a pregnancy until the physician had pointed out the possibility to her. The suspicion proved well founded. After the first shock Ida maintained her self-control in remarkable fashion. She made very realistic plans for the future, carefully assayed the extent to which her condition would interfere with her other plans, began to save against the expenses to be anticipated, and spoke of her child as if it were a foreign object that must first be removed from her and then put somewhere else. To her it was a matter of course that her child would be adopted by someone and that she would have no further concern in the matter. She thought affectionately of her parents but saw no reason to be reconciled with them; her interest in George had totally vanished; she said she was happy that he had been drafted and that he did not and must never know anything of the whole affair. She was concerned only by the thought that the people among whom she would have to live and work might one day learn that she had had an illegitimate child. She confided to Mrs. D. and the doctor that she had decided to confess the truth to her parents when concealment was no longer possible and that she was preparing to resolve her problem in a practical manner.

Later she had to admit that this "realistic" attitude had not been sincere. She had had terrible fears before her confinement; she had been certain that she would die and she had even begun to pray, even though in recent years she had stopped believing in God and going to her father's church.

Almost to the very end she thought of her child as something alien that she wanted to be rid of as quickly as possible. It was only after she had left Mrs. D.'s house and was alone with her almost-born child that she began to imagine how good it would be to have a baby. The content of these fantasies was full of tenderness but she regarded them as impossible of realization. At times she cherished the idea of keeping the child and going back to her parents with it. She said that both her mother and her father loved children and would certainly find some way of resolving her problem; then she rejected this idea as ridiculous and once more sought refuge in her indifference and her "realistic adjustment" to the situation. When she was admitted to the maternity hospital she declared that she would not nurse her child and would give it out for adoption at once.

After the delivery she found her little boy "marvelous" and began nursing him, but, after each episode of motherly pleasure, she asked that her child be taken away from her as soon as possible because she could not keep him; she said that she wanted to have nothing to do with him, that he meant nothing to her, and that she was afraid that he might mean something. But at the same time she thought in terms of postponing the child's adoption. As the time neared for her to leave the hospital, she felt weaker and had intervals of fever. She felt safe in the hospital. There life was centered on her and her baby. Now she wanted to keep him but she recognized the difficulties that were entailed. She showed keen interest in what happened to her child and the kind of home in which he would grow up; she wanted to be sure that he would be happy there and that he would be properly taken care of.

With Mrs. D.'s help she abandoned the idea of adoption and the child was placed in a foster home. Ida went to see him there and was greatly disturbed; she asserted with tears in her eyes that she missed him terribly, wanted to keep him with her, but did not see how this could be managed.

Mrs. D., who was a really motherly woman, then suggested taking the child into her home and giving Ida the pleasure of having him near. Ida's reaction was quite remarkable. She roundly rejected her employer's suggestion and refused to discuss it, saying that this would be the same as giving the child to her own mother and that in this way she would not only lose him but herself fall back into a new dependency.

She was worried about her career, which had been a matter of so much concern to her and her parents, and about the reactions of her new environment—the environment of her ambitions and aspirations—to her unsanctioned motherhood. George wrote to her from the army, though he knew nothing of his new fatherhood, and suggested that he come home and marry her.

Ida rejected his proposal with curious haste. If she married him now it would be only as a sacrifice for her child's benefit.

Even after her child had been placed in the foster home, she emphatically reiterated that she had no feeling for him, and she renewed her request that he be adopted. Now she looked on her child as she had done during her pregnancy—as a burden of which she had to relieve herself; she had not the slightest sympathy for George and often left his letters unopened for days.

When Ida finally made up her mind to cut off George and the baby, she plunged herself into her work. But she lived in constant fear lest someone discover that she was an unmarried mother. She made excellent progress in her work, earned the respect of her fellow students and professors, and received a scholarship. Yet at each step forward in her career she was haunted by the same secret fear of what would happen if her secret became known.

This is the set of facts. Let us first of all try to explore the organization and "coherence" of all these statements, actions, and decisions on the level of reality. The first phase of the story, from the beginning until the sexual relations with George, is relatively simple:

Ida's relation with her parents offered her no satisfaction. Undoubtedly spoiled as an only daughter and at the same time constrained by the strict moral and religious obligations by which the parents were governed, she had reacted against these constraints very early. At the age of puberty this reaction took the form of aggression toward her parents in the guise of ostentatious atheism, well calculated to wound them in their cherished beliefs and anger them on the social level.

Simultaneously, then, developed but unsatisfied affectivity, nostalgia for early childhood but without religious training, rebellion, aggression against religion and against parents subject to that religion. All this can be summed up in a few words: *Hate and aggression against frustrating barriers;* whence a first vicious circle, for the parents' reactions (resentment, increase in restrictive pressures with the aim of gaining submission) intensified the aggression in direct proportion. The consequence was a painfully tense family situation that increased steadily and to which the only outcome under such conditions was a rupture.

The open revolt was manifested in the declarations of atheism and, when the parents forbade the marriage on the ground of their religious scruples, the same attitude was expressed in sexual relations with George: Ida's declaration of independence. George was the lever that enabled her to declare her independence, and, by performing the sexual act, which shattered the parental interdict and the religious taboo, she appeased her aggression, accomplished the rupture, and committed the "unforgivable sin" that liberated her from her environment by placing her indubitably outside it.

In this first phase, everything, including George, had meaning only in relation to the central attitude of hatred and aggressiveness toward the parents' principles, experienced as frustrating obstacles.

Phase two began with the sudden eruption of a new way of perceiving the situation. Undoubtedly because of the

TABLE II

Phase 1

discovery of the reality of the sexual act, quite different from idealized love, and because of the collapse of tension resulting from the accomplishment of the rupture, Ida seemed to find herself facing a guilt and a moral loneliness that were now present and imposed their weight as irreversible reality in no way conforming to expectations. At one stroke George lost his former significance and was vested with the responsibility for this lack of satisfaction, and Ida turned against him, ran away from him without explanation, and took refuge in the home of a girl friend in whom she confided. She immediately undertook her *redemption* by deciding to devote herself to preparation for a profession of which her parents approved, but without asking them for help; this is a solution that derived simultaneously from the consummation of the rupture and from the desire to redeem herself better by assuming a supplementary self-punishment. Her exemplary work for Mrs. D. showed that she embarked resolutely on this course.

The central theme then is *guilt-self-punishment-redemption*. So it is understandable that, from this center of meaning, the plan to marry George no longer had any value. It is possible, indeed, that there was a prior self-punishment in the abandonment of this plan (and of George), in addition to the new guilt-creating quality acquired by George's presence.

It is only on the foundation of an attitude of this type that the various concomitant expressions can be understood. Nevertheless, in order to understand how that attitude can be created under the shock of an experience, given the earlier attitude that led to undergoing that very experience, one is compelled to investigate *in what affective climate the first theme was rooted in order that the second could be connected with it*.

It appears that the second could come into being only as a potential background of the first, hidden by it during the acute crisis of opposition to the parents' religious principles and emerging naturally after the extinction of the first. This

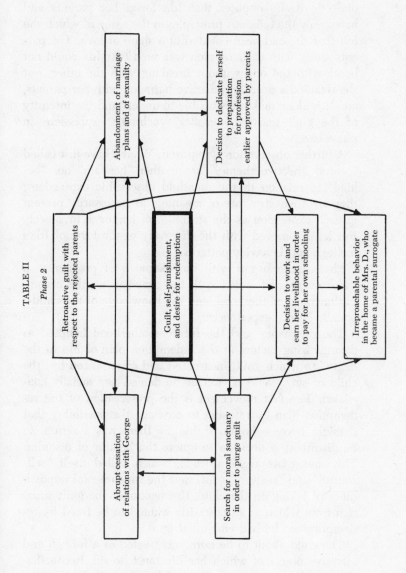

TABLE II

Phase 2

dialectic itself supposes that Ida loved her parents and hated only the religious principles in the name of which she felt that she had been cheated of a share of love. The parents' unity with their religion was such that Ida could not break with the one without breaking with the other, but she retained a need for affective harmony with her parents, and this alone makes it possible to understand the intensity of the guilt reaction and her synchronic expressions in phase two.

A further observation is required: What I have just called "central affective themes" are neither "beneath" nor "behind" in relation to the manifold observable expressions; they are their structure of meaning, as necessarily present in each expression as the structure of language in speech. But let us proceed with the discovery of the logic of Ida's feelings and behavior patterns.

Phase three began with the diagnosis of pregnancy, a shock event, and ended with the confinement, the accomplishment of motherhood, and the knowledge of the child— equally crucial experiences.

The pregnancy and the future motherhood irrupted as disorganizing factors in the redemption plan of life to the degree to which guilt, incarnated and materialized by "the child of sin," could no longer be denied nor socially concealed. The first movement is the preservation of the redemption plan by refusing to envisage the possibility that it might become impracticable. So there was a refusal to be disturbed, a decision to ignore this creator of disorder. This immediate rigid attitude, which called itself "self-control" and "realism," expressed the fundamental impossibility of taking on the child, the symbol of the guilt situation from which at all costs Ida wanted to be freed by redemption as she had embarked on it.

The child about to be born was treated as a foreign and intrusive object of which her life must be rid. Reconciliation with her parents was impossible before she had accomplished her redemption; George was rejected like the child

TABLE II

Phase 3

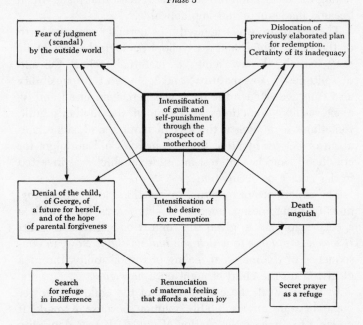

and on the same ground. Her concern was social scandal as an obstacle to her professional plans, in which she had invested her moral rehabilitation.

In fact the guilt was intensified in disturbing fashion with this certainty of maternity. The first guilt was aggravated by that of being an unmarried mother and then by a third, which came from the plan to give up the child, and finally by a fourth that grew up round George himself, from whom she was concealing the truth. The fear of death, which thrust her into prayer, symbolized the fear of an absolute punishment (death in childbirth) for this accumulation of guilts. The fantasy of a reconciliation (returning to her parents with her child) was rejected as absurd because it excluded the project of redemption.

What dominated this phase, then, was a profound mortification arising out of the intensification of guilt and entailing the dislocation of the earlier redemption plan, which became inadequate and impracticable.

The last phase was triggered by a normal event, the birth of the baby, which had a psychophysiological effect of its own, namely, the awakening of maternal feeling; the end of solitude, a new maturity, and a sense of responsibility also emerged. Hence the baby was perceived in an ambivalent fashion, sometimes as a sign of the mother's guilt, sometimes as a sign of the fact of motherhood, sometimes as an object for identification, given Ida's old nostalgia for childhood (and her interest in children, which was invested in her choice of occupation).

The experience of maternal satisfaction (loving the baby, nursing him, finding him sweet, etc.) was lived with a special significance, given the context of aggravated guilt: *It was a happiness to which she had no right.* Now, in consequence of the maternal feeling of responsibility, the idea of giving up the child brought on a new guilt.

In this context, the consignment of the child to a foster home became an acceptable solution because it made it possible to appease the tension of guilt: Ida was depriving herself of her child through self-punishment but avoiding culpable desertion. It seems that it was this same self-punishment that made her refuse Mrs. D.'s offer, which tended to recreate a simulacrum of reconciliation with the parents and a sharing of the child with them. George, now made responsible for her miseries and the symbol of her revolt against her parents, was completely abandoned and rejected.

Intensive preparation for her examinations became the only acceptable refuge, and self-punishment was satisfied by the sacrifice of her maternal feelings, but the fear of being rejected as guilty by her professional environment (fear of being unable to redeem herself, no doubt allied with a new self-punishment that impelled her to reject herself as guilty) became the background of the picture against which her redemption through work in a career formerly approved by her parents stood out.

Thus the certainty of having no right to happiness dominated the situation as a whole and organized the meanings of events and decisions. (Cf. Table II, Phase 4.)

Let us linger a moment here and ask to what level of consciousness the structured wholes that we have tried to

TABLE II

Phase 4

represent belong. They are absolutely *not conscious* as such in Ida. Her consciousness is wholly occupied, if one may say so, by perceptions of events, by day-to-day requirements, by considerations on behavior to be adopted, by attention directed to what is happening to her, all marked, too, by various sentiments. At the same time these combinations express the affective structuration of Ida's experience, and, though they are not present to thinking consciousness, in a certain way they are present in permanent fashion as *the very structure of her consciousness and her behavior* in the successive phases of this period of her existence.

But let us go farther. After this attempt at a formulation of structures that are relatively synchronic by phase, we have still to formulate what diachronically determines and organizes the succession of these groups—in other words, the form of their development.

Let us work first at the level of organization of the sequence. The hypothetical phases are punctuated by real events: Before phase one, one must from this point of view take note of the constricting attitudes of the parents on the pretext of their religious principles and the advent of adolescence (the age of opposition) in Ida; before phase two, there is the accomplishment of the sexual act; before phase three, there is the pregnancy; before phase four comes the birth of the baby. These realities of the world and of personal history are experienced (perceived and assimilated) in terms of a preexisting affective-motor structure, but in turn they modify that structure, and in a manner that is neither irrelevant nor random.

The successive dynamic structures that have been proposed are these:

1. hatred and aggression toward the parents' principles experienced as frustrating obstacles;
2. guilt—self-punishment—desire for redemption;

3. intensification of guilt, self-punishment, and desire for redemption;
4. conviction of having no right to happiness.

We have already remarked that, in order that the second theme emerge after the collapse of psychological tension resulting from flight and the realization of the sexual act, it must be supposed that Ida loved her parents, sought affective harmony with them, and felt cheated of some part of love only because of the parents' adherence to their religious principles. In this only child the parents' religious devotion was therefore perceived not only as a source of moral demands but above all as a frustrating force at the level of the parents' very presence, as if Ida had been *jealous of God,* who diverted her parents from her, occupied their time and their thoughts, and informed their behavior. In all her verbal revolts of puberty, it seems, she wanted to alienate her parents from their God, and she put their love to a test. This testing was inevitably intensified in direct proportion to the resistance of her parents' religious bond, and she had to "kill God," at first through verbal denial (affirmations of atheism) and then by the "deliberate" accomplishment of irreparable rupture (a free sexual act as a major sin) in the fantastic hope of recapturing her parents in their absolute concentration on her as she had experienced it in early childhood, and no doubt in a thoroughly satisfying manner. In order that the experience of "sin" culminate in inextinguishable guilt instead of leading to the consummation of the affective rupture with her parents, it must necessarily be supposed that she wanted to sever the parents from God and not to sever herself from them. Hence she killed God symbolically and then she was anguished at what she had done and at having also vitally wounded her parents by the same act. This was the inception of her plan of redemption, which became more and more exigent in proportion as succeeding events (pregnancy, then birth) emphasized with increasing drama and implacability the irrevocability of the act of vengeance.

Here then we confront the fundamental form in which the permanent operation consists; on the one hand, giving meaning to what occurs, and, on the other, organizing the multiple forms of behavior that seem to respond to events: *assure the monopoly of exclusive love by killing the divine Rival and winning forgiveness for this aggression by punishing oneself.*

This general matrix is graphically represented by Table III:

TABLE III

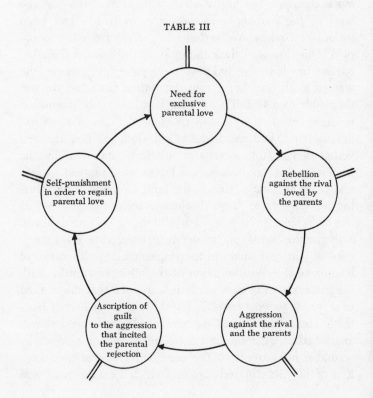

It is a simple form, commonplace enough in psychology, but peculiarly intensified in this case by the fact that the rival is the God of the subject's religion. The dominant themes of the successive phases analyzed above are directly shaped by the form. As such it is not "anterior" to the structures by phase; it is their constant and dynamic matrix, and this dynamic generative form (if the double pleonasm be forgiven) is Ida's unconscious.

Let us absorb the lesson of these few observations. An organization exists on the affective level that thematizes situations, events, and interpersonal relations for the subject-who-is-involved-in-them. From a certain point of view this organization is itself the expression of a way-of-being-in-the-world and of experiencing the world. This existential reality produces numerous imaginative, verbal, even rational constructs, gives them a form and a meaning, and also expresses itself in behavior, decisions, actions, yet without being the object of thinking consciousness.

In contrast, on the level of thinking consciousness an important superstructure can indirectly express this affective center of diffusion of experienced meanings. The conception of life and the world on a rational, philosophical level can reveal its exigencies. Nietzsche emphasized this bitterly in *Beyond Good and Evil:*

Even the historians, the theologians, and the philosophers . . . make a pretense of having arrived at their opinions through the spontaneous development of a cold, pure, divinely indifferent dialectic, . . . whereas at bottom a prior thesis, a suggestion, most often a heart's desire, abstracted and put through the sieve, is defended by them and supported with laboriously assembled arguments.

This systematization is something quite different from a combination of associations of ideas, images, or emotions. "The existence of *themes of thought*," Binet said,[7] "cannot be explained by the automatism of associations. . . . In order for a theme to develop, there must be an appropriation of ideas, an activity of selection and rejection that goes far beyond the labor of association. The latter is intelligible only if it is directed; reduced to its own resources, it uses any resemblance, any proximity, and so it can produce only incoherence." In contrast it may be said that it is the "theme" in its capacity as "organizer" that determines the relations and results of association. To seek to go back through a supposed chain of associations to "sources" that might be the key to "depths" is as if, by following the turns in a road, one were to hope thus to arrive at the geology of the territory covered. Similarly the development of the embryo is regulated and harmonized by an active "organizer" of which one always sees only the effects without ever seeing its mode of action or, perhaps, even its nature.

Consequently it is absurd to compare *contents* that are seemingly comparable from one consciousness to another. For every consciousness implies an unconscious system in its representations, in relation to which reality takes on an experienced meaning without being able to recognize by what this meaning exists.

The unconscious, the latent formal structure of consciousness

Having taken into account the facts that the affective life includes an organization, that it is thematized, that its various expressions include relations with one another and with one or more of the latent themes, we should proceed further into the structure of affectivity, and thus we shall finally be introduced to the organization of the personality and behavior.

We have already had occasion to point out, in dealing

with the examples given earlier, that a number of formulations, series of decisions, diverse behavior modes, numerous postural or verbal expressions can manifest a formal constant that is present and active in these different "contents." By reason of its presence (it is always there in its various expressions) and its dynamism (it intervenes actively in experienced and perceived meanings), this form has nothing of an emotional or affective halo; it is an agent of the structuration of experience and of behavior without the knowledge of the consciousness.

We cannot refrain from recalling here the statements of Claude Lévi-Strauss in connection with the methods of structural anthropology:

Tracing behind the chaos [of observable fact] a single pattern, present and active in its various local and temporal contexts . . . the underlying structure common to many formulations, enduring through a series of events. . . . This pattern could not possibly correspond either to a particular model of the institution (let us say here the observable facts) or to the arbitrary grouping of a number of given contents. . . . In every case there is something that is preserved and that diachronic observation makes it possible to individuate progressively through a kind of filtering that permits the elimination of what might be called the lexicographical content . . . in order to retain only the structural elements . . . and arrive . . . at the logical architecture of the (observable) developments that may be unpredictable but are never arbitrary.[8]

In the matter of psychological understanding, what is required is to make the effort to formulate the organizing principle or principles that impose their forms on the multiplicity of what is experienced, felt, acted out. Now there is obviously no way of arriving at such principle or principles except by accumulating the many and varied expressions in all their modes of production and with all their contents and then filtering out the "lexicographical contents" in order to keep only their "structural elements." Then it is observed that numerous contents are *isomorphic*

—that is, they have a common structure—just as situations varying in their historical character and their conscious or social repercussions may present *formal analogies* that it is a matter of grasping and that the subject's consciousness cannot grasp by itself.

Freud, discussing the symptom,[9] makes a curious statement that shows how sensitive he was to the phenomenon described here though without being able to define it on the basis of his elementarist and associational system: "Her symptoms," he wrote of one of his patients, "went back to events that had made a deep impression on her and that had occurred during the period when she was nursing her ailing father; hence these symptoms had a meaning and corresponded to *residues or reminiscences of those affective situations.* . . . As a general rule, the symptom was not the precipitate of a single one of these traumatic scenes but the result of *the accumulation of a great number of analogous situations.*" We will come back to the symptom, and here it is important to us only to emphasize the ideas of *residue* and *accumulation of analogous affective situations.* If these words are pulled together, the idea of structuralism leaps forth instead of the physiological image of an accumulation of stimuli or the image of fragments of recollected memories. What is this *residue of the accumulation of analogous situations* if not indeed the common structure that makes them *analogous* in spite of the variety in circumstantial contents?

In one sense this structure is empty, since, by hypothesis, it is emptied of contents, but in another sense it is full, for in it there is summed up a bearer of meaning capable of being expressed in quantities of meanings that will never exhaust it. In other respects it is more *general* than the contents, which are always particular or particularized. And it is *nonconscious.* Here we come back to a law of structural anthropology: "Transition from the conscious to the unconscious is accompanied by an advance from the special to the general."[10]

For a half-century the "unconscious" has been psychology's warhorse, and it has gone into popular speech as the lair of obscure and generally unavowable "impulses." One of the anything but negligible effects of this conception has been to paralyze observers of behavior into impotence, for they were never again certain of being able to determine, among the signs offered to their perception, which of the mysterious impulses might appear and, if it should appear, what indecipherable and enigmatic mask it would be wearing. As a result the right of being a psychologist was limited exclusively to those who had the key to the mystery, the rules for decoding: the speleologists of consciousness, the specialists in depth psychology initiated into the symbols.

There was, however, no lack of voices to cry out against the hoax of "depths." Jung wrote: "It must not be thought that the unconscious is always buried under numerous layers and can be discovered only through a painful and deep excavation. On the contrary, it is continually insinuating itself into conscious psychological activity." [11]

And Goldstein wrote: "To us nonconscious phenomena have a character completely different from that ascribed to them by psychoanalysis. They are not repressed conscious phenomena whose secret mission it is to seek to reoccupy the areas forbidden to them by consciousness. We avoid the erroneous hypostasis of configurational events into separate propulsive forces, an error so characteristic of the Freudian doctrine. Thus we remain clear of the inaccurate theory of impulses. . . ." [12] In one of his most recent publications, taking up again ideas that he first set forth as early as 1927, Goldstein severely criticized Binswanger for having refused to erect a counter-psychoanalysis, saying: "To attempt to reconcile Freud with the existential point of view is to doom oneself to the obfuscation of problems."

"The existential point of view," with Binswanger, Merleau-Ponty, Minkowski, and so many more, has in fact supplanted the notion of the unconscious with those of "misinterpretation" and "latency." The "new model" unconscious is nonconsciously present *in all the expressions of personal life.*

If this conception is correct [Lévi-Strauss wrote], it will probably be necessary to reestablish between the unconscious and the subconscious a more marked distinction than contemporary psychology has accustomed us to making. For the subconscious, the storehouse of the memories and images collected during one's life, becomes a mere aspect of memory; at the same time in which it affirms its permanence, it implies its limitations, because the word *subconscious* is related to the fact that memories, although retained, are not always accessible. In contrast, *the unconscious is always empty;* or, more precisely, it is as foreign to images as the stomach is to the food that goes through it. An organ with a specific function, *it is limited to the enforcement of structural laws,* which exhaust its reality, on inarticulate elements that come from elsewhere.[13]

What comes to us acquires significance for us, just like all the information that we seek in our *Umwelt,* only to the extent to which our unconscious organizes it in accordance with its laws. One cannot help thinking of the well-known remark by Boas on language (and all the more since phonology has served as the "wet nurse" to all structuralism): "The structure of language remains unknown to him who speaks until the advent of a scientific grammar; and even then it continues to shape his speech outside the subject's consciousness, imposing on his thinking conceptual frameworks that are taken as objective categories."

In fact linguistic structures are unconscious for the speaker, even though they are indispensably present and active, since, without their having been set in motion, speech would be deprived of intelligible meaning and would become an incoherent series of sounds or of shards of meanings. Similarly the unconscious is the whole of the structures present and active in our personal life, organizing, regulating, and determining the expressions of our existence. That is why there is and *there can be no language of the unconscious* in the sense that the unconscious *is* a language. This notion of an unconscious language is the result of a mistaken transposition of the laws of phonology into a magic conception of the unconscious. This last conception, according to which "unconscious activity is an activity that has all the characteristics of conscious activity except, specifically, consciousness," [14] makes the unconscious a second or obscure consciousness that speaks in enigmas. As for the transposition of phonology and linguistics, it forgets that unconscious structures are never meaning, any more than grammar is speech, although there can be no speech without grammar.

Fantasies, symbols, and dreams

It is advisable to review some natural modes of expression of structures with a view to allowing ourselves to be guided by these access roads toward the very reality of these structures before we study their origins.

Initially, in order to schematize, I will distinguish four modes of expression: words, images, dreams, and symptoms. There are two other major divisions—feelings and behaviors—that deserve to be studied separately.

1. Words. In "the psychology of feelings" [15] and "the creative imagination," [16] Ribot, attempting to define the "fundamental elements" of affectivity, said that it was a matter of *emotional-abstracts*. He made these into "generalized sentiments" and "extracts of previously experienced analogous emotions or direct affective recollections charging certain *words* with subjective *value*." In Chapter IV of his *Logique des sentiments* (*Logic of the Emotions*), Ribot grouped *emotional-abstracts* with symbolic poetic words. "These emotional-abstracts," he said, "would be expressed in the essentially subjective value that we give to certain words."

The old scholar had in fact grasped a relationship between (intellectual) concepts and (affective) values, in spite of the open opposition that he set up between reason and emotions, and he had sought their convergence at the level of consciousness in the *affective value of words*. It is quite true that in many cases and many subjects certain *words* somewhat comparable to those "suitcase-words" that are attributed to schizophrenics carry an intense, so to speak, concentrated meaning that summarizes and expresses a whole affective complex, a whole existential concatenation. To transpose Ribot's formula, I am tempted to say that it is a problem of *affective concepts* that are expressed for a given subject in key words, witness words, symbol words.

A. discusses spiritual love with me in terms that are peculiar to him. "It is a feeling whose power frightens me," he says, "and makes me want to run away. It is demanding and it deprives the beloved of his freedom; it implies my submission, it binds me, it paralyzes me, it suffocates me; it is draining in its essence, and, what is more, it suffocates with good conscience on the part of the lover, because everything he does he does 'out of love.' So immediately that stigmatizes the beloved with ingratitude: it is he who does not want to acknowledge the worth of love . . . and then with guilt: it is he who wounds love by not submitting to it or who gives the lover grief by seeming to refuse his love."

Through these statements one can establish that A. puts himself into the position of the beloved and not that of the lover. He makes himself the victim of a love that acts on him like a net flung on a free animal, like an octopus enveloping its prey (note these "images" that might equally serve as expressions). He insists on the inevitable guilt of him who "does not submit." The filigree of the subject's elaborations reveals the demanding love of a grasping mother, admirable in her devotion, against whom the son cannot defend his freedom of initiative and action without incurring the moral reproach of disobedience and ingrati-

tude. For such is the "model" of this conception: This is
what the word *love* means to Mr. A. And this *nonconscious*
model subtends everything that he says as he attempts to
explain to me what the word embodies for him.

If I add that A., who is forty-two years old and unmarried, is currently involved in a relationship with a woman,
it will be understood that his behavior with the woman who
loves him is not simple.

J. talks to me about *authenticity* and, since in my paraphrase
I translate this as *spontaneity*, she springs at me, for, she says,
authenticity is exactly "the opposite of spontaneity." She adds:
"This is the more important because the word *authenticity* sums
up the objective of my existence, just as it sums up all values.
Spontaneity is abandonment to the lures of the moment, letting
oneself go without scruple in the lowest impulses, wallowing
immorally in unbridled sexuality, living on a selfish, animal level;
it is shutting out thought, self-control, unselfishness, devotion;
it is the loss of every human feeling (J. is in a remarkable state
of passion as she says these things); it is unchaining the instincts.
Authenticity is exactly the opposite. It is rigidity of morality,
self-sacrifice, abnegation, virtue."

Here again her word is a key word, and my initial mis-
construction (while it inevitably betrays my own conception of spontaneity) clearly shows that, to the subject, its
content is individual; it summarizes something very important on the level of experience. Her personal drama, furthermore, is immediately definable, for it arises out of the
fact that she is attempting to sacrifice *her* spontaneity in
herself (investing it with the utmost opprobrium)—in other
words, to purge herself of every desire for personal satisfaction in order to live on a moral level of impersonal rigidity. Her "model" is to kill in herself something living that
she regards as noxious, hoping that thus she will have performed her duty.

If, here again, I add that J., who is thirty-eight, constantly tortures herself in the effort to amputate anything in
herself that has a personal aspect (desire, love, femininity,

momentary pleasures, even intellectual interests, need for
pocket money, etc.), it becomes clear in what way and why
authenticity is a key word for her, because it dooms her to
stand guard over herself and every day to kill any sign of
pleasure in living, which is immediately suspect of betrayal
of duty; and duty thus is seen as absolutely negative, self-
destructive, an empty, imperious abstraction that brings
death.

Through these examples, and innumerable others that
one can easily find all round one, it will easily be seen
that the affective structures are bound up with affective-
concepts, possessing a peculiar "semantic domain" individuated in the field of experience, and they are expressed
in key words.

At the same time, it is no less apparent that these words
are not the only modes of possible expression of the reality
to which they introduce us.

2. *Images* (stereotypes, fantasies, and symbols). We
have already encountered images as expression. When they
are charged with affective value, images are like dramatized key words, and here again we come back to the
thinking of Ribot, who attributed to *poetic words*—those
that create images—a value of expression of emotional ab-
stracts. An image can embody a conception of existence, a
way-of-being-in-the-world. Bergson thought that for every
philosophy a central image possessed, in its unlimited po-
tentialities of expression, the secret of all the philosopher's
discourses, and he gave marvelous examples of this.[17]
Similarly, poets have often translated their conceptions of
the world or society into images. One has only to recall
Baudelaire's famous *Albatross*.

In his psychological studies Gaston Bachelard has shown
the value of images capable of representing "the obscure
soul" because of their evocative power. "We live images
synthetically in their initial complexity," he wrote,[18] "often
giving them our unreasoned allegiance."

We feel strongly that images, as expressions of powerful

affective structures in a human subject, contain something that goes beyond simple illustration, simple transposition in a poetic form, and assume a superior dimension, that then they become image-forces (Fouillée would have said "idea-forces"), fantasies, symbols, or myths.

Analyzing his behavior with women, a man said to me: "In the sexual act I do not become involved; affectively and psychically I remain aloof; I am completely rational, I procure satisfaction for my partner, but personally I remain quite controlled." Then suddenly he supplied me with an image that, he said, had just flashed through his mind: he had thought of an observation by Paul Claudel that, he said, "had an immediately illuminating meaning for me on the very first reading. It is this: 'Woman's belly is the abyss in which man's spirituality is lost.'"

This image goes further than the preliminary verbal statements; it gives an almost direct explanation of his sexual behavior, to which it is the key. The image itself is obviously something other than a comparison or an illustration; it is the immediate expression of the way in which the subject views the relation between the sexes. The development of this image is sufficient to lead us to a series of experienced but never verbalized certainties, such as: "in the sexual act the woman pumps or drains the man's intellectual energy," or, still better: "through the sexual act woman feeds on man's cerebral substance and, if he lets himself go, she would leave him empty or emptied."

Let us for the moment leave aside the logic of the behavior in relation to these magic convictions (actually, in this context, "rationality and control" clearly emerge as a "retention" of intellectual energy, a resistance to absorption by the woman), and let us look more closely at these new statements. They in their turn express what is called a *fantasy:* here the fantasy of "the cannibalistic woman devouring the masculine brain by absorbing it through the penis-tube during the sexual act, which places the man at her mercy."

A fantasy is a creation of the imagination, shaped without visible relation to objective reality or magically transforming some fragments of experience or knowledge, and invested with a large affective charge. Fantasy has a form, and for this reason it can be confused with the affective-motor structure itself: "Fantasy," J. B. Pontialis [19] wrote in discussing the ideas of Bion and Melanie Klein, "is indeed a certain structured, active reality, capable of informing not only images or dreams but the whole field of human behavior."

In fact it is an expression of the structure; in certain nervous states it can assume a hallucinatory value, and even in its most ordinary state it is beyond the reach of critical thought; it is experienced as a belief that is never challenged. It is more than a "representation," it is more than imaginary, it is quite different from a "psychic element"; it is a node of meanings, a condensate of potential affective and motor patterns, all invested in an image that perhaps seems metaphorical to the observer but the implications and quality of which are felt in an immediate, visceral way by the subject involved.

Mrs. D., a twenty-six-year-old wife and mother who is now pregnant, suffers from anxiety attacks. On my request she describes the situations that give rise to the anxiety and it is seen at first that the constant common to all of them is separation (distance) from her parents. "It is actually among them, in the house of my childhood," Mrs. D. says, "that I feel security, and nowhere else." Anxiety attacks began when she was seven or eight years old and one or the other parent was absent or far away. Memory images recur, such as that of the burning of the town of S. during the war (she was then four years old). The more her husband, an industrialist, talks to her about industrial competition and the struggle for existence, the more frightened she becomes.

Then one day, when during her visit she was discussing loneliness as an anxiety-provoking situation, she recalls a "stereotype," what she calls "a very precise picture. There is a little girl seen from the back, in an obscure, dark, black setting; a

little stretch of road and, very close, a black wall. All round
there is nothing; a void rather than annihilation." As she describes this stereotype-image, Mrs. D. immediately suffers an
anxiety attack and struggles in vain against tears.

This time we are dealing not with a fantasy but with an
image of another kind, a *stereotype* that perhaps has its
roots in memory-images but that is not experienced as such.
It is a picture that has the function of a symbol, and it too
contains a tremendous affective charge. This stereotype-
image symbolizes *loneliness,* and even, Mrs. D. tells me,
after that comment, "it symbolizes *absolute* loneliness, with
the feeling of being nailed to the ground, powerless, surrounded by nothingness, reduced to nothingness."

Let us point out by the way the light that this discovery
throws on the combination of the subject's behavior patterns: She makes it quite clear to us that the infantile attachment to the parents is an effect and not a cause, a
behavior of escape from the anguish of solitude, the parents
being "always there" whereas the husband is not always
there and she perceives her existence as one of exposure
to dangers. But let us concentrate rather on the value of
the image: It summarizes anguish and it represents loneliness, but, beyond this meaning, it serves the function of a
symbol for the subject ("absolute loneliness") to the degree
to which *the* theme of all her anxieties is expressed in it,
the center on which her existence is focused, *what gives
everything meaning* (for Mrs. D. at a nonconscious level,
"that is life").

And this brings us naturally to the symbol, about which,
it seems, everything has been said without any clear definition of it.

There is a broad meaning to the word *symbol* that
cheapens the term and through which anything could become a symbol of anything else provided that there were
a relation of indirect meaning. To say that words are symbols, or that the conventional signs of a science are symbols
(mathematical or chemical symbols), that a way-of-speak-

ing in images or metaphors is symbolic, or that a riddle is a succession of symbols is to condemn oneself to have no idea what one is talking about for lack of a vocabulary. The nomenclature of the rhetorical figures of a language should help article writers here and foster a greater precision in expression.

Indeed, very specific conditions are required if one is to be able to speak of *symbols* in the strict sense.

"The essence of the symbolic relationship," Freud wrote,[20] "consists in a comparison. But a haphazard comparison is not enough to establish this relationship. We suspect that the comparison requires certain conditions although we cannot say to what class these conditions belong." In other pages of other works he was to say no more about the subject on the theoretical level, but he was to give many examples in which the symbol seemed to be expressive of a latent meaning, a hidden meaning that has the characteristic of being refused by the consciousness of the subject involved. Considering the examples and methods of psychoanalytic interpretation, Ricoeur wrote: [21] "Certainly, in the Greek sense of the word, the symbol is an enigma, but, as Heraclitus said, the master whose oracle is at Delphi does not speak, he does not dissemble; he signifies. The enigma does not block the intelligence but arouses it; there is something to be unwrapped, to be disentangled in the symbol; this is, specifically, the double meaning, the intentional focus on the second meaning through and in the first." In an earlier passage,[22] he had said: "In my view, the symbol is a linguistic expression with a double meaning that requires an interpretation, interpretation being a labor of understanding that seeks to decipher symbols."

It seems to me that, in order to make the matter totally clear, three cases must be distinguished: First, the *double meaning*, which requires an interpretation in the strict sense, or at the very least a transcendence of the immediate *datum*. But this double meaning is a very broad category of expressions, ranging from ambiguity (deliberate, as in

the pun or the witticism, or unwitting, as in the misunderstanding and the mistake) to "cyphered" information that
presupposes a cryptographic code without which interpretation is impossible (password, code message).

Then there is *simple symbolism*, which requires a special
relation between *two* terms, of which one is evident and
the other is secret or hidden. The special relation required
is that the so-called manifest term express in a typical
fashion, though in a different concrete whole, the essence
of the second term in its own context. Here we are in psychoanalytic symbolism in the strict sense, which, furthermore, is the only symbolism possible in an associational
theory. For instance, *the spot* (the spot that one removes,
washes out, erases) symbolizes the soilage of the sin or
the moral impurity of an act of which one accuses oneself.
Thus Lady Macbeth saw a spot of blood on her hands and
attempted compulsively to wash them; here one will recognize the symbol of "blood on the hands" (in this example
the subject sees it in a hallucination) and also the *symbolic
conduct* that signifies her remorse for the murder that she
has caused to be committed.

Here is an example of the same kind:

Mrs. G. tells me this story: "The other day, late in the afternoon, I saw my son (nine years old) come home in a terrible
state; he must have had a fight or been playing in the mud, because he was caked with it, filthy, ragged. I don't know what
got into me but I flew into an uncharacteristic rage, grabbed
him, undressed him, dragged him under the shower, and
scrubbed him furiously with a rough bath mitt, paying absolutely no attention to his howls of pain and fright. I came out of
this curious state a moment later, feeling vastly relieved."

In order to "interpret" this symbolic behavior, one must
know that early on the same afternoon Mrs. G. (a pretty
woman in her thirties) had committed her first adultery,
after long weeks of desires and moral scruples. She had
done so during a walk in the woods, and she had gone home

a prey to the tortures of guilt. Her son's "filthiness" had suddenly taken on a symbolic meaning for her.

In an extreme case simple symbolism establishes a relation between two objects or two types of realities: In the alchemy of psychoanalysis, the key would symbolize the penis, a vessel would symbolize the feminine genital organs, the extraction of a tooth would be one of the many symbols of castration, etc. "A great number of animals that mythology and folk lore have used as genital symbols serve this same function in dreams," Freud wrote; [23] "the fish, the snail, the cat, the mouse . . . but above all the one that essentially symbolizes the male member, the serpent."

When one works with psychoanalysts (and, worse still, with psychoanalysts' apprentices), one recognizes their standing interpretation by which every action, every word, every thought is avidly "analyzed"—in other words, taken as a symbol. One really sees at work the full scope of the exigencies of the coding and decoding system that is at last capable of interpreting anything, the interpreter's artificial subtlety becoming the mark of his competence and his subject's "resistance" enhancing his certainty, in accordance with the postulate that, the more the subject resists, the more the second term of the symbolism is "unconscious" and therefore "deep"!

Let us, finally, get down to the *symbolism of wholes*. In this theory the symbol by itself represents a whole conglomerate with which it maintains a significant relation, a relation of expression. This relation seems to vary between two extreme limits, one being socio-affective representativeness (and it is in this sense that the totem symbolizes a clan; the Cross, the Christian religion; a flag, a nation) and the other being the structural expressiveness of personal affectivity. It is this latter case that concerns us here.

We have already seen that it was essential to the symbolic relation to maintain an *analogy* between symbol and symbolized reality. In structural expressiveness the symbol, through and in its own concrete structure, epitomizes the abstract general structure of the whole that it signifies.

In fact it is because some aspect of this structural relation exists in simple symbolism that in certain cases it impresses us by its value and its obviousness. In the example described earlier, Mrs. G.'s symbolic conduct was such only because, in a significant "purgative" action, it materialized her present manner of feeling existence, of relieving herself of an intolerable guilt. Just as in the example of Lady Macbeth, so in the case of Mrs. G. the stereotype in itself signified her fundamental (and pathogenic) existential situation. If *The Trial* or *The Castle* teems with symbols of Kafka's universe, it is precisely because the author's affective universe was the bearer of a structure expressed (and, in a sense, "simulated" by reason of an underlying analogy) by the image of a doomed man seeking vainly and tragically to know the offense for which he was condemned.

Thus the symbol is more than a double meaning and it is equivocal only for the observer. It summarizes, condenses, and at the same time concretizes a structure, a system of experienced meanings, an affective universe, a thematized whole. Thus it manifests something that overflows it on all sides, and it conceals a virtual infinity of complications. To understand a symbol is not to seek its hidden meaning, for it has no really hidden meaning; it is what it signifies—that is, it refers without ambiguity to an isomorphic universe and an understanding of its structure of meaning is sufficient, without any other associational activity, for the discovery of the structure of experience that it expresses.

Here is the explanation for the fact that many facts of consciousness, many tales or legends (when the symbol is collective it ceases to be a symbol and becomes archetypical, in Jung's sense), words, numbers, images, stereotypes, fantasies, gestures, myths can acquire the value of symbols when their relations with the whole signified are those of the structural model in relation to the indefinite variety of the analogous situations experienced by the subject. Hence the subjectivity of the symbol.

To you as to me an orange peel is an orange peel. As such it is a fact of the world of the senses. If I dwell on "what is an orange peel," I can easily associate it with *memory-images* (like that of the orange wine that my grandmother used to make) or go back to the classical medical comparison with the premonitory *sign* of cancer of the breast, or place it in the broader *concept* of peelings. But now suddenly a subject gives "orange peel" a special value: "What is thrown away, thrown out, what my torturers try to make me eat by force every day, garbage, detritus, rottenness, filth, my own repulsive filth." [24] Thus he makes it a symbol to the extent to which at the same time it signifies to him the leitmotiv of his obsession.

So one can say with Dalbiez, criticizing the Freudian use of the word *symbol*,[25] "that there is no causal relation implied by the relation between a symbol and what it symbolizes," and that it would be more advisable to replace this idea with that of "expression." Let us add that what is meant is an expression of a special type, the enormous affective potential of which for the subject involved we have seen.

3. Dreams. From images to fantasies, visions, and symbols, we will logically go on to dreams, "the royal road of access to the unconscious," in the famous phrase of the author of *Die Traumdeutung* (*The Interpretation of Dreams*). They concern us here as expressions of the structures of experience and we shall devote a fuller study to them in another place.[26] What is striking when one examines the work of interpretation that Freud carried out on certain dreams is the fact that he operated in two successive phases: a phase of free associations starting with the images in the dream and a phase of grasping the relationship between the dream (thus enhanced by these chains of association) and the subject's biography.

The second phase is not discussed for lack of a theory

by which to justify it and formulate its methodology, but
the first phase, in contrast, is very detailed for the excellent
reason that it is a favorite domain of Freud's elementarist
associationism.

We will ask the dreamer to discard the impression produced
by the manifest dream and to direct his attention to the various
elements in the content of the dream and to tell us, as they present themselves, the associations that these fragments bring to
life. In what order should the patient explore the fragments of
his dream?
A number of ways is open to us: we can simply follow the
chronological order as it has appeared in the account of the
dream; this is, so to speak, the classic and the most rigorous
method. Or we will ask the dreamer to select the residues of the
day in his dream, for experience has taught us that some residue
of memory or some allusion to one or more facts of the preceding
day has slipped into almost every dream. . . . We can also tell
the patient to talk first about the elements that seem most important to him because of their sharpness. . . . What is important is to bring out the associations, and it makes little difference
which method is used in order to arrive at this goal.[27]

What results is a "mass of images and ideas, of memories
and admissions" that the psychoanalyst is supposed to use
in his labor of "interpretation." Here one might think that
the second phase has been reached, but this is not the
case: With these series of associations the psychoanalyst
"fills in the gaps that remain among the dream fragments,"
"makes their strange combination understandable," gets a
better comprehension of the manifest content "by noting
the relations that obtain among the associated images and
the dream itself." [28] The real work is still to be done, and
it is supposed to lead to the formulation of one of the nonconscious dynamics of the subject's personality. If the
"latent content" were not on this level, the dream would
not be "the royal road that leads to the understanding of
the unconscious." [29] And here, routinely, comes the "leap"
that, when it succeeds, falsely validates the association

technique; this leap is the transition from this mass of information to the unconscious dynamic of the subject's personality, the only valid objective.

Structural psychology, which regards the dream as one of the expressions of the unconscious structures, may perhaps make it possible to explain this essential second phase better than does the associationist theory, and even, in consequence, to cast a new light on associations themselves.

Everything in fact proceeds as if the structure of the dream were nothing other than one of the affective-motor patterns of the subject, or a nonrandom combination of patterns in a small number. The structure of meaning of the dream and the unconscious dynamic of the personality are one and the same thing. Nevertheless, and still because of the individual values of certain symbols, fantasies, stereotype-images, or key words, there are instances in which this structure of meaning cannot be located without recourse to commentary on the components of the dream.

Let us begin with simple cases in which the affective structure, the real *stage director of the dream drama,* is immediately transparent:

G. is twenty-four years old, unmarried, and living with his parents. For weeks he has been haunted every night by a nightmare at the end of which he awakens with a start and sweating: "I dream that I am waking in my bed and that it is morning: I decide to get up. I do so, and, as I lower my feet from the bed, I feel that they come to rest not on the rug but on a corpse. I know that this corpse is my father's."

The structure of the dream situation is simple; it can be summed up in this statement: "My father's death is there like an obstacle that prevents me from fulfilling myself or like something that I must cross in order to be."

In fact the nightmare had begun about a month after the father's death, which had occurred under peculiar conditions: After much nagging the young man had prevailed on his father to lend him the family car for a long journey, and the father, who had heart trouble, had during his absence taken a rather long walk, during which he suddenly died of an embolism.

Hence the affective structure is illuminated by the light of the dream: The young man is haunted by the conviction of his own guilt and he no longer feels that he has any right to live his own life.

This case is as simple as that famous dream of the lady who strangled a little white dog, a classic dream described by Freud, in which the structure of meanings is quite simply this: "Determination to rid herself of a familiar person, in spite of the natural repugnance at doing so, and with the impression that it will be easy."

Not only is there no need for series of associations in cases of this kind, but it may even be said that the formulation of the dream's *Gestalt* orients the subject toward the nonconscious manner in which he is currently living his life or an aspect of it, or toward past situations analogous in structure.*

Now here is a dream with somewhat more body:

A thirty-two-year-old teacher in a high school, married but childless, told me the following dream: "It is a very simple dream. I am walking in a city and then in the country, then in another city. The only problem is that I am a giant or else the houses are minuscule, for from all appearances, in spite of my desire, I cannot enter any of them; they are too small and I am too big." When he awakened, the dreamer remembered no special personal impression experienced either during or after the dream.

* Let us point out here that Jung had had an intuition of this phenomenon and had incorporated the principle into his method, though without arriving at a strict formulation. "His method," Mrs. Jacobi wrote,[30] "is distinguished from free association in this, that the dreamer is not alone in bringing his contribution to the associations but the physician has his part too. Indeed it is often he who, through the analogies that he supplies, determines the orientation that the patient's associations are going to take."

The structure of the situational image presented by this dream is equally simple: one can identify three themes: *

1. The subject is not in a normal relationship with his environment.
2. Adaptation is impossible for him but it is a fact and he is compelled to acknowledge it without understanding why.
3. He can find no rest, no surcease, no refuge.

Amazed, the subject in question recognized this structure as a constant in his existence, a constant of which he had no rational consciousness. This was the more the case in that he was maritally and sexually happy. Spontaneously he evoked two images after the structure of the dream had been stated: one was the "exquisite personal joy" that he felt when he opened the door of his apartment with his keys on his return from work, and the other was the painful recollection of childhood years. His parents were divorced and he was constantly going from his father's to his mother's to his grandmother's house and never knowing in which of these he was at home. The lack of adaptation to which the dream testified was felt by him, when he thought about it, as "the permanent feeling of looking for one's place in society and not finding it, and perhaps not wanting to find it."

He said that he had found it difficult to establish himself in the successive social backgrounds in which he had sought to play a vocational part and that were "always too restricted."

Now here is a rather more complicated dream:

Miss S. was harried by this repeated dream: "I see myself walking on a dirt road between pieces of ground that seem to have been burned. I see a few charred tree trunks and, as far as the eye can see in all directions, there is no vegetation, no

* The word *theme* is used to represent the affective aspect in the sense of experienced-not-thought and the word *pattern* to represent the affective aspect in the sense of the nonconscious organizer of behavior responses.

living thing, nothing except, quite far from me, a white house that I would like to go to, somewhere in the black expanse. The road on which I am is filled with viscous mud in which my feet are mired. I try to go forward, and I do so, but with tremendous fatigue, progressing only a few yards. I am laboring, suffering, I am going to fall . . . and I wake up in the grip of a feeling of anguish."

From these dramatized images let us derive the general significant components of the situation; let us construct the "pattern" of the situation experienced by the dreamer. This pattern establishes relations among five themes. (See Table IV.)

1. The subject is alone, without help or recourse; she feels this loneliness.
2. There is nothing round her; she is surrounded by nothingness because everything has been annihilated.
3. There is a desired objective but it is beyond reach.
4. She is exhausting herself in vain in her current efforts.
5. She feels anguish as a result.

Let us add that this woman is forty years old. Since she was sixteen she has been kept by a married man who is now sixty-five, a father, and in fact a grandfather. She is

TABLE IV

blindly in love with him. She does not work. Her present situation deprives her of any family or social help. She lives quietly but in concealment in a small apartment where her friend goes three times a week to spend a few hours. She recognizes that she has wasted her life and that she will never have a house of her own. Nevertheless she savagely fights against her anguish and refuses to face the situation as her dream shows that it is really being lived. She is under treatment for lumbar pains gradually leading to a paralysis that her specialist diagnoses as "lacking an organic basis" and that resists all treatments.

A study of the graphic representation is enough to show the functional connection of two dominant themes: solitude (at once endured and sought) and destruction of normal social relationships—themes rejected by the subject's thinking consciousness because they would entail an accusation against the man whom she loves and to whom her existence is absolutely attached from every point of view (if she left him now she would have nothing left at all: no work, no house, no money, no husband).

When the structure of the dream was disclosed, Miss S. told me all the foregoing and admitted that she was in an insoluble situation from which (for the reasons stated above) she did not want to emerge, while at the same time saying (and this brought on an anxiety attack): "I should have liked a house of my own, a home, and children. Soon I'll reach the menopause and then I'll know . . . that everything's over." The relation between the dream (and the psychosomatic illness) and the total situation experienced by Miss S. is clearly understandable.

Before going on with a still more complex dream, let us attack one of the examples offered by Freud so that we may compare the structural method with the associationist method in a case selected by the latter. In his *Introduction to Psychotherapy* [29] Freud devotes ten chapters to the theory of the dream and gives many examples. At random, let

us take the one on page 216,* which concludes a chapter
and leaves the reader's hunger unsatisfied. The first para-
graph of what follows is the account of the dream; the rest
is the whole of Freud's commentary, giving prominence to
the famous free associations:

The dreamer is traveling on a train. It stops in open country.
He thinks that there has been an accident, that he must take
steps for his own safety; he goes through all the compartments
of the train and kills everyone whom he meets: conductor, engi-
neer, etc.

This is connected with the recollection of a story told to him
by a friend. A lunatic was being moved on an Italian train, in a
reserved compartment, but through negligence another traveler
had been allowed to enter the same compartment. The lunatic
killed him. The dreamer, then, identified himself with the lunatic
and justified his action by the obsessive notion, which had been
tormenting him from time to time, that he had to "eliminate all
the witnesses." But then he found a better motivation that
formed the starting point for the dream. The day before, in a
theater, he had seen the girl whom he had been supposed to
marry but whom he had dropped because she made him jealous.
In view of the intensity that jealousy could attain in him, he
would really have gone mad if he had married this girl. This
meant he regarded her as so unreliable that he would have been
compelled to kill everyone whom he encountered in life, because he would have been jealous of everyone. We know
already that the act of going through a series of rooms (here,
compartments) is the symbol of marriage.

In connection with the train's stopping in open country and
his fear of an accident, he told me that one day when he was
actually traveling by train the train had suddenly stopped between two stations. A young lady sitting next to him said that
there was probably going to be a collision with another train
and that in that case the best protection was to raise one's legs
in the air. These "legs in the air" also recalled the many outings
and excursions that he had had with his girl during the happy
interval of their early love. This was further proof that he would
have had to be crazy to marry her now. And yet [Freud con-

* Of the French edition.—Translator.

cluded] my understanding of the situation enabled me to state that the desire to commit this madness was nonetheless still strong in him.

Now let us go through this dream from the structuralist point of view. The structure of this dream, directly analyzable through the three lines of the story itself, is this: *"It would not take much for me to lose my mind and (through impulsiveness or lack of thought) do some crazy thing that would have grave consequences."*

Let us point out that, in broad outline, this structure is present in Freud's conclusion, although not expressly related to the content of the dream.

But what is most curious is that the dreamer's four chains of association, apprehended through structural analysis, come down to repeating the same form four times; they are four variants of the same pattern (see page 167).

It happens quite often that the repetition of the pattern takes place on the level of the dream itself, as if the director (the affective-behavioral or dynamic structure of the personality) were having the same pattern acted out a number of times with different contents and actors and certain individual aspects complemented one another. Here is an example:

Mrs. B., who is thirty years old and childless, tells me the following dream: "It takes place in a room that looks like a bedroom because there is a bed. I am with my husband and his brother, but in the dream I am not married to my husband. He is urging his brother and me to marry. I do not reject this idea at first because I think that my husband will see for himself that it is ridiculous and his brother 'won't go along.' Since that seems not to be apparent to my husband, and since I see that he seems to insist on it, I make every effort to show him that his idea is ridiculous. I try very hard; he doesn't want to hear about it, and I don't know to whom to turn. The brother goes out and I am alone again.

"Then there is a new episode. I am in the same room, hidden behind the door; in the corridor, which is like a narrow street,

TABLE V

Overall pattern	It would not take much (a mere incident).	To make me lose my mind.	And (through impulsiveness or thoughtlessness) commit some crazy act that would have grave consequences.
var. 1	The train stopped in open country.	I thought there must be an accident and I ought to think about saving myself.	I went through all the compartments and killed everyone I met.
var. 2	Through negligence a traveler was admitted to a compartment.	In which a lunatic was being moved and	The lunatic killed the traveler. "All the witnesses must be eliminated."
var. 3	(If I marry this girl)... ...on the slightest occasion...	My jealousy will reach such intensity... ...that I should be jealous of everyone	And I should be compelled to kill everyone with whom I came into contact.
var. 4	The train stopped between two stations and	My neighbor said there was going to be a collision and flung her legs up into the air.	I have often profited by legs raised in the air but one would have to be mad to do so in these circumstances.

var. 1	I am not married to my husband. He is trying to "foist me off on someone else," who might be his substitute.	I do not go along with this. I hope that he will recognize that it is absurd.	My husband does not even reply to my attempts. He finds natural what I find abnormal.	I wrestle with this problem all on my own.
var. 2	Persons pass by who try forcibly and deliberately to take me along with them and make me leave my place.	I do not want to do this and I protect myself as well as I can.	(My husband is not present.)	I resist on my own and "it keeps on."
var. 3	A meddlesome, "leeching" character suddenly invades my life.	Finally I find him a "pest." I must prove to my husband that I want no part of this character.	My husband is an observer and does nothing: I do not know what he is thinking.	I resist the "pest" without any help.
Pattern	**1** *Impression of an offensive aloofness on the part of the husband and increasing risks entailed by this.*	**2** *Desire to prove to the husband how unsatisfactory (painful and dangerous) this attitude is.*	**3** *Acute feeling of incomprehension on the husband's part.*	**4** *Solitude in the resolution of the conflicts thus created.*

there is a rather quick Indian-file procession of persons whose
assignment it seems to be (I am certain of it when I hear them,
as I can because I am hidden) to get me to join their band and
make me go out of the room. Some of them try to seize me by
the arm. I disguise myself as much as possible, with a very unpleasant impression. This scene goes on and on and the procession never ends. I resist, with growing painful tension.

"When I think that the procession has ended, I go out and
enter a room next door that is a kitchen and dressing room at
the same time and that opens on this corridor-street. I prepare
to do something, but a strange-looking, excited character comes
in and buzzes round me like a bee, trying to get my attention.
At this moment I feel the presence of my husband in the room
and I tell myself that I must make him understand that I am
trying to get rid of this leech character. I defend myself. I say:
'Let me alone, get the hell out.' I open the door for him to leave,
and I wake up with a feeling of suffocation because the situation
is so complicated; I do not see how it is going to end or what
exactly my husband's attitude is or whether I can get rid of the
pest."

In this dream there are three sequences, which I could
summarize and distribute on the basis of four statements in
each instance (see page 168).

Or, again, one can summarize by this statement of the
structure of Mrs. B.'s present painful existential situation:

*She is led to wish to prove to her husband how unsatis-
factory, painful, and dangerous is the affective estrangement
that he evidences toward her, and yet she is certain that
she has no chance of success in this undertaking, given her
husband's lack of understanding of what she is going
through.*

The two other data of experience are in the one case a
"cause" and in the other a consequence. Hence the final
pattern would be illustrated by the table on page 170.

It would be important to point out here that this dream
(the structure of which was checked over and accepted by
the subject during a consultation), on the occasion of the
existential situation that it expresses, sets in motion affective-

TABLE VIB

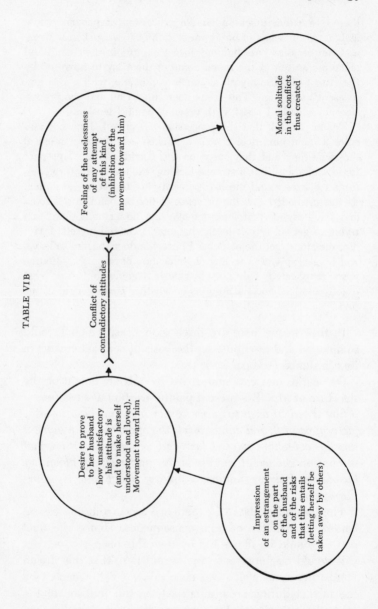

postural-behavioral categories without the operation of which the existing state would be unintelligible. I mean that, in order for this dream to occur, the present situation must have been lived on a nonthought level as it has just been described, but that, in order that this situation itself come into existence, *a constant and fundamental affective category* of the subject must have been brought into play. This can be only the category "being loved—being accepted —being understood," expressed in extreme sensitization to contrary situations or situations of rejection (affective rejection, refusal, incomprehension). It is important not to be misled on the precise significance of this category and not to see in it the trite expression of the "need to be loved," for the structural relation is specific among "being loved— being accepted—being understood." Confronted with this structure, Mrs. B. recognized it as her own and then spontaneously related that, as a child and an adolescent, she was already saying to her mother: "If you don't understand me it's because you don't love me," an attitude associated with reactions of rebellious pouting.

It would be easy to point out the biographical indications that would give this category the historical context in which it was constructed, a context that was revealed to me subsequently, the structural analysis of the dream having preceded these confidences.

Through these different examples, and although space precludes a complete study here, it will be understood that, in conformance with the statement of the psychoanalysts, the dream is a significant expression of the unconscious. However, it is in relation to the unconscious defined in a specific manner that the dream is expressive. It dramatizes the experienced structure of the dreamer's present situation and this goes back to a still more general structure, which can be grasped only through one of its aspects—in other words, by one of its investments.

4. The symptom. I shall be able merely to sketch once more the lines of research of structural psychology in connection with the understanding of symptoms. The work of psychoanalysis on this subject has accumulated all the materials that could be desired, and it is proper to use them. The symptom is a particularly important object of study in clinical psychology because it is typically a *signifier* to which the patient does not have the key and of which he does not understand the meaning.

Expressing, as will be shown presently, a combination and even "a cluster" of structures, the symptom shares with them the characteristic of nonconsciousness, but, through its constituted presence, it imposes itself on consciousness and the ego, for which it means nothing. Thus the symptom is a nonsignified signifier. It is experienced as absurd, and the conscious ego suffers it as a parasite independent of its will. But its roots in the structural architecture of consciousness clearly prove that it has a meaning, even though this meaning eludes the subject's intelligence even as it unremittingly claims his uneasy attention.

It will be understood that, in order to reduce this obsession of absurdity (which somehow manages to double the very obsession of the symptom) and to assimilate this painful reality (the symptom is real, inasmuch as the subject recognizes it as a foreign body), the patient sometimes constructs an "explanatory system" that is more or less rational or magical and that in his eyes acquires a certainty (though illusory) based on the symptom-fact.

In this section, obviously, we shall be dealing with psychic or psychogenetic symptoms or psychic illnesses, which can equally well be "psychic" (like an obsession) or psychosomatic (like genital impotence or an organic functional disease) or psychosocial (like compulsive stealing or asocial behavior of psychopathological origin).

Freud wrote somewhere that one must "peel the neurosis." Everyone who has worked in the field of psychopathology must have learned the truth of this statement in his practice, for, if one embarks on a trail one day, starting with the symptom, and if on that trail one succeeds in discovering a meaning (by linking the symptom with a traumatic structural situation, for instance), one perceives in the next interview that, starting from the same symptom, one can commit oneself to another track, and so on. This fact gave rise to the notion that the symptom is a crossroads at a center of convergence or intersection of structures, and that therefore it is always *overdetermined*. Whence, furthermore, a resistance factor arising out of the fact that pathological and pathogenic structures persist, whether because they have not been brought to light or because there are still others, unexplored, that still support the symptom in which and by which they are expressed.

A second fact, underscored by all teachers of psychopathology, is that the final, and the greatest, resistance comes from the *subject's own resistance to cure*. I will limit myself to notations on both these points.

H. P. is a thirty-five-year-old husband and father who is in treatment for sexual impotence of the premature-ejaculation type. This symptom has always existed, he says, but now it is being aggravated by tendencies to total impotence. He is now very anxious, having never considered that the first type was equally abnormal. At first sight Mr. H. P. complains of nothing else and intends to localize his problems on his genitality. Subsequently it will become clear that the whole of his behavior is affected, particularly his social-professional conduct, characterized by especially embarrassing difficulties in self-assertion, given his responsibilities as an executive in an organization. Although he is attracted by women, he cannot engage in seductive behavior toward them or even pay them compliments, and this is all the more the case because they are the more seductive and "exciting" to him. Whenever he gets into one of these situations he falls into a kind of erythrophobia (obsessional fear of blushing). In addition he has a phobia of darkness correlated with a fear of being blind, which seizes him when he is suddenly plunged into darkness (when he turns out his night light, for example). Moreover, he has a compulsive fear of being rejected by any person with whom he has anything to do, whatever the nature of the relationship, even if it is professional. Finally, he has a horror of every external symbol of virility (beard, pipe, mustache, even a cigarette) while at the same time he complains that he has a feminine face and is overly sensitive.

His biography is rather checkered. An only child, he was a witness to his parents' quarrels before he was three years old, his age when they were divorced. Since his mother was obliged to work, at a very early age he was sent to live with his grandparents, and he looked forward with anxiety and hope to the end of each week, because every weekend his mother traveled some hundred miles in order to spend a night and a day with him. At such times he slept in her bed and experienced "the height of happiness and security."

Very gentle and very quiet, to such a point that during his infancy he was taken for a girl, he had always endeavored to gratify his mother; his school record was that of a good pupil, trembling with fear lest he fail to please her and she reject him. A shock was experienced at the age of five when a neighbor died of a uterine hemorrhage, which in his perception (as a result of vaguely understood tales) was connected with her husband's "inconsiderate" sexual activity. An "unpleasant memory" dates from about the same age: Seeing two dogs copulating in the country and ending in *penis captivus,* he had hurried, though he did not understand, to apprise his hosts, and they had gone out to investigate and then made uninhibited fun of him. A more serious trauma dates from about his tenth year, when an exhibitionist with an erection asked him to touch it. Another came at about the same time with the discovery of blood-stained sanitary napkins (his mother's, thrust into a basin).

All these facts emerged slowly during a number of interviews and are presented here much condensed.

The symptom of sexual impotence, which disappeared after thirty-five sessions—a cure that was accompanied by the disappearance of all the other behavioral problems—lay at the point of intersection of at least seven combinations, the forms and sources of which follow:

1. Inhibitory block of masculine behavior or of the integration of masculine models through the remote effect of aversion-flight with respect to his father, who beat the

mother while the child tried in vain to defend her (fantasy of the virile person as the frightening aggressor).

2. Aversion to his own sex (his being-a-boy) in fear of being rejected, like the father, by the mother, the only source of security in an uncertain universe.

3. Simultaneous curiosity and guilt about sexual matters, the guilt arising from the discovery of his mother's napkins and also from the discovery of animal sexuality made under the conditions described. Let us add, obviously, his moral education, the shock produced by the exhibitionist, and the results of the nights spent in his mother's bed until he was well advanced in age.

4. Fantasy of the sexual act as aggression and of the penis as capable of causing death by hemorrhage as a result of penetration. The origin here is the trauma of the exhibitionist added to that of the story of the neighbor's death.

5. Fantasy of the feminine sex organ as one of extreme fragility, like an endlessly open sore in danger of hemorrhage at the slightest penetration. This fantasy was joined with the preceding one, which it reinforced, and it arose from the same causes, to which was added the discovery of the mother's napkins.

6. Adoption of feminine behavior models, associated with the desire not to be a boy, with imitation of the mother, with high evaluation of submission-gentleness-desire-to-please, which are not only the contraries of the aggressiveness linked in fantasy to virility but also the product of fear of abandonment by the mother.

7. Fantasy of the sexual act as copulation triggering ridicule and sullied by "animality." Complementary image of love as pure sentiment (model of mother-son love, which excludes sexuality).

In the graphic presentation that follows I have attempted to show the organization of these patterns that combine in the rejection of masculine sexuality as well as of any male self-assertion.

From this table one can understand the overdetermina-

TABLE VII

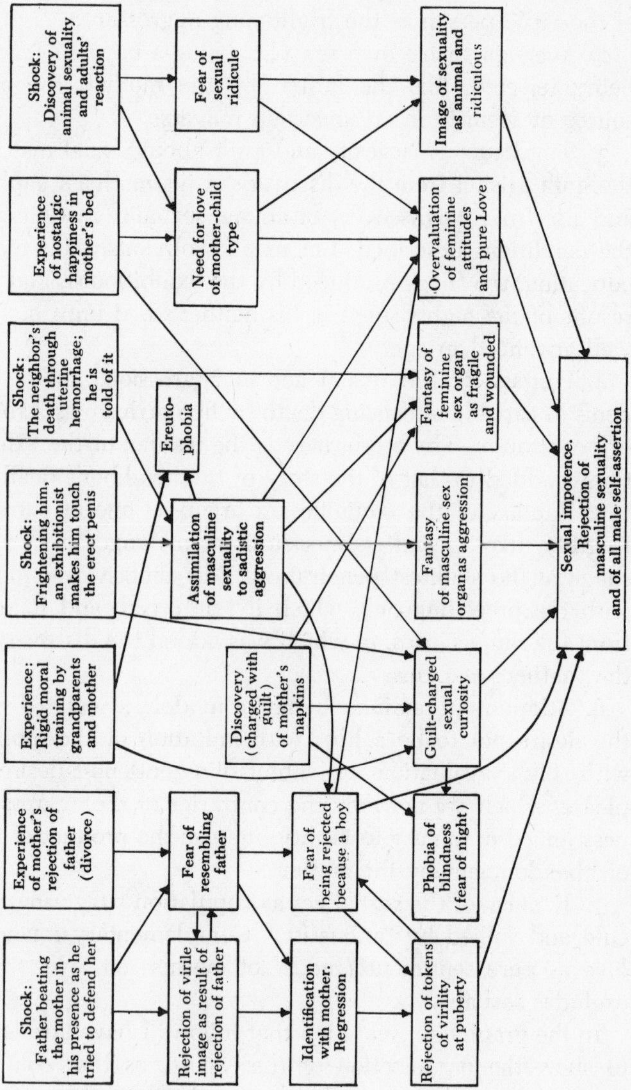
Shock: Father beating the mother in his presence as he tried to defend her
Experience of mother's rejection of father (divorce)
Experience: Rigid moral training by grandparents and mother
Shock: Frightening him, an exhibitionist makes him touch the erect penis
Shock: The neighbor's death through uterine hemorrhage; he is told of it
Experience of nostalgic happiness in mother's bed
Shock: Discovery of animal sexuality and adults' reaction
Rejection of virile image as result of rejection of father
Fear of resembling father
Discovery (charged with guilt) of mother's napkins
Assimilation of masculine sexuality to sadistic aggression
Ereuto-phobia
Need for love of mother-child type
Fear of sexual ridicule
Identification with mother. Regression
Fear of being rejected because a boy
Rejection of tokens of virility at puberty
Phobia of blindness (fear of night)
Guilt-charged sexual curiosity
Fantasy of masculine sex organ as aggression
Fantasy of feminine sex organ as fragile and wounded
Overvaluation of feminine attitudes and pure Love
Image of sexuality as animal and ridiculous
Sexual impotence. Rejection of masculine sexuality and of all male self-assertion

tion of the symptom by the fact that, in current life, it is
virtually impossible that a single structure or relatively independent structures should be precipitated (in the chemical sense of the word) in a symptom that expresses and
summarizes them at the same time.

The "unlocking" of behavior, then, requires patient anal-
yses without any surprise in the therapist if he starts afresh
from the same point or comes back to it by different roads.
The symptom as a summary of the convergences of structures is at the highest point a repetitive automatism: repetitive because an automatism, neither more nor less than a
structure, but with a rigidity derived from the fact that it
is a quintessence of multiple automatisms expressing themselves in its unique mechanism.

Here is another case, in which the trigger or symptom is,
historically, a commonplace remark made by a third person. This phenomenon affords the opportunity to take the
full measure, if it were still necessary to stress it, of the
extent to which affective structures operating as dynamic
categories can give massive significance to commonplace
information. An apparently fortuitous phrase, or one whose
pertinence does not go beyond the immediate, can in this
way "plant a neurosis," to use Hesnard's expression, and
suddenly crystallize a neurotic symptom that immediately
becomes a parasite on consciousness, destroying its capacities for the apperception of the present as such and its
adaptation to reality.

E. L. is twenty-four years old and a law student. He is
afflicted with a serious and progressive obsessional neurosis: he
is continuously afraid that he will lose his trousers while he is
in the street. As a result he is afraid to go out any longer and
tends to live in the seclusion of his room, wearing sports outer
clothes.

Moreover, he is convinced that his spinal column cannot support his body, that it is collapsing, "going slack," and that at
the same time his abdomen is "deflating" and sagging forward,

and he connects this to the vexatious tendency of his trousers to fall.

In the effort to understand how these neurotic beliefs are hinged together, one finds that E. L. does in fact fear that the falling of his trousers in the middle of the street will let everyone see that his spinal column is collapsing and that his abdomen has sagged. Needless to say, E. L. shows no actual anatomical problems. He is an excellent athlete almost six feet tall and weighing one hundred eighty pounds, with a baby face and a gift for language. As in all neurotics, perception of social incomprehension and the moral isolation that results from it is creating reactional and aggravating behavior problems. E. L. seeks to increase the number of his friends and acquaintances in order to explain himself, but this is not without its complications. His story is ordinary enough. He is the elder of two children (his sister is four years younger) whose father owned a small ceramics business. The father's character was relaxed, bohemian, careless, accommodating to the point of weakness, but good, and the mother, who was more authoritarian, enforced order. They lived in a small country town where they enjoyed a high social standing.

Very early, it seems, for reasons that are not known but that undoubtedly had to do with the attitudes of those round him, E. L. was extremely jealous of his sister, who, taking the defensive and enjoying exaggerated parental protection, complained about him as soon as she learned to talk, and this led to outbursts against him from the mother at first and then from both parents.

It would be legitimate to suppose that E. L. suffered a psychological trauma at the birth of his sister as a result of the general conditions of his life and his environment (an only child for four years, physically made much of and at the same time affectively frustrated by a mannish mother, poorly prepared for the birth of his sister, sent to nursery school at that time, and therefore resentful of his exclusion). This structure of the experiential situation (frustration—exclusion—rivalry) led in E. L. to aggression with respect to his parents and his little sister and hence a reactional pattern of rebellion, an attitude that, far from bringing about the restoration of the former nostalgic situation (as children magically hope), had obviously produced an aggravation of the exclusion.

Subsequently, round the age of ten to twelve, employing in his strategy those parental observations that adjured him to be "more reasonable," E. L. acted in two ways: He was the one who set the example, who "ought to" set the example, and for this purpose he conformed meticulously to everything that he perceived as the "rules of conduct and good manners" in his parents' comments on anyone. If the parents said of some workman that "he doesn't look nice with that twisted mouth," E. L. concluded that one must be careful to keep one's lips straight. If the parents told his sister not to slouch, he took pains to hold himself very erect, etc.

At the same time he became the little girl's censor and called attention to every fault in her behavior and every lapse in her general appearance: at table, in the car, at play, in school work, etc. He himself was an excellent student.

This second organization of behavior was first of all a kind of readjustment of the earlier attitude. The same nervous tension continued, but the experiential objective of reincorporating the affective environment and obtaining approval took other means. Aggression against the sister slipped into a meticulous personal conformism (already obsessed with "rules") to principles and values in the name of which he now had (or thought that he had) *the right to judge his sister and procure her condemnation.*

This climate, which developed from his tenth or twelfth year until he went away to school when he was about seventeen or eighteen, had become quite neurogenic for E. L. and he obsessively developed his system, although without on that account gaining the approval of his parents or bringing about the exclusion of his sister. His exasperated parents were themselves "conditioned" to every observation by E. L. against his sister, who developed her own revenge aggressiveness and deliberately put E. L. into ambiguous situations of pettifogging trickery or else played two parts, one before her parents and the other before her brother in order to irritate him.

It may be supposed that by this time the situation of conflict was sufficiently crystallized for E. L. to have brought together all the conditions for a neurosis. His orientation toward the study of law was the result of the same drive for superiority in the knowledge of the rules that would simultaneously assure him of the right to judge-and-condemn, power without the appearance of aggressiveness, and the affective approval of his parents because of his excellence in reason and in juridical competence.

But his parents seemed not to fall into line as the adolescent desired. Then he cherished an obsessive bitterness, inwardly reproaching his father for the latter's weakness ("if he had been a man he would have understood and found it easy to take my side against the two women"). Still meek, careless, and tired, the father shut off any dialogue with this pettifogging son.

When E. L. was about seventeen he was sent away to school in order to complete his secondary studies, in which he had been brilliant. During this period he discovered his physical strength and began to engage enthusiastically in athletics, especially the use of dumbbells. His physique was well adapted to this. During both short and long vacations he went back to the family home and his sister, who now queened it there to the great (inner) wrath of E. L.

Now his obsession seemed to have been completed. His behavior was wholly determined by the primitive *Gestalt* but the latter had engendered more peculiar patterns: for one thing, a stubborn hatred of his sister that had extended to his mother and, still more envelopingly, to any sentimental view of problems; for another, the concentration of the demand for approval and justice (the justice that he wanted to dispense but that he also wished dispensed to himself) on his father; and an orientation of his will to power toward physical strength. In this last connection, the choice of the dumbbells, determined by other physical reasons or the school environment, had none the less an undeniable psychological significance: the triumph of pure brute force. It may be suspected that the conflict with the father was going to assume the aspect of a "man-to-man explanation."

Within four years E. L. had won honors in the university (law) and athletics (dumbbells). His obsession had now become localized: he must have a major "explanation" with his father. He must "settle accounts," put an end to his childhood and adolescence. E. L. had the feeling that, in order to make his career as a man, he necessarily had to have done with the problem.

When he was about twenty-two he felt that the favorable opportunity was at hand during the long vacation. On a number of occasions chance incidents caused him to "put off" the big explanation. He had decided to "bring his fist down on the table." He held all the advantages but at the last minute his heart always panicked. Several times his mother had to tell him: "Let your father alone, he's very tired." In fact he was extremely tired. Furthermore, he suddenly died of an embolism at the family table just when E. L. was for once attacking.

The father's sudden disappearance, occurring in E. L.'s existence dominated affectively and posturally by the structure the development of which we have traced, now determined a reorganization in it round nonconscious self-accusation for the father's death. It was all as if this death had at one blow robbed him of the law and the power obsessionally built up for the defeat and domination of his father in order subsequently to dominate and rectify the primal and permanent situation. The whole construction crumbled, and it was as if the ruins of the unique structure were awaiting a new form.

In the beginning things went relatively well. E. L. no longer made any demands and left the management of the business and the family to his mother. He went back to the university. Six months later, when he was performing some routine dumbbell exercises in the usual place, the coach said something that was to have great repercussions: "The curve of your hips is amazing, you have a woman's line." In three months the neurotic symptoms were complete and the phobias described at the outset of the case appeared.

The influence of the "trigger" is quite clear here. The remark is shocking only in relation to a structure ready to "take as a whole," so to speak. Its influence, seemingly, consisted in fixating a structure under construction precisely in this thematic orientation and in diverting its significant potential toward a part of the body (in other cases it is toward an idea, an image, a class of objects, a kind of animal, or a class of persons), which, however, was not fortuitous. *The symptom has a significance.* In the instant case, it will be easy to understand this significance, which, as always, refers to the structure or the organization of structures that it summarizes, unites, or concretizes. Here is the verification of the psychoanalytic proposition that there is a relation between the symptom and the unconscious; but we will say that the symptom *expresses* the structures in a certain way and it is for this reason that it is *symbolic*.

In the preceding example the symptom was sexual impotence and it appeared as the expressive consequence of the convergence of a number of connected structures. In the present example it is also symbolic of structures, but it takes rather the aspect of a fantasy since it is a question of an imaginary problem.

Its symbolic value goes back to the structural psychological significance: He is "deflated," he can no longer hold himself erect (he can no longer throw out his chest), he is a woman (he is not a man), he will never again be able to be a man (he can no longer wear trousers), his body has betrayed him and is the cause of his failure, but at the same time he is doomed to failure. Through these metaphors we attempt to grasp the *Gestalt* of the symptom-symbol: *The affirmation of self as will to power is wrecked because he could not take (and henceforth he can no longer take) a manly attitude.* Such, in E. L., is the significance that is concretely vested in the obsessional contents.

The contents as such besiege the ego. The latent structures of meaning remain beyond the grasp of consciousness, although it is through them that these contents mean some-

thing. The ego experiences the symptom as an undetach-
able, exhausting, ridiculous parasite because consciousness
cannot reflect its own structuration, which is its unconscious.*

Now let us have something to say of *resistance to cure*,
which is characteristic of psychic illnesses. Here we are not
dealing with the well-known "resistance" introduced by
psychoanalysis, which is at the same time an artifact of the
method and a transposition of the doctrine of repression,
itself associated with the conception of that zoo, the unconscious.

Nor are we dealing with the therapist's opinion in the
face of the frustrations or the delays of his analysis (we
have seen to what an extent the symptom has multiple
roots).

True resistance, which one observes during treatment at
the crucial moment of the dissolution of the pathogenic
structures, seems to be the product of two correlative phenomena: one is the stable economy represented by the
neurosis, the other is the subject's own idea of the cure.

The first phenomenon is an apparent paradox, since the
neurotic condemned to indefinite repetition does not enjoy
the present and has no future (does not conceive a future
in his mind), and in addition he suffers (anxieties, fatigue,
lack of adjustment, difficulties of social existence, lack of
attention span, problems with those round him, etc.). He

---

* Reacting to this absurd assault, the ego, as I have said earlier,
can construct an intellectual edifice that "explains" or "justifies" it.
This artificial construction, centered on the contents, obviously has
nothing in common with the discovery of the structures.

That is why self-analysis is difficult and above all this is why introspection can only chew over the contents and corroborate the intellectual system created by secondary rationalization.

In certain anxiety neuroses, for example, the theme of death
classically imposes itself as desire for death and fear of death, and
this is linked to self-punishment, itself bound up with a fantasied
guilt requiring absolute expiation. This neurotic phenomenon is well
known. It seems that the famous conflict between a "life instinct"
and a "death instinct," which recurs regularly in all anxiety and guilt
neuroses, is a secondary rationalization of this type.

should want to be cured, and his conscious thought sin-
cerely desires it; he wants to gain help, to rid himself of
the parasitic contents of his consciousness or his behavior;
he feels ill. But the neurosis is his existence. He has organized his system of meanings, through the neurosis he has
avoided *some reality that he could not face.* In one sense it
is *a refuge;* it enables him to dispense with an impossible
confrontation refused by his whole being.

Indeed the cure is directly referred to the reality (or supposed reality) that the patient has always sought to avoid.
The image of cure is bound up with an impossible type of
existence. That is why it is extremely important to analyze
at the right time *what meanings the patient gives to his
cure.* There is a *fantasy of cure* that acts as a powerful curb
on the progress of consciousness and that is capable of nulli-
fying the effects of the therapy if it is not itself treated.

All this seems to me to be relative to the great law of
structural psychology according to which the structures of
meaning *are* structures of behavior. In the case of Mr. H. P.,
for example, premature ejaculation, a pathological symptom as a type of sexual impotence, was a mode of sexual
behavior avoiding the dreaded situation of aggression that
might cause a fatal hemorrhage with all the guilt attached
to that blood in other ways. It is obvious that, at the outset
of the treatment, the image of cure (easy to define here as
normalization of the patient's sexuality) induced an irrational psychosomatic panic as if he were therefore going
to be compelled to behave like a murderer.

If a given patient has built his existence on a structure
the axiom of which is "no one cares about me except insofar
as I am ill," any progress toward cure creates the conviction
that henceforth she will encounter only indifference. Experience itself is powerless because the information that the
patient derives from it is coded in a manner that is not
transparent to us; I mean that, if such a patient *by being ill*
established that, far from being loved-cared for, she is
arousing hostility and irritation in those now round her, her

behavior "adapted in relation to the pathogenic form structuring her existence" will consist in *making herself worse* in order to produce the awaited love. From this she may arrive at the catastrophic conclusion that "one must die, then, in order to be loved," and this fantasy (*the others round my beloved corpse*) can be wholly vested in patterns of behavior leading to death or can aggravate an intercurrent organic disease.

Once again it is meanings-for-the-subject that must be understood, with their organizing principle (which we have called *structure of meaning*), in order to penetrate into the subjective universe of the forms that determine perceptions, experience, emotions, and behavior patterns. The various *expressions* of this universe as they have been sketched in this chapter are approach roads to the understanding of the latent structures of experience—in other words, to the unconscious.

FOUR

Formulating the Laws of a Science

Every emotional state has a blindness and a natural insensibility to all facts that contradict it. —William James, *The Varieties of Religious Experience*

The primitive archetypical mechanisms

"Magical thinking," Claude Lévi-Strauss wrote,[1] "is only a start, a beginning, a draft, part of a not yet realized whole; it forms a well-articulated system, in this respect independent of that other system that will be constituted by knowledge, except for the formal analogy that connects them and that makes the first a kind of metaphorical expression of the second."

This magical thinking, which Lévi-Strauss calls savage thinking, is regarded as a logic comparable to scientific logic (calling into play the same functions, and particularly the process of conceptualization) but applied to "a different universe." Here too one finds the attempt to name, to define, to classify, to group similar things by establishing their similarities with the natural goal of understanding and action, but these operations are not undertaken on the basis of the same groups of meanings.

For scientific knowledge what is sought is the relation of phenomena with one another, and so what is involved is the investigation of abstract-objective structures. In magical thinking the significant element is in the relation between the phenomenon and the subject, and the structures in which it results organize the meaning of the *experienced* universe.

Let us accept this idea as our guide for the time being in our endeavor to grasp the nature of unconscious structures. What justifies this method of approach is the obvious kinship that exists with the processes of concept formation. They are linked by a formal analogy, an isomorphism. Matters proceed as if a single categorizing function were capable of mediatizing reality in order to apprehend it in a certain form, or even, more simply, to apprehend and memorize the *Gestalten* of the real. When it becomes a matter of the real as an experienced situation, this function seems capable of perceiving its form and fixing it in a recollection without memory-images but without loss.

The essential function of nervous activity, as we have seen in the case of animal psychology and the operations of the brain, is to inventory and categorize forms in the field of experience, on the basis of innate structures that organize the relation between the organism and its *Umwelt;* but also to construct and fix other forms in terms of the experience and influence of the earlier forms.

We have seen that this modern conception, which incorporates the advances of linguistics, cybernetics, and research in concept formation, as well as in habit formation, makes it possible to revise the understanding of the old ideas of instinct, need, drive, tendency, and unconscious.

During the years of early childhood, until the appearance of analytical intelligence capable (at least potentially) of carrying out the decentration necessary to the apprehension of objective relationships, a *conceptualization-generalization* is at work on the purely affective or experiencing level, exploring and fixing situational forms in order to organize and stabilize the conditions of reactional behavior.

When conceptual and analytic intelligence and consciousness of the present begin to function (after the age of six), a major revolution takes place in the general organization of relation with reality and with other persons. The process of conceptualization-generalization is then put to work for the analytical intelligence and consciousness as a function of the present. In the section of this study devoted to the operation of thinking consciousness I will outline the conditions of this change of the universe and the types of relations that are established between the two ways of perceiving and experiencing the world. Meanwhile an initial structural level develops, corresponding to what has been called *affectivity*.

Erected on the foundation of an initial specific structuration of relationship (in other words, starting from what used to be called the newborn human being's instinctive and reflex equipment, to which are added the congenital qualities of character, sex, and ethnic origin), structures are developed and differentiated, at once affective and postural-behavioral, by reason of the very fact that the organism is striving to survive in its environment. The perception of the signals, the formal constants, the situational analogies in terms of which the organism should act by using its basic structures of response and differentiating them in turn: this is the elementary biological imperative of adaptation and the culmination of the nervous system.

Structural psychology will probably be brought to study the neuro-physiological bases of this primal quest for information, as well as the archetypical mechanisms available to the human organism in order to differentiate forms, distinguish among patterns of response, and then employ these first differentiations as categories for the sorting and coding of the next situations, and so on.

To the mechanisms of generalization and inhibition, objects of the researches of psychophysiology, and to the mechanisms of structuration of perception, the objects of the researches of experimental psychology, one should add researches in the organizing and regulating mechanisms of the organism's offensive-defensive reactions. Some of these mechanisms have been recognized by clinical psychology and erroneously incorporated, in the framework of psychoanalysis, as "ego defense mechanisms"; others have been defined, in the framework of differential psychology, in connection with the study of "nervous types," characters, and what is called today "individual styles of conceptualization."

Hence there should be a certain arsenal of specific organic, structured resources available to the organism in its commitment to the real—this real being its life environment, with all that this implies of the ecological and the sociocultural for the human being.

Let us give a few samples of these functional mechanisms that organize and regulate the relation to experience, as certain researches, in the present state of means of investigation and working hypotheses, have been led to formulate them.

We have already (in Chapter Two) discussed generalization and internal inhibition as a function of differentiation of the forms of life situations; we have described the automatisms for the detection of signals and successive types of signals triggering and orienting the specific behavior patterns; we have mentioned certain differentiated reactional mechanisms according to the degree of probability of the satisfaction sought. This domain is still vast.

Substantial general interest inspires current investigators in the study of the mechanisms of conceptualization. Under the influence of the researches by the great pioneer, Jean Piaget, and through cybernetic applications, there has been a great rise in work on concept formation, and in the course of this essay I have alluded to the importance of these procedures for the understanding of categorization, as well as the formation of affective-motor structures on the foundation of information. The consequences are quite important in the degree to which they rejuvenate the conceptions of learning and the methods of teaching.

We shall have occasion to come back to this in the next section, when we study the formation and operation of *patterns* in the concrete personality.

Studies on memorization (especially those of Paul Fraisse and those that he has inspired) endeavor to clarify the relation among memory, the apprehension of structures of meanings in the perceptive field, and the integration of the structures into the growth of the personality.

The mechanisms of conditioning, in addition, make it possible to understand the conditions and modalities of what used to be called the "association of ideas"—that is, of connections established between components of the total situation (thus becoming "signals") and that situation itself as a significant structure and as a trigger of types of behavior-responses. Many investigators are clarifying more limited aspects of these general processes; here are some examples.

Zeigarnick's experiments, confirmed by other authors since 1927, have shown that the sudden interruption of an activity-that-achieves-satisfaction by an outside agent creates a continuing tension and, through memory, a fixation of the interrupted situation as well as of the image of the satisfying object (the Zeigarnick effect). In other words, satisfactions are forgotten faster than lack of satisfaction. Studied in connection with intellectual tasks, this effect discloses a more general mechanism going into action at all levels, and this would explain why *situations-that-generate-tension* (failure, frustration, anxiety, and, more generally, all situations of lack of satisfaction or uneasiness) create an *affective sensitization* to the structure of the concrete situation that produced this result, an affective sensitization that arises out of the persistence of the tension itself.

Goldstein, for his part, in his *Psychopathologie organismique,* has shown the existence of another general mechanism, which he calls "post-effect." He has written:

Every activity of the organism leaves a repercussion (post-effect) that modifies subsequent reactions, their progress, and their intensity. . . . The post-effect is reinforced when the same stimulus-situation attacks the organism afresh. . . . When the development is normal, it consists in an uninterrupted formation of new structures, making the old forms inoperative because they are of a different architectonic type. But, if the conditions of maturation are bad, abnormal post-effects disorganize behavior and hamper the subsequent development of the child and even the life of the adult.

Under the name of "ego defense mechanisms," [2] psychoanalytic researches have recognized and identified general defensive automatisms that appear in the organismic perspective no longer as "ego defenses" against the disturbing force of "impulses" but as forms of the human being's resistance to situations of unsatisfaction or vital threat (e.g., insecurity).

Every organism shows a psychobiological resistance to situations that threaten it with frustration, unsatisfaction, insecurity, or destruction, and this resistance is expressed in defense mechanisms. Experience shows that these mechanisms differ with the intensity of the tension.

It is known, for example, that the lack of parental affection (experienced by every child as lack of food-love and as insecurity at the same time) incites a child of a certain age, at an early stage of intensity, to a behavior of fixation and maximal approximation (the child is perceived by the parents—or by one or the other of them according to their significance to him—as "clinging"); this reaction develops (aggravation of frustration and reduction in probability of satisfaction) toward demands for attention; at the second stage of aggravation, the reaction is aggressive demands progressing in turn toward open and lasting aggression; at the third degree, when the lack and the improbability are still mounting, the response is escape behavior with negativism, remoteness, and withdrawal into self progressing to autism (intensification of the life of the imagination and search for self-satisfaction in the imaginary), leading to a rupture of contact with the real and with other persons.

Spitz [3] has described this aggravation, in the case of complete lack prolonged by separation, in the child during his first year of life (Spitz' hospitalization syndrome), and in it he sees, at this barely differentiated and almost vegetative stage, three successive phases of aggravation: attachment to any substitute, agitation, progressive shock with arrest in development.

When completely differentiated, the classic "defense mechanisms" * might perhaps be classified according to three groups in a progression corresponding to the increase in the gap:

Group 1. Persistence of tension (persistence of the need with conversion of its object, the direct source of satisfaction setting off the avoidance):

—Displacement mechanisms (tendencies toward a substitute having a direct analogy with the source of satisfaction).

—Compensation mechanisms (search for analogous satisfaction in a different concrete domain in which the source of satisfaction is accessible).

—Sublimation mechanisms (search for analogous satisfaction in a higher domain: social, intellectual, esthetic).

Group 2. Reduction in tension by discharge, direct or indirect:

* It is well known that S. Rosenzweig in his work has investigated what are the *individual styles of resistance to frustration*—that is, the personal structures of response to situations of imposed unsatisfaction (*patterns* of the affective reactions and the reactional behavior types).

—Aggressive-destructive mechanisms (against obstacles and then against the object).
—Aggression-displacement mechanisms (substitute-objects, scapegoats).
—Mechanisms generalizing aggressive demands.

Group 3. Reduction in tension through negation of the "need" of the real and of self:
—Reduction-negation-of-need mechanisms (withdrawal into self, isolation).
—Projection mechanisms (attribution of denied personal needs to others).
—Regression mechanisms (flight into an archaic stage of existence).
—Denial-of-reality mechanisms (autism, imaginative life, indifference to the real and to others, flight from reality).
—Mechanisms turning aggression back on oneself (self-denial, self-accusation, self-destruction).

It is important to add that there are also contrary mechanisms, those of growth and assertion of the ego (such as identification) or those of social assimilation (such as imitation).

Let us end our examples here. What was essential was to show that, prior to any personal experience, specific organic mechanisms are called on to enter into action in order to assure the handling of situations that will be created by personal history in the environment of existence.

The creation of affective structures in individual lives

During the first six years of life, on a level that excludes thinking consciousness—in other words, on the level that we shall agree to call affectivity—the relation with reality and with others is organized in a certain way by bringing into play the general mechanisms that we have discussed.

This results in the construction of those structures that we have called affective-postural-behavioral structures, the system of which will condition the subject's affective existence: it is understood that this level of existence can be assimilated to a magical or mythical mode of knowledge and action.

On this subject too the discoveries of psychoanalysis are to be incorporated into structural psychology, in particular those of the "primacy of childhood," the basic part played by the individual's history, and the fantasy "interpretation" of events experienced during the earliest years. "The necessary analytic work," Freud said,[4] "never stops with the events of the period when the problem appeared, but always goes back to the subject's puberty and earliest childhood. There it finds the determining events and impressions." This statement recurs in all the texts and today it is rightfully accepted by all clinical psychologists. Speaking in another book [5] of the psychological traumatisms that definitively mark the unconscious lives of human beings, Freud wrote: "All are to be found in earliest childhood, up to about the fifth year."

It is also important to take over from psychoanalysis the point that the situations experienced in this period are not "understood objectively" but "felt on a fantasy level." Through the many examples in Chapter III we have already demonstrated the truth of this phenomenon, although there is no reason to believe in an "interpretation of reality," given the fact that the child lives his magical reality with his own system of categories and can give the events, the situations, the persons, and all the components of his *Umwelt* no meaning other than the one that he does give them. We will return to this essential aspect of the pre-self-conscious universe.

In order to explain the "determining" influence of situations experienced in early childhood that generate structures of affectivity, structural psychology will have to avoid at the same time the Freudian and the Behaviorist hypotheses.

According to the first, the impressions experienced by the child are "forgot" and thus fall into the unconscious, where, through a kind of mysterious force, they are associated with others and arouse images or actions on the conscious level at a distance. The "model" for the Freudian conception is very easy to guess: At the time of his discovery of psychology under Charcot and Bernheim, Freud had been struck by the phenomena of post-hypnotic suggestion during which the subject, receiving a delayed-execution order while he was in the hypnotic state, carried it out after the stipulated interval and in a state of waking consciousness, without any recollection of the order and always with good conscious reasons to justify his conduct.

It was this model that Freud transplanted into his interpretation of the influence of unconscious memories. From the depths of the unconscious (whence "depth psychology") the fantasy-memories that had been forgotten determine ("motivate") ideas, opinions, reasons, and forms of behavior.

As a result, the rediscovery of the "forgotten infantile memory" would be, for psychoanalysis, the means of eliminating the permanent pathogenetic influence of the unconscious image, extirpating the disease, so to speak, and restoring to the conscious ego the responsibility for influence in the sector previously determined, apart from it or in spite of it, by the nonconscious "force."

According to Behaviorism the procedure is different. The determining influence of impressions experienced in childhood supposedly arises from the fact that they create a *conditioning*. Any element of the situation, after a certain number of repetitions or as a result of the fixating traumatism, would have the capacity to engender the original overall impression or to recreate the experienced situation, as well as the behavior forms that corresponded to it at the time.

Thus the association of one element to another, or the connection (concomitant or successive, direct or mediate) between an element and a whole would enable that element to bring on the original reaction. Since conditioning does not need consciousness in order to take place (it is on the psychophysiological level), conscious memory plays no part in this relationship. Here the "model" is the theory of the conditioned reflex and that of the "chain" reflexes.

Before we outline the structuralist explanation, let us emphasize that in both hypotheses the *automatism* of the feelings and reactions thus determined is explicitly recognized. All the obscurities of these theories come from the fact that they are the prisoners of contents and that they cannot fight free of the fascination of contents in order to discover the forms without whose influence one cannot explain how contents that are analytically different or composed of quantitatively and qualitatively different elements have the same existential significance.

In the study of the historical formation of these determining structures I will restrict myself to emphasizing four basic aspects: (1) the mythic significance of experienced situations, (2) the fixation of forms at this level, (3) the detection of formal analogies, and (4) the assimilation of experience.

1. *The mythic significance of situations experienced* during infancy is mythic only for the so-called intelligent and objective adult, ideally purged of all affectivity. For the child, the situation as he lives it and the impressions that he gets from it are *reality*, and the sole reality. What he perceives cannot be superimposed on what we perceive. In his field of meaning he singles out combinations that are specific.

If a child of eighteen months, three years, or five years is present during sexual relations between adults, it is certain that "he will not understand" if he is placed at the point of view of the significance of the situation for the adults (and for the parents, who in this way justify their belittling of the child's presence); but it is no less certain (and the proof of it need no longer be undertaken, so abundant are the clinical observations) that he "understands" something in his own fashion. For example, if the adults are his father and mother, that the father is killing or devouring the mother, throwing himself into an attack against her. This is the child's reality and this is his "experience" of the situation. A series of experienced impressions is linked with this: night, for example; his own fear . . . fear of night, fear of the aggressive father, fear of being attacked and devoured in his turn, fear of being deprived of his mother, fear of the sounds that accompany the mystery, etc.

Here is a commonplace example taken from another aspect of child life:

Yvon is a three-year-old whose mother works as a maid. There is no special need for her to work, but she wants to "earn money" and she cleans houses from eight in the morning until noon. When Yvon was very small she left him at home in his bed; later she placed him in a playpen in her closed (and empty) garage.

Once he was two years old, she took him with her because he used to get out of the playpen and "make messes" in the garage or the house. In the apartments in which she worked, Yvon's mother put him into a corner and forbade him to move "so he would not get in her way while she worked or irritate her employers." Yvon was quite well behaved. He always hugged a thoroughly dirty old Teddy bear to his chest and refused to be separated from it day or night. Ashamed of this "old toy," and enraged by Yvon's "precocious stubbornness," she took the toy away from him one day and burned it. Then, because she thought of herself as a "good mother," she bought a brand new doll for Yvon "to take its place." Yvon wept a long time; he refused to have anything to do with the doll; since then his sleep has been very irregular and he has had night fears.

Obviously the situation experienced by Yvon—that is, *his reality*—can in no way be superimposed on his mother's. The dirty old Teddy bear, which had become his security in his fear of loneliness and abandonment by his mother, was snatched away and destroyed by her, and she was perceived as the "wicked witch" who created insecurity and who could inflict the same treatment on him. This was *the only reality that Yvon had experienced.* Moreover, we should understand that that reality was quite as real as the money earned by Yvon's mother or the social position of her employers.

There is no need to multiply the concrete examples. There is nothing imaginary in children's "fantasies": They themselves are existential meanings, the reality of children's experiences.

The child's experience can be constructed only on the basis of his primitive modes of relations to reality. How could an "object" (objectively) emerge from his impressions? "His memory," it might be said in a transposition of an observation by Guillaume,[6] "can bring to each new experience only what already existed in the old one." Let us add, as has been said already, that the universe of infancy is egocentric—in other words, everything has meaning only in and through its relation to self. By very definition there can be nothing objective.

2. *The fixation of forms*—that is, the stabilization of the structures of experienced situations—is undoubtedly accomplished by the operation of conceptualization-generalization in perception itself, through the succession of similar experiences or in the traumatisms created by events. Hence it would be through the repetition of experiences or the persistence of an "existential climate," or else through the very impact of a shock situation, that structure was individuated and stabilized. A situation experienced for the first time is already perceived by its structure, but this, if it is not traumatizing, should have a margin of meanings, or a number

of probable structures, or a simple value as *orientation* of the subsequent stable generalization. Laboratory experiments in "mediated generalization" [7] make it possible to understand how and why a given subsequent structuration of an experience is facilitated by prior experiences that were not determining but orienting.

Many experiments made with children between the ages of four and seven years have shown that in an experimental chaos of figures devoid of significance they created significant combinations on the basis of *resemblances* and that they perceived by assimilation. In Chapter II we attempted to establish that the determination and stabilization of forms are accomplished by an activity inherent in perception itself, proceeding by analogy. Whether it be *the continuation of an existential climate* (such, for example, as an atmosphere of violence between father and mother, or anxiety resulting from the natural infection by the mother's anxiety, or a chronic fear arising out of an anxiety-creating ambient situation such as bombardments, etc.) or *the repetition of situation* (for example, deprivation of certain foods enforced by a specific diet that the physician has recommended to the parents for the child,* or an exclusion-punishment inflicted by the father at every meeting, or an aggression by an older brother as soon as the child is alone with him, or an increase in affectionate attentions whenever the child is ill, in contrast with the customary indifference, etc.), or even a *traumatism*—that is, a shock-event that disturbs the existential balance (such as being present at adults' sexual activities, seeing a murder, being hurt, suf-

---

* In a case of this kind, disclosed during the psychological examination of a five-year-old, the parents had thought it advisable, in order to avoid food temptations for the child, to lock him away in another room while the rest of the family ate. The child had obviously developed a fantasy of condemnation to death by starvation and exclusion while his food was devoured by his brothers, under the protection of the magic power of the parents: the-rejected-person-condemned-to-death (and therefore guilty) by the powers that order the universe.

fering an amputation, being chased by a sadist, being
caught in an unusual and anxiety-creating event like a
bombardment, a fire, a shipwreck, being separated from
a beloved security figure, etc.)—what does the child retain?
Perhaps—and in a manner that increases with age—there
is a fixation of the memory itself, without its precise locali-
zation but in its content and with the fantasy dimensions
that the situation had; what on the other hand is certain is
that, in another manner, something is fixed that corresponds
to the *kind of situation*—in other words, the formal structure
of the situation or situations perceived as analogous—and
also to their mythic meanings.

3. *The detection of formal analogies* is found again on
the level of elementary impressions to the extent to which
a detail has been able to assume a genuine *signal value* in
relation to any one of the outstanding situations and thus
to summarize in itself, as has been observed in animal psychology, the presence of the situation as a whole. Facts of
this kind abound in clinical psychology and all the observations of the Behaviorist and associationist psychologists
are so many proofs of the fact, apart from the theoretical
interpretation of it that is offered.

In Mrs. P., thirty-five years old, the *Gestalt* of black (or dark)
eyes immediately sets off reactions of flight and panic. If she is
compelled to remain where she is, as happened during her first
psychotherapeutic interview (with a therapist who had such
eyes), she is in the grip of an unremitting uneasiness and feels
an "instinctive antipathy." Only much later—six months later—
was she to bring out the analysis of this reaction and the admission of this *Gestalt*, a reaction strong enough to have brought on,
immediately after the end of the first session, an active search
for a protective love in the shelter of someone close.

Spontaneously, in connection with this reaction, she recalled
a very distant memory of panic fear experienced with a doctor
"with black eyes" whose image was associated with an aggression. On the other hand, the *Gestalt* of blue eyes was always
the determinant of a reaction of sympathy-approach. It was

associated with the recollection of her mother (the subject was seven years old when her mother died) and of her maternal grandfather, who had to serve as a substitute mother.

In this illustration the signal is overdetermined because here it is at the intersection of the patient-doctor situation and the existential contrast of blue-eyes-black-eyes. It is well known that in many children the "white coat" can become the signal of "danger of aggression" if they have ever undergone surgery.

Here is another curious example, taken from the everyday life of a normal subject:

The subject, a twenty-eight-year-old woman, refused to taste a slice of watermelon, but without the slightest apparent emotion, saying simply that she "didn't like it." Since in other respects this woman had shown the greatest gustatory curiosity about many exotic fruits and vegetables, her companion insisted that she try the watermelon.

This brought forth a disgust and an avoidance-refusal behavior that increased in proportion to the other's insistence (defensive, aggressive-defensive, flight, nausea). She was asked for an image association, but at the moment, in spite of the halt in the experiment and the accepted orientation toward the past, her relaxation was not sufficient. When the relaxation did come, memories surged up with which the present perception had strong but latent analogies.

First memory: "I think first of a picture by a Spanish painter in which there is someone offering a watermelon, and this person makes me think of *The Man With the Club-Foot* and *The Beggar* by two other Spanish painters. I can see again [here a pantomime of repulsion] the ugliness of the people and their expressions. I have an exact image of the gesture of one of these persons. . . . That gesture . . ."

Second memory: "That gesture makes me think of something different, a picture that was in my bedroom when I was a child, opposite my bed, and that I had plenty of time to contemplate for many years. This picture was a 'Sacred Heart of Jesus' and its Jesus, with the same gesture, was offering a blood-red or blood-covered object, which was his heart. This picture always made me want to vomit, but I certainly was in no position to say so, or *a fortiori* to remove the picture. . . ." [Silence]

Third memory: "This makes me think that since that time and—I recognize it now—because of that picture, I have always had a horror of rare meat, then of any red meat, and that this was a constant subject of quarrels and pressure on the part of my parents. . . . On the other hand, I adore veal. . . ."

It is curious to observe *the extension of the chain of analogous relations* in this example; the association of these images is neither fortuitous nor accidental, beginning with the fortuitous and accidental circumstances of their point of departure (disturbance brought on by the traumatizing picture offering the spectator a bleeding human heart). Starting from this, the physical trouble seems to have taken as its *index* or *signal* of the original situation the color red (essential, in fact, because of its significance of heart and blood). The color would then serve as an analogical support for the chain of associations. But through the succession of memories a closer *analogy of structure* emerges: "Jesus offering his red heart," "the persons in the pictures, one of whom is offering an opened watermelon," "parents compelling her to eat a rare steak," and "the luncheon companion offering a slice of watermelon for her to taste." The analogy of form is striking, it is this that establishes the connection and the "transfer" of the reaction from the first experience to all the others. Let us stress that the significance of this first experience (or, rather, its structure of meaning) is wholly subjective, and it is also a subjective analogy that constitutes the connection.*

On this subject I cannot restrain myself from quoting here an observation by Guillaume [8] criticizing Fechner: "Fechner wondered whether the sight of a human smile as a regular predecessor of unkind treatment, or that of a harsh countenance preceding caresses, could assume in a child's

---

* I have often found in a certain social category of subjects traumas brought on by images, pictures, stories, or narratives, and at adolescence, about three times in ten, brought on by reading.

eyes meanings contrary to those that attach to these expressions in normal life. This amounts to the supposition
that anything can become the sign of anything else." It is
normal that in the name of the theory of form and against
Fechner Guillaume should contend, on the contrary, that
"we perceive directly certain properties of meaning that
are inherent in objects"—in other words, the "smiling face"
or the "harsh face," "unkind treatment" or "caresses" are
perceptions-conveying-immediate-meaning and their meaning does not come from some possible association. This, as
we have seen, is confirmed by experience, and indeed it is
in the conflict of experienced situations that enforced association, accomplished in the laboratory, leads to experimental neurosis by making the corresponding behavior reactions telescope. At the same time it must be recognized
that, when meanings are not conflicting, the margin of
possibilities of "association" is quite large, although, contrary to Guillaume's theories, the structure perceived is
nonobjective and one must always be wary of personal contexts, subjective relationships, and mythic analogies.

This, furthermore, leads us to some comment on the assimilation of experience on the basis of previously erected
structures.

4. *The assimilation of subsequent experience* is carried
out on the basis of structures of meaning thus constituted
and acting, as Piaget said, as operative categories employed in a nonconscious fashion for the incorporation of
the facts of experience, in a manner quite comparable to
the operation of our concepts in naming and understanding
intellectualized items of information.

Thus, though in another way, one can understand the
observations made by Ribot [9] on "the unconscious work
equivalent to a series of value judgments and proceeding
by analogy, prior to an imaginative construction composed
of associations radiating out in various directions but uni-
fied by the unconscious situation of a predominant desire."
There is indeed an integration of the structures of perceived

(and experienced) situations as a result of analogies of form, which are constructed and differentiated under the influence of experience itself to the degree to which the subject remains "established" in the experience and the automatic calculation of probabilities of meanings—in other words, of structure—is operative.

Everything is constructed within this dialectic and it is precisely for this reason that repeated isomorphic traumas dangerously fixate a structure; "dangerously" because it becomes so "full of implications" that henceforth it can "distort" anything in order to recur everywhere.

Among Rosen's current ideas,[11] there is at least one that seems to me important enough to claim the psychiatrists' attention; namely, that it is paranoia and not classic schizophrenia that should be placed nosologically at the center of the group of schizophrenias, and furthermore that the paranoiac, during his earliest infancy, was brought up by a mother or father who denied him and who was therefore experienced as "wishing his death." The antiquity of this structure of relationship and its continuity in a persisting climate would end in paranoiac delirium and, in other cases, in other types of schizophrenias as effective realizations of death in life.

In connection with the implications of significant forms, we have already seen, in dealing with a concrete case, the influence of the "trigger remark" producing the massive taking over of experience by an exclusive structure that disorganizes behavior patterns of adaptation to reality.* The converse too exists; then the trigger remark is a trauma phrase that very slowly and quietly executes a kind of progressive thematization of the whole affective existence, a

---

* Minkowski [10] gives a typical example of this in a case of paraphrenic psychosis (delusions of grandeur): "During the war and even well before it the patient had had what he called strange ideas about himself. One day, when he was lying down, a noncommissioned officer passed by and said: 'Look, there's Napoleon lying on his belly.' Under the influence of this jest the ideas that he already had took on more and more body; he said to himself that he might indeed be the descendant of some great man."

thematization that at a certain stage of systematization also makes the subject veer off into mental illness.

In their quality as extreme cases these clearly show the operational method of a structure that has become an instrument for coding information. The "significant phrase" is the key that organizes everything perceived into meanings, almost as if, after one has read a number of fables with different contents, but structurally similar in a manner that is not apparent, one clearly stated *the moral of all these fables:* this would at once reveal their structure—that is, *their common structure of meaning.*

Functioning as organizing principles of situations in their experienced meanings, and erected in subjective experience, in individual existence in the course of what happens in each person's singular life, these structures of our affective relationship to the world and to others therefore do indeed come from the past. But the past has two modes: First, the past that our memory encounters either when it attempts to reconstruct it or when it emerges quite of itself in our dreaming; and then the past that, through the structures of our affectivity, shapes our experience lastingly. If the rule of the first mode of the past is forgetfulness, since, as Minkowski said, "everything in the past suffers the erosion of time, everything in it is inevitably doomed to be forgotten," [12] the second mode of the past, in contrast, is unforgettable without ever being remembered, it is *always* there, and, in this sense (only in this sense), a constituent of our present even though it is so in an absolutely unconscious fashion.

Structures, patterns, and attitudes

The structure of a human subject's affectivity is not the current state of his affectivity or even the current distribution of his emotions—positive, negative, shaded, mixed—of his desires and aspirations, of his fears or his regrets, etc., in the whole of his field of living. When a subject agrees to talk to us about his existence and the meanings of his present experienced universe—in other words, about his affective life—he begins to describe current feelings—in other words, everything in which his affectivity is invested, as well as the personal emotional reactions that are peculiar to him. He gives us the current, historical content of his affective life, the constellations of objects or persons in relation to which he currently places himself, each of these experienced realities being more or less inscribed in a movement that comes from the past and that is directed toward projects. In a description of this kind, one always observes that there are foregrounds and backgrounds in relation to which the foregrounds take on certain values, and that there are central zones and concentric or marginal zones of different affective intensity. One could construct the topography of this current state, and the experienced realities are organized in a certain way in this "snapshot" of personal history. Very marginal areas are subconscious, and certain emotions are even, as it were, "asleep."

But, in spite of its living character, this picture is relatively too static to take affectivity into consideration. Beyond its current sedimentation, affectivity appears as what, in the person's confrontation with the "outside" world, with events or circumstances, *governs* that relation or that interaction on the conscious level. Out of the continuing encounter with "what happens to us" surge up emotions, sentiments, reactions that are the expressions of the active way in which our affectivity experiences and charges with meaning these events, these circumstances, these accidents of our lives.

Thus a subject can describe the current state of his affectivity; he can lack the desire to speak of certain sentiments difficult to express in his fear of others' judgment; he can neither hint at nor state some obscure or remote sentiment, or one that is very simply unutterable because

he lacks the words with which to characterize it; but always
he restricts himself *to the historical content,* to the facts of
his affective existence here and now or there and then.

He cannot, unassisted, take cognizance of the dynamic
forms that continually "digest" fact in order to turn it into
personal experience, and from this point of view the structures of his activity are always operative in his vital field
and at the same time always unconscious. It is these forms
that structural analysis makes it possible to uncover.

If one starts with this description, even directing one's
attention not to the content of what is described, not to the
"text of the argument," but through this text, and necessarily through it, to the *structures of meaning*—in other
words, to what might be called the *implicit general postulates* of what is exposed to us—then in the opposite direction one carries on the same operation by which these
postulates, veritable *a priori* forms, organized the circumstantial and contingent content, the direct object of description—in other words, experience or observable behavior.

From this point of view the slightest expression of experience presupposes the setting of these structures in
motion, just as the slightest employment of reason presupposes, beyond its content and the definitions employed, the
setting in motion and the operation of a certain number of
axioms.

Let us take a simple sentence quoted by Rogers in his
work in mirror-reformulation. A little boy says to his
father: "All the other kids in my class have bicycles." Rogers
writes that the *meaning* of this statement is to be sought
in a grammatical reversal revealing the implicit idea: "I
am the only one who does not have a bicycle." Unfortunately, Rogers stops there and believes that this new formulation lays bare the meaning of the sentence, and this
is true. But let us rather set ourselves the problem of determining what structures of meaning make this sentence possible and are expressed by it or in it. Let us draw up a
schedule of the formal principles that it reflects, not on the

level of its grammatical organization but on that of the structure of the child's relation with his *Umwelt*.

If it is translated in terms of "feelings," five of these immediately appear, and I will state them thus, without any effort here to speak in the child's language:

1. I have the feeling of not being like the others from the point of view of Having or from the social point of view.
2. I have the feeling that my father possesses the power to wipe out my inferiority and that this depends solely on him.
3. I have the feeling that I cannot directly rebel against him and that I must take precautions.
4. I trust my father, at least up to a certain point (I can establish communication with him).
5. I must now do something to put an end to my existing social situation, which creates an inferiority and is intolerable.

How the psychological analysis is oriented becomes clear; it sets out in quest of the feelings expressive of certain structures that are in fact *signified* by the sentence if one is willing to take it at face value and wonder "what it means" no longer in its chance content but as *general feelings* the presence of which is required in order for it to have a meaning. Let us proceed at the level of an even more rigorous analysis. These feelings, in turn, are organized into three basic attitude-sentiments:

1. Sensitization to the social distance between oneself and others (comparing oneself to others in order to be assimilated into the group).
2. An accusation-rebellion against the father, inhibited by
3. Dependence on the father.

From here one goes on to determine the structure of the child's relations to the group and to his father as the *formal characteristics* of his present existence and what actually determines his experience and his behavior. We are confronted with three affective-postural-behavioral structures (that is, engendering feelings in connection with experienced events, as well as attitudes or behavior modes).

The "structural reformulation," then, would lead to this: *"You would like very much to be like the others; it is because of your father that you are not like the others, but you are relying on him to remedy this."*

Here we are far away from the current content of these structures and yet they are here, present, *contributing meaning,* to such a point that to restrict oneself to the content alone would be to doom oneself to understanding nothing.

Furthermore, if the father replies to his son: "What difference is that supposed to make to me?" we will say that he has "understood nothing." Nevertheless he has replied.

Let us take that same response. The child would take it for what it means, which is: "I refuse to concern myself with your problems; you can't count on me." This is its structure of meaning, revealing the formal structure of the father-son relation as the father feels it. This experience in turn will influence the child's affective-motor structures according as it is or is not confirmed, and it will more or less modify his relation with his father.

So the question: "What does this mean to the subject?" compels us to go back from the content to the foundations, which introduce us into the structures of his affectivity and which, so to speak, are its *axioms.*

A body of laws becomes the objective of the analysis: We have to understand the relations that support axioms among one another.

Thus the affective life appears as *a system,* determined by more or less independent (and even, in certain pathological cases, contradictory) axioms not challenged by the subject, given the fact that he experiences his affective existence without any consciousness of the principles that organize it, a system operating as a set of categories for the coding or decoding of continuing information—in other words, for the perception of the meanings of the *Umwelt*, meanings that the subject believes to be objective.

Axioms, body of laws, formal organizing principles: in all these words there is no doubt something shocking. After he had contrasted, as we have seen, *system* of personal experience and *structures* of the universe objectivized by science, G. Granger wrote that "the translation of subjective experience into a body of laws is impossible."

It is clear from the epistemological point of view that this transformation would be impossible because such an operation, as the purest formulation of the universal exigences of reason, cannot be performed on what is eminently individual, subjective, and irrational.

But clinical experience proves the contrary, and I think that one is entitled, at the completion of a structural analysis, to speak of structures and axioms, for every individual's affective system is *a coherent hypothetico-deductive system* dependent on definitions (affective-concepts), postulates (unchallenged principles), and operational categories, all of which can claim the name of axioms, since the whole organization of existence at the level of experience is rigorously governed and directly modeled by their continuing operation.

And this, furthermore, is indeed the impression produced by the effort at genuine understanding of others. Listening to someone else tell us his story, describe his existence, his feelings, his perceptions of those round him, we have the impression of a coherent universe from the moment when we understand his individual identifications of groups of meanings and the regulating principles, unique but *constant*, that determine his actions.

The entire construction is totally irrational, absurd, bizarre, perhaps inconceivable for the observer, but intrinsically it is regulated and regular as a geometry. Going back to Russell's famous remark on mathematics conceived as a hypothetico-deductive system, one might say: "One never knows what it is talking about or whether what it says is true." This was justified by the fact that the mathematician is free to set up his axioms (postulates and definitions) and the relations among axioms (his axiomatic, or body of laws, properly so called) as he thinks proper. But in the architectonics of affectivity, as in the hypothetico-deductive system of mathematics and modern geometries, once the axiomatic has been fixed then nothing is any longer arbitrary.

The work of the psychologist, like that of the epistemologist who would attempt to discover the style of conceptualization and the axioms of a mathematician on the basis of a random chapter from the man's work in which there was nothing but completed calculations, consists in grasping, in and through the sole fact at his disposition (a slice of affective existence and of observable behaviors), the dynamic categories and formal constants that structure the experienced relationship between the subject and his world.

This idea of structures of the subject-world relationship has been hinted at by all psychologists, but it is the modern idea of "*pattern* of personality" and "*patterns* of behavior" that comes the closest to it. A pattern is a model that models, a constant form of active structuration.

It has not been possible for the theoreticians of psychology to explain the nature of patterns completely because a theory, whatever it may be, even if it acts in conformity with the general laws of structuralism, employs a system of coding experience that is founded on the basis of certain determining experiences that resist change as soon as it has been established, so that it becomes incapable of incorporating other experiences without distortion.

Precisely through their vocabularies, however, as well as their interpretations, one encounters extremely suggestive observations among the earlier psychologists. Thus Pierre Janet, for example, in his *Automatisme psychologique* (1894), had derived from his clinical experiments the thought that affectivity evolves without consciousness of an "ego" or an "I" and that in this area sentiment, image, and orderly progression of a form of behavior express a single, identical psychic reality; according to him, realities of this kind, constituting automatisms, were capable of organizing in a coherent and repetitive fashion a "level of conduct" that excluded consciousness, the sense of the present, and intelligence, brought together differently under the name of "function of the real."

There was also Albert Burloud, who in his *Psychologie des tendances* (1920) masterfully propounded the schematization and thematization of "tendencies," psychophysiological postulates that, in his view, acted not as elementary forces but as abstract dynamic forms (in other words, *formal*) recognizable in the *kinds* of meanings perceived, in the *themes* of memory or imagination, as well as in the *schemes* of reactional behavior.

We have already seen that Ribot, exactly like Binet, opposed the contingency of the associationists with the observable reality of those themes endowed with a capacity for selecting and orienting perceptions and behaviors. As we know, Ribot had suggested the concept of *emotional-abstract*, which, moreover, was taken up by Burloud, to designate the dynamic forms of affectivity: "The emotional abstract," he wrote in *La logique des sentiments*, "is a condensed residue of analogous emotions, a general and generalized sentiment, taking part in the process of generalization of the ideas that accompany them."

Freud too had observed two phenomena that, if one separates them from his system, acquire a peculiar value: On the one hand, what he called "the automatism of repetition" and, on the other, what he called the "transference," both these phenomena appearing as two aspects of the same psychic reality.

Every individual [he wrote] through the concomitant influence of a natural predisposition and facts occurring during his childhood, possesses a personal, determined manner of living his [affective] life. Thus one derives a kind of *stereotype* (sometimes more than one), a stereotype that, in the course of existence, repeats itself a number of times, reproduces itself when circumstances and the nature of the accessible (affective) objects permit, and can to a certain degree be modified by subsequent impressions. . . . Current (affective) investment attaches itself to these *prototypes* in conformity with one of the stereotypes already present in the subject under study.[13]

Elsewhere [14] he wrote: "One cannot help admitting that in psychic life there exists an irresistible tendency to repetition." On this subject Freud always spoke of the compulsion to repeat. The *transference* itself, in its strictest sense, is essentially defined by the fact that, in the affective relation with the therapist, the patient *reenacts* a type of relation that he has constructed in his past. "The patient incorporates the physician into one of his *psychic series* that he has established in his past. . . . Sometimes it is the paternal *imago* * that sets the standard for this incorporation, but the transference is not bound to this prototype and can be achieved also following the maternal, fraternal, etc., images. . . ." "The patient repeats (in his present situation) with the analyst psychic events that he has already experienced. . . ." [15] "The patient has *no recollection* of what he has forgot, he merely *translates it into actions*. . . . The patient obviously repeats this act without knowing that a repetition is in question." "He has *transferred* onto the analyst psychic attitudes that were already prepared in him and that were in intimate relation with his neurosis. And thus, before our eyes, he repeats his defense reactions of that time. . . . What he shows us is thus the nucleus of his intimate history; *he reproduces it in palpable, present fashion instead of remembering it*."

Even more than Freud, Jung, thanks to his dissident conception, according to which the unconscious is structured (an observation derived from the comparison made among the myths, tales, and legends of all eras that demonstrate

---

* The famous term *imago* is used here, as we see, in the precise meaning of *model* and hence corresponds to *pattern*. Later Freud used the word *image* in the same sense.

in their varying contents the presence of constant *archetypes*), has endowed the "complexes" with a definition that
is already almost structuralist; through the labyrinth of his
cloudy thinking one can define *the complexes as networks
of affects and reaction paths* that, except in pathological
cases (in which a given complex, proliferating like a cancer,
invades affective life and behavior), are normal components
of our being-in-the-world, a version that could accompany
the incisive definition given by Marie Bonaparte: "The complexes are the organs of our psychic anatomy." [16]

Among the modern concepts that tend to express the
reality of structures and patterns, let us go back again to
that of *attitude*, which on sound ground has acquired a
great importance in contemporary psychology. It is remarkable that all studies undertaken from very varied channels
of approach have thus led to the focusing of a structuring
reality the effects of which are manifested on the affective
level as well as on the perceptive and behavioral levels.

For some fifteen years a number of students [17] have ex-
perimented on the *types of apprehension of the real*, or
preferential individual methods of organization of experience. They have called these "perceptive attitudes," or
styles of cognitive verification (one can see the relationship with Rorschach's *Erfassungstypus*—type of understanding). But, as soon as experience has been widened somewhat, one sees that these *perceptive* attitudes are in correlation with *characteristics of behavior*.

Moreover, in the same line of research, we know what is
called the Lesser and Kagan principle (the methodological
applications of which are immediate in the interpretation
of the Thematic Apperception Test), according to which
"there is isomorphism between the themes of the imagination and the structures of observable behavior."

Mira y Lopez erected his famous *myokinetic psychodiag-
nosis* on a similar finding: "Every mental attitude," he
wrote, "is accompanied by a muscular attitude as a consequence of the unity of the living creature." Through his
method, he said, he wished to "contribute an objective

standard for the measure of dominant tendencies in the personality as they are expressed in the individual's fundamental *attitudes of reaction.*"

In a general way, in fact, an *attitude* is a constant formal structure that shapes the manner of being, of understanding, of reacting, and of judging, and that consequently functions as a special apparatus for the coding or decoding of information. On the intellectual plane one would say that it is "the personal point of view" that one adopts in order to understand or know, or the customary method that one adopts in the face of problems to be solved; on the affective plane, one would say that it is the factor of thematization of experience and feelings; on the behavioral plane it would be a "pattern of postures and reactions."

In the present state of psychology, one can say that structures, whatever the name given to them, are regarded as significant centers to which all the modes of expression of a personality refer.

Goldstein makes the notion of *attitude* the key to his structuralist conception of the organization of the personality, and in the work of Schilder, one of the pioneers (with Lhermitte, van Bogaert, Head, and, once more, Goldstein) of the concept of the *body schema,* one finds this remarkable sentence written in 1931: "I think that in one way or another we can read in the postural model of the body what are the individual's strongest desires, and, whenever we discover a disturbance in one of these partial desires, we hope to find its trace in the postural model." [18] But the idea of structure, through its greater flexibility, makes it possible to go farther than does that of attitude. Not only does it recall the essential aspect of "*a priori* form" or "category" in the Kantian sense,* but it can serve at every stage of generalization because each structure of meaning

* It is obvious that the Kantian meaning referred to here envisages only the operative and transcendental essence of the category as active structuration of experience and that it is necessary to eliminate its meaning of *universal form of human experience in general.* Here, in fact, these "categories" are *individual* and their totality constitutes the dynamics of the personality.

detected in a sentence or in a mode of behavior is organized with a broader structure, which itself enters into a structure of structures, and so on. Such seems to be the complex edifice of interdependent forms, all *unconscious*, for consciousness grasps only current contents and never spontaneously its timeless structural invariants.

The methods of discovery

The aim of concrete psychology, then, is to discover the structures of the relation between the subject involved and his universe of experience—in other words, the structures of meanings that constitute his existential field (which he believes to be objective) and at the same time the affective-postural structures of his personality, since these two realities are one and the same thing.

It is obvious that another problem is clearly raised, and to this I shall devote the next section. This is the determination of the relation between the level of affectivity and the level of thought. Here let us make a few remarks on the first direction of study and the means of arriving at it.

1. *Analysis of the subject's verbal expression,* of his descriptions of his feelings, his opinions, his beliefs, and his affective or affective-motor reactions is an important method of approach for the psychologist. The well-known psychoanalytic objection—that consciousness of self reaches only an infinitesimal part of the vast domain of the "psychic" and that the most determining realities are "elsewhere," in the unconscious—cannot be taken into account if it is demonstrated that the formal unconscious is already present, as the latent structure of what he is expressing, in the subject's most trivial utterance dealing with his personal existence.

Behind what he says one should look not for what this means in itself, *or even what it means to him in the literal sense,* but for the structural signifier that is implicit in it after the conscious current content has been filtered out.

This is a very natural place for theoretical discussion of the *stage of comprehension* proposed by Carl Rogers. Reserving the right to develop elsewhere the method of psychotherapy that is to be inferred from structural analysis, I will say here only that the restatement of meaning-for-the-subject is absolutely essential to the objective of penetration of his universe of meanings. Without it one is doomed to "interpret"—that is, to superimpose *our categories* on what he wants to make us understand—and therefore to fail irreparably in the discovery of his (to say nothing of imposing ours on him by suggestion).[19]

It is important to know that the most serious errors are committed—that is, that one arrives at an interpretation and not at an elucidation—if one does not closely relate the structures of verbal expression or of the affective-postural reactions to the *significance of the experienced situation for the subject himself,* including especially the significance of his very relation with the psychologist here and now.

Mr. D. is a thirty-seven-year-old bachelor living with his widower father and working in a factory. In the first session he describes homosexual impulses in great detail. Although he has never practiced homosexuality, he describes himself as certainly a potential homosexual, but remarkably vicious. Changing the subject, he details his behavior toward his father, which he regards as unsuitable for a son. He no longer speaks to the older man, does not look at him, does nothing for him, reacts with sharp physical impulses to whatever he says, slams the door when leaving, etc. . . . Then, a moment later, he spontaneously embarks on his problems about his own penis, which he considers ridiculously small and badly shaped, etc.

There seems to be an abundance of psychoanalytic "material" and yet attention to the structure of what is said and concentration on the formal constant of the three types of confidences are sufficient to make it clear that Mr. D. has done only one single thing all along: *He has accused him-self and endeavored to have the therapist find him abnor-mal.* What significance does the therapist assume for him? What is the relation between this experienced significance and the affective-postural pattern that is brought out? To what existential system does this structure belong? None of this is yet known. But that this is the significant form of what is already known is absolutely certain. This *Gestalt* can and should be the object of a *formulation* in the strict sense of "put into a formula and formulated." The subject receives it from the therapist with a substantial and surpris-ing emotional impact; he recognizes it as his, in a manner that excludes any "resistance" because it is present and recognizable in what he has said *without the addition of anything further, even his own elucidation.* And, recogniz-ing it as his own, he takes cognizance of it as of a "general tendency" or, as we would say in our vocabulary, as an axiom of his existential system.

2. *Analysis of the expressive action.* "We are all aware that every individual has typical movements," J. A. Precker wrote in the remarkable chapter of his *Manuel des tech-nique projectives* given over to expressive movement:

We can recognize a friend a hundred yards away by his car-riage, or even, without seeing him, we know that he is in a room crowded with people simply from the customary quality of his voice. The psychologist who studies expressive behavior is concerned with two questions: (1) Is this behavior stable? *
(2) What is the relation between this behavior and the depth of the personality?

We establish the postulate that a person's movements are not accidental or determined by chance but are logical according to varying environmental conditions and are connected with the fundamental motivations of the organism.[20]

* *Stable* is to be taken here in the sense of *constant* or *containing an invariant.* From this point of view any "unstable" behavior (agi-tated, vacillating, volatile, suggestible, etc.) can be *characterized as such* in stable fashion: in other words, its character is clearly deter-mined and established.

We have already indicated that, however astonishing it may seem at first glance, attitude, posture, or movements themselves express what a subject feels here and now in the total present situation as he is living it. There is no point in indulging in any "interpretation." The subject who locks himself away in silence is quite simply signifying that he will not or cannot participate; the way in which one shakes hands is also significant. To again quote Precker: "The man who, on the level of conscious intention, thinks that he is warmly congratulating an opponent whom in fact he loathes betrays himself in his smile or in the movements of recoil and withdrawal that accompany his formal simulation."

If one examines the structure of the expressive movement, one observes that dissimilar movements, different in their contents, can have the same structure; this relieves us of the hypothesis of "symbolism" or "projection." Here, *mutatis mutandis*, the problem is the same as that of the transfer of learning: the same form is invested in different contents and, strictly speaking, nothing is transferred. Since every affective attitude is by its essence affective-*motor*, the movement is directly expressive of what is felt. It does happen that, as a result of social or cultural constraints or others arising out of the educational environment, behavior patterns corresponding to the expectations or the pressures of the environment hamper the full motor expression of the feelings. This phenomenon gives rise to a "tension" (which seems to have its neuro-physiological accompaniments, as is proved by the studies of "parasite" movements during exercises in relaxation) through the conflict of behavior patterns, a tension that can have actual effects of irradiation if it continues.

This would also explain the relief resulting from "displacement" behavior or similar substitutional behavior, the "release" of which is a special case, and to which one can relate movements or hints of actions brought on by certain techniques that clinical psychology calls projective, as in the construction of the village in the Imaginary-Village Test.[21]

A number of studies are currently being undertaken on bodily expression, some in order to study its significant structures as a means of diagnosis, others in order to organize methods of psychotherapy through the overall resolution of postural tensions (methods of relaxation).

The great hypothesis of Felix Deutsch is confirmed through these investigations and justifies them: "Postural attitudes reflect or replace . . . precede or accompany . . . the verbal expression of the unconscious material. In repose every individual has a characteristic basic posture, to which he returns whenever he is taken out of it." [22]

The psychology of types of movement (extent, orientation, form), of the total movements of the body (walking, working, resting), of the kinds of postural-motor reactions, of carriage and rhythm, of the voice, of style in speaking and writing, of graphic movements, of pictural movements, of hand movements, etc., shows signs of becoming not only an important branch of general typology but also and particularly a major orientation of the observation of subjects during examination through tests.

3. Psychological tests. It has been said since tests were invented that none of them could claim to evaluate a function or an aptitude *separately* from the whole of the personality. Alfred Binet himself said that the experiment of tactile discrimination through the two points of a compass (a classic laboratory experiment for the measurement of the threshold of perceptible divergence) was more a method for the study of the subject's whole personality than a method for the exploration of his "sensitivity." And this was not a jest. In his famous work on the intelligence he showed the extent to which observation of the subject in the total situation is richer in information about him than is knowledge of his performance in intelligence tests properly so called.

In spite of the often vehement attacks by persons un-familiar with psychology or by amateurs of dubious good faith, test technicians agree in believing that taking a test is to be considered as *a total situation* in which a subject is placed, and his reactions are significant in relation to the situation as he personally experiences it, the presence of the observer being a part of this whole.

The test itself, then, is a constituent of a vast situational datum; in other words, for the subject "taking a test" as-sumes a determined, subjective meaning that is articulated with the meaning given to it by the observer, with the sub-ject's total impressions of the place in which he takes the test, of his spatial position with respect to the observer, of the weather, of the aspect of the material with which he is confronted, with the meaning that he gives to the instruc-tions, etc.

Given all these facts, "performances" can be evaluated only in the framework of the psychologist's total compre-hension of the subject in the situation.

Whatever the conditions and circumstances in which the test is taken, the fundamental principle of structural psy-chology justifies the confidence and the working methods of those psychologists who seek to determine *the patterns of actions and reactions* through reference, on the one hand, to the objective structure of the test (the purified and vali-dated situational model) and, on the other, the significance of the total situation for the subject himself. Hence psy-chologists simultaneously seek patterns and departures with respect to norms (which are sometimes averages, some-times the aggregate of signs of adaptation regarded as "normal").

In the arsenal of diagnostic weaponry, certain techniques are more specifically directed toward achieving the revela-tion of the structures of affectivity, or, in the common phrase, of the depth personality. These are *the so-called projective techniques,* the postulate of which follows:

If, through appropriate instructions,

1. *one excludes, relatively, the effect of a certain activity on a conscious level, characterized by critical control, reflection, intelligence in its function of realistic adaptation to the solution of practical problems, and*
2. *one offers the subject relatively unstructured stimuli the structuration of which he has to complete,*

then in what he does we should necessarily discover the traces of the operational activity of the affective-motor structures that constitute his depth personality and his existence on the level of conscious experience.*

Whatever their *a priori* theoretical orientations, all students have been led by their experimental work and what it has shown them to formulate *the structuralist hypothesis,* most often without daring to give it this name, which would have contradicted the sacrosanct idea of "projection" in the Freudian sense and which would tend to replace it with that of "expression."

"Every spontaneous act," Rapaport wrote,[23] "an individual's expression or response, his movements, his perceptions, his feelings, his verbalizations, his motor actions, in some way bears the stamp of his personality. The important postulate, according to which *an individual shapes his personal productions in accordance with the dispositions of the active matrix of his personality,* has been specifically regarded as the projective hypothesis."

By way of a concise review of the projective techniques currently employed it is easy to show that the patterns of personality (of the subject-environment relationship on the level of experience) are always grasped in their operation *at the perceptive level and at the expressive level* in a closely bound fashion, although the techniques are designed to bring out this or that specific aspect according to their creators' intentions.

---

* It was precisely this level that Frank, in the little book that established the theory of the projective techniques in 1949, decided to call "the private universe."

A. THE PROJECTIVE TECHNIQUES THAT
SHOW THE STRUCTURES OF PERCEPTION

It is worthy of note that perception thus considered—that is, in its significant structuration for the subject—acquires in projective psychology the names of *apperception* (active grasp of the perceptive datum by the subject), *misperception* (perceptual distortion), and *dynaception* (perception patterned by the dynamics of the personality).

1. The tachistoscope experiments. When viewing of the perceptive datum is shortened in order to reduce the quantity of pertinent information and the pressure of meaning exerted by the context, there is an increase in the part played by the subjective structuration of the datum and the subject should derive the significance from within himself. Thus one learns the orientations of his apperception.

2. Jung's word-association test. If the subject is given a list of ordinary words and asked to speak the first word that comes into his own mind in association with each "inductor word," the latency intervals and the differences in response words on the second exposure to the test will show which words have to do with "complexes."

3. The sentence-completion test. (There is an abundance of material by different authors.) These consist in offering the subject the initial words of sentences, or even mere grammatical subjects, and asking him to complete the sentences. The forms of his constructions are organized in terms of the ways in which he perceives the beginnings and of the significant affective themes induced (or provoked) by such perceptions.

4. The story-completion tests (for example, Duss' fables). These make possible a broader development of the principle of the sentence-completion tests and are related to the TAT.

5. Weil's affective-diagnostic test. This is based on the detection (through the measurement of the psychogalvanic reflex on the psychogalvanometer) of the subject's nonconscious emotional reactions at the apperception of more or less abstract stimuli (from words to geometrical shapes). In this way one can detect certain thematized "areas of sensitization."

6. *Murray's Thematic Apperception Test.* This and a number of allied techniques (Bellak's CAT, the Symonds Test, Schneidmann's MAPS, the Tridimensional TAT,* van Lennep's Four-Images Test, the ORT, etc.) present the subject with starter-stimuli on the basis of which he has to construct an organized story with a beginning, a development, and a conclusion.

There is an abundance of methods, many of which attempt at all costs to treat the production as a dream with the *a priori* interpretations of psychoanalysis, with the "symbolism" of the "elements" in the content, and with the hypothesis of the narrator's self-identification with the hero of the story that he tells.

The most valid results are those that are arrived at through the study of the thematic constants in the stories, each of which represents a circumstantial variant (with due allowance, in a certain way, for the inducing images) of a few *structural invariants* among which the stories are divided and that correspond directly with the narrator's affective system.

7. *Rorschach's psychodiagnostic test.* An exemplary technique, this, as everyone knows, consists in showing the subject in succession ten reproductions of ink blots, some of them grey and black, some red and black, and some in a variety of colors. The impressive number of publications discussing this test had brought to light many varying methods of employing the test, and research has led even to the designing of new blots (Zülliger, Holtzmann, etc.).

The Rorschach test makes it possible to observe the sub-

---

* This test, in which the subject is presented with three-dimensional masses of ambiguous and blurred significance, has been successfully employed by my collaborators and myself as a projective technique for the blind in the Psychological Laboratory of La Persagotière in Nantes.

ject's structures of perception in operation, and in this domain the *formal codifications* introduced by Rorschach himself and developed by his successors are completely structuralist in spirit.

The recognition of the "sensitive areas" of the past, examined on the basis of the observation of "shocks" from certain ink-blot patterns, has in addition led to the closer examination of the value of each plate in evoking a particular situation or the relation to a factor of the experienced environment. Let us take the first plate, for example. In view of the facts that it is the first, that the subject has just received his instructions ("What can this represent, in your view?"), and that the plate is relatively easy to apprehend (a grey spot with considerable white space), one can legitimately consider that *the total situation* is defined thus: "Type of situation in which the subject should assert himself or show what he can do while being watched by others and in the presence of another-as-judge in a relatively simple task but one that is unfamiliar and creates a certain surprise."

If this is the "specificity" of the plate, the structural analysis of the responses, the behaviors, the succession of responses, and the overall reactions should make it possible to detect *the structure of the behavior and the impressions experienced* by the subject *in every situation of this type*. A specific case of self-assertion, but a typical case, this situation, through its very general structure, necessarily determines, on the one hand, the particular meaning inscribed in this general framework that the subject is going to give it (e.g., an opportunity to make a showing, or an anguishing danger of failure and pejorative judgment, etc.); on the other, the personal postural-behavioral patterns that he sets in motion in order to respond to it and that at the same time define the meaning of this situation for him.

A methodical analysis of his production from this point of view makes it possible to infer the one and the other and guarantees generalization—that is, the attribution to the subject of these ways of perceiving and reacting no longer in *this* test situation but in *every* analogous existential situation: situations with the same form.

Experimentation fully confirms the hypothesis and suggests that this method of diagnosis be extended to all the plates.[24]

By way of this dimension the Rorschach test goes beyond the framework of techniques that reveal the structures of perception and becomes more a technique of expression.

B. THE TECHNIQUES THAT SHOW
THE STRUCTURES OF EXPRESSION

As has been shown earlier, the question is one of techniques that place the emphasis on the analysis of means of expression but that necessarily bring into play the perceptive structuration.

1. The free sketch. In this technique it is the expressive movements (types of movement, orientation of gestures, utilization of pictural space, behavior during the work, means employed, etc.) and the themes selected that are studied as manifestations of the affective-motor structures of the personality.

2. Finger-painting. First employed as a method of relaxation and then currently as an occupational therapy or a means of release, finger-painting is a way of studying personality patterns, especially through the analysis of the movements made during the successive productions.

With the palm of the hand covered with paint, the subject has to cover a horizontal surface of special prepared paper (and the whole surface), selecting the color, its consistency, and, obviously, the manner of working. Then he discusses what he has done.

Observation of the expressive hand movements (smearing, rubbing, scrawling, pushing, pulling, patting, clapping, scratching, removing in little dabs), of the rhythm, of the texture, and of the method, and analysis of the verbalization make it possible to probe the postural and reactional patterns in their most general forms.

3. *The myokinetic test of Mira y Lopez,* its author says, is a way of studying muscular attitudes and expressive movements in their relation with "mental attitudes." The subject is supposed to draw lines following a model, without support for his hand and with his eyes blindfolded.

4. *Margaret Lowenfeld's Mosaic Test.* Margaret Lowenfeld (who is also the creator of the World Game, later revised by Charlotte Bühler) wanted with this test, even more than in the World Game, to give her subjects the most extensive means, and the least significant in themselves, for the expression of their affective-ideo-motor *Gestalten.*

With 465 small pieces of six colors (black, white, red, blue, green, yellow) and five shapes (three kinds of triangle, the square, and the diamond), as well as a box that serves as a frame, the subject is asked to make "whatever he likes." In their studies evaluating the Mosaic Test, Diamond and Schmale wrote: "The basic hypothesis is that in the Mosaic Test major defects in the creation of a recognizable *Gestalt* are in correlation with . . . and reflect . . . significant defects in the structure of the subject's basic personality." [25]

5. *The Imaginary-Village Test.* Derived from Lowenfeld's World Game, Bühler's World Test, Bolgar's and Fischer's Little World Game, and Arthus' and later Pierre Mabille's Village Test, The Imaginary-Village Test * provides the subject with all the means of expression of the structures of his affective universe.

With three hundred pieces, some of them representational (charged with a potential affective value by the designs that ornament them or by their shapes) and others nonrepresentational (left to subjective significance), the sub-

* As published by Editest, 94, rue du Général Capiaumont, Brussels.

ject is asked to build "an imaginary village in which he will live" starting from a specific spot on a square platform.

Through the materials, the expressive movements of construction, and the space arrangements of the pieces within the designated area, the subject structures his production in a way that reveals his affectivity and the possible disturbances in his relation to the world.

6. *Rosenzweig's frustration test.* Here twenty-four situations are presented, all of them variants of a particular structure: a situation of frustration for one of the characters in them. The subject is supposed to examine each situation, to identify himself with the person who, as the case may be, is suffering material or moral injury, is blocked by an obstacle, or is deprived of an expected satisfaction, and to express his reaction in verbal form.

From the *formal* analysis of each reaction and from the evolution of the reactional pattern through the *successive* frustrations, Rosenzweig derived what he called the *personality patterns* of characteristic types of reaction, with their constants of direction and significance, as well as the measure of the gap in relation to a "standard of conformity" to the average reactions of the group.

7. *The role game.* In his article, "Psychodrama as a Projective Technique," [26] Moreno himself makes it possible to speak of his methods here as a means of diagnosing postural-behavioral patterns of the relation of the subject to others. Earlier, when he originated the Situation Test, he had thought of studying "role behavior" in individuals by having them enact situations representing aspects of everyday life, whether their own or fictive scenarios. From other sources we know the place occupied in the development of his ideas by the Impromptu Theater before he arrived at the therapeutic measures of psychodrama and sociodrama as means of relearning or readjustment of roles (for Moreno personality was defined in terms of roles). The concept of role, which must be understood as a made-up person, as in

the theater, represented for Moreno *a structure of adapted socioaffective relationship* that is available to the subject and that he can therefore employ in his handling of a social situation that requires it. The ability of changing roles means that the subject has preserved sufficient *spontaneity* not to be the prisoner of any one role, but it means also that he has available a range of behavioral patterns that makes possible the adjustment of the interpersonal situation.

In the Projective and Expressive Action Test, Moreno and his collaborators went back to the situation test and elaborated its sociodramatic procedures as well as the methods of evaluation. The test consists in nine situations "the operations of which are planned in advance and objectivized, but in which the subject has full latitude to express his personal reaction and his ideational contents." After a brief interview and an initial free play intended to create confidence and "warm up" the subject, he is introduced into the nine prepared situations, one after another.

Instead of describing this test, the details of which the reader will find in the article cited, I should prefer to say something about role-playing as a projective technique. The method that has given me the best results is this:

Individually or in small groups, subjects are asked to create simple scenarios involving one, two, or three characters, with no detail beyond the identification of the characters and a description of the situation in which they are going to be placed. Hence the scenario stops with a presentation of the imaginary protagonists and their situation. Then the group is asked to choose the first situation among all the available scenarios to be acted out. When this has been done, the experimenter asks for volunteers who "see the roles clearly and would like to play them."

The actors then go out separately. The director (experimenter) then introduces them one by one and, in a short interview intended to create an easy atmosphere and warm up the subject, asks each one to explain to the spectators how he "sees" the total situation and how he expects to play his part step by step. This phase is necessary too in order to put one's finger on what will emerge later as the difference between the *a priori* conception of the role (in the imagined progression of the situation) and the part actually played (in the concrete unfolding of interpersonal relations).

When the actors (without communication among themselves) have thus individually and separately presented their ideas on their parts and the situation, the acting-out begins.

Thus organized, the role game becomes a veritable *simulation model* through which the subjects will necessarily disclose the affective-postural-behavioral structures that govern their behavior. Structural analysis of each one's role-playing, looking into the general modes of reactions registered in turn in a constant structure, will have to be placed *in relation*, before any conclusion can be drawn, *with the structures of the situations* as they have been subjectively felt by the subject during the drama.

This means that, after the enactment, each actor must be interviewed in order to understand what the concrete phases of the acted situation generically signified to him. One sees then that each has lived his experience in a unique manner and it is in relation to the structure of this lived experience that the behavioral patterns acquire a meaning.

Then, with surprise (if the results are disclosed to him), the subject recognizes that without knowing it he has invested the enactment with his *chronic* ways of perceiving and reacting. His understanding is enriched by the discovery of the meaning of the other persons' reactions and of the chain of processes that has governed the interactions. He also measures the gap that may have been produced between his way of understanding the present and the present itself. But through this dimension the role game ceases to be a projective technique and opens into a psychotherapy and a sociotherapy.

Consciousness

We have still to situate self-consciousness in relation to the structures of the affective level. From the genetic point of view, a second level of consciousness is created after the age of six years, bearing a potential revolution in the relation to the world. This level implies the possibility of performing a *decentration*.

Thus far psychological consciousness was comparable to a *vigilance* with respect to the surrounding world, and the information that was perceived, analyzed, and generalized directly concerned the relationship between the organism and its vital environment, without any possibility of grasping "objective" relations among things themselves. Everything existed only through and in its relation with the self, through and in those situations in which the subject was involved through his organism. It is this level, as we have seen, that is constituted as a level of experience or as affective universe.

Now this consciousness as vigilance in a universe of an ecological and egocentric type undergoes a quite rapid metamorphosis after the sixth year of life in normal subjects (this takes two to three years) and becomes capable of taking a position *at a distance from itself* (thinking consciousness) as well as *at a distance from the world* (constitution of the objectivity of the world and knowledge, at least potentially).

This revolution, the secrets of which are far from having been fully discovered, seems to determine (or to be determined by) the entry of new processes into action. They include:

1. *Perception of the objective relationships among things,* which makes it possible for the functions of analysis of the content of information, coding, categorization, and percep-

tion of forms to be applied in a new manner that carries within it *abstract and conceptual knowledge*—in other words, that enables the intelligence to develop in a prodigious bound toward rational understanding, the culmination of which is scientific knowledge.

2. *Perception of the present as such.* It seems that a process that Minkowski, picking up a term used by Pierre Janet, called the "process of presentification" [27] appeared to upset being-in-the-world and transformed vigilance into consciousness of the *here-and-now*, or consciousness of the present as such.

It is this that represents the influence of the process that Pierre Janet described as a function of the real and of which he said: "The final expression of the function of the real, which probably sums up all that preceded it, might be a mental operation that is unfortunately very little known: the constitution of time, *the formation of the present moment.*"

By carrying forward the implications of this phenomenon, the alterations of which in the unhealthy consciousness were described by Minkowski and Janet (alterations to which, it seems to me, the famous "illusion of *déjà vu*" might be linked), one would come to consider, in the perception of the present as such, the effect of a process of *individuation* the expressions of which would be many:

—the possibility of perceiving any situation no longer in relation to the forms of past experience but "in itself" and, so to speak, in its individuality and its uniqueness;
—the possibility of *consciousness of self* simultaneously as individualized ego and as consciousness of the present;
—the possibility of situating the past as past and the future as indeterminately to come, and therefore a revolution in the perception of time;
—the possibility of constructing through a method (and no longer through the automatic influence of patterns) the resolution of situations, which makes feasible a *realism* hitherto impossible;

—the possibility of purging the present individualized in the ego-here-and-now of everything that is not itself, by differentiation.

3. *The inhibition of the affective-behavioral patterns of the lower level of consciousness.* This new inhibition is a function of self-control, a capacity to stop and suspend, linked to the function of presentification and intellectual perception of the situation. No doubt it is also the expression of that possibility of standing off at a distance that we suggested above as origin or condition of the *thinking consciousness.*

4. *The formation of the consciousness of moral values properly so called,* or the possibility of taking a position at a distance from oneself and judging one's own actions in relation to abstract general rules or non-personal values, a further consequence of decentration: the possibility of sacrificing something of oneself for others or for the group, inhibiting egocentration; and the awakening of the sense of personal responsibility.[28]

After this digression by way of genetics let us go back to the normal consciousness. These four principal processes are developed together in normal evolution, although prepared by the earlier stages; they burgeon after the second stage of childhood in a way that makes one think of a veritable mutation. The possibilities of the *intelligence* in particular undergo a metamorphosis, as Diénès' experiments in the formation of the concept have demonstrated, arriving at Piaget's conclusions from another point of view.

Confirmation can also be found in psychological studies dealing with defectives. Investigators saw that in defectives consciousness of self, consciousness of values (apart from conformist conditioning), self-control, and the sense of the present and of Time suffered a delay or an arrest proportioned to the deficit of intelligence as a "symbolic function," insofar as this is classically understood to mean the perception of objective and abstract relationships. "Defectives, like children," Minkowski concluded, "since they do not sufficiently detach themselves from their desires, their plans, their joys, and their sorrows, have only an incomplete knowledge of themselves, subject to the degree to which from this point of view the development of their personalities has attained. This being the case, it is easy to understand that they could have only such knowledge of their fellow-beings as was proportionate to their own degree of awareness." *

Thus two levels of existence are brought into being, of which the first (the level of experience or affective existence) is completely marked by the egocentric experience of the unthought past and the second is an indefinite possibility of objectivity. These two levels, which bring into play *functions that are analogous* but radically different in their results, structure our consciousness of the present and our behavior in the present.

It is as if, in the healthy state of inner calm and intellectual detachment, normal adult human subjects were capable of perceiving the information of their present by coding it with intellectual categories. In such cases they can finally take different points of view and even envisage a number of aspects (all this being absolutely impossible when the affective structure is dominant); they give their reality a relatively objective meaning, and they can react in an adapted fashion to the situation in the here and now.

But it may happen that this realism of adjusted intellectual operation, functioning in the present, is put out of action by affective and postural patterns. This amounts to charging with experienced meanings the perception of a present clouded by the return of an unrecognized past.

Between these two extreme instances our way of being

---

* Let us state also that, if their affectivity seems overdeveloped, this is the result of an illusion arising from the pertinacity of their very primitive need for love and security; their insecurity is enhanced with the impression of having no "grasp" on the world and with the reactions of anxiety as well as hostility on the part of those round them.

in the world and toward others oscillates constantly and often it mingles the two levels of structures and meanings. More precisely, it seems that in day-to-day existence there are regions or kinds of situations in which our "objective" perception may be impossible or, at the very least, difficult.

Maturity and emotional stability, like the "strength of the ego," are in direct relation with the resistance of the "consciousness-of-self—consciousness-of-the-present-reality—objectivity" level to the tide of affective-motor meanings.

These, which are always present, are not necessarily in direct conflict with common sense and with critical-thinking-consciousness, since, fortunately, they often provide the affective support for commitment and action. Their potential, however, can divert thought or, more subtly, establish itself under the cloak of reason and intellectual justification.

It is the discovery by the thinking consciousness of its own *deception* that constitutes the lever of psychotherapy. Consciousness and the ego are indeed gulled to the extent to which they feel objectivity in meanings expressing the affective structures or the fantasies of the private universe.

One has often wondered through what mystery psychotherapy could free consciousness from the implications of the unconscious structures. There is no mystery, it seems to me. When attention—in other words, thinking consciousness, with its power to inhibit and arrest—is directed to the affective structures that without its knowledge determined the meanings of its existence, the ego recognizes simultaneously the validity of the observation and its own deception. It was in fact induced, by its blind captivity, to treat the here and the now as an eternal repetition of the past, and this deprived it at once of the reality of the present and of any future. It placed in action behavior forms with chronic patterns corresponding to primitive meanings. Through the recognition of structures—and not necessarily through the recollection of original situations (as Alexander has observed)—and through a series of *redefinitions of its false concepts* in the light of the present regained, the ego restores, and becomes capable of mobilizing in a more stable fashion, the level of objective (or more objective) relations with the real and with others, with its own past, in short, with respect to which too it *takes on some detachment.*

It is always the same facts of the world that seem to strike the receptors, but something has altered in the system of coding and categorization, and as a result the meanings are no longer the same. The liberation of consciousness is matched by a mutation of universe.

FIVE

Conclusion

The representation of the "psychic apparatus" that we have
been led to make for ourselves can no longer, in the late
1960s, be that proposed by Freud in 1896 or even that
elaborated by him in 1920. The model of that era, strongly
marked by the fashion of post-hypnotic suggestions and the
physiology of impulses and instincts, can no longer serve
for the understanding of the new mass of observations that
psychoanalysis itself has unleashed.

Phenomenology from Husserl to Merleau-Ponty and the
existential analysis created by Binswanger have broadly
demonstrated that our universe is integrally and uniquely
composed of meanings, of which, consequently, we are the
prisoners. . . . Animal psychology, rejuvenated by the work
of Lorenz and Tinbergen, has discovered that functions that
are similar with respect to the higher functions of man
but acting on the level of the ecological *Umwelt* centered
by the organism itself in its vigilance for survival enabled
the animal to code specific information and to adjust forms
of behavior to stabilized situational forms. . . . The psychology of human learning lost the ideas of generalization
and transfer here, but it gained pedagogical methods by
trying to achieve formation at the level of structures themselves, and this was developed by the so-called simulation
methods with the help of models.

All these contributions, in turn, were confirmed and en-

riched by the theories on information, necessarily concomitant with the advances of cybernetics, which is the leading
employer of them. The methods of automatic analysis of
content and coding in different code systems could be realized in electronic brains as well as in translating machines
or in robot animals. . . .

General linguistics and phonology, for their part, developed the concept of unconscious structure in a new direction, in consequence rejuvenating the methods of the study
of man; structural anthropology, with Claude Lévi-Strauss,
found in this the source of fruitful principles for research
and comprehension. This notion of structure, thus reinvigo-
rated, restored to *Gestalt* psychology a different immediacy
and an enrichment that Goldstein had predicted and prepared.

Structural psychology, then, is "in the air," and by now
one can trace its guiding lines. It carries the seed of an
advance in psychology, and new concepts have to be created. It is interesting to observe that, *in terms of the very
laws of conceptualization and of information coding, the
outmoded theories can no longer "read" the new findings*
and the numerous contributions of unanticipated experiments; one may also predict resistance by the old structures
and the archaic coding system to the advances of knowledge that call for a new examination of schemes constructed
in the past and adapted to a certain level of apprehension
of the real.

General psychology can no longer keep up the compart-
mentalization of faculties. The convenient psychoanalytic
trilogy of id, ego, and superego is no longer valid. Similar
functions structure two levels of experience, one ego-cen-
tered, the other decentered and objective. The unconscious
dynamic structures of consciousness, under the influence of
which meanings appear in the universe, are, like those
meanings themselves, either of the system of the preobjec-
tive and organismic level, affective-postural in essence, or
of the system of the objective level properly so called, that

of thinking consciousness and rational relationships. Consciousness, then, is not the direct giver of meaning; meaning comes from forms and formal signifiers, assimilating and coding information on the two levels simultaneously. The structures of meaning are found on both these levels, that of concepts and that of affective schemes. The latter organize subjective elements, most of the time mistaken because fantasied, deceiving the intelligence of the subject, who is their dupe. The neurotic clings to them out of fear of the truth and cherishes his fantasies, which condemn him to a world of his own that is unreal. In all human beings affective meanings are commingled with the perceived world, and we have more or less to suffer from them, correction being feasible only through the recognition of the distorting structures, which are always present, significant, and motor.

Freedom, then, is perhaps only a continued liberation of consciousness, imprisoned without its knowledge by its structures that determine meanings as much as behaviors and that have been developed in continuing intentionality toward the world at historical moments of adaptation.

Every organism conceals its structuration, every individual being like every society; but it possesses also what is life itself: the possibility of changing its structures within specific limits linked to the range of development of the organism itself and to the natural resistance of the already erected structures. No living thing could survive without organization; none could survive with an immobilist organization, but no more could any survive in a permanent revolution that would be the illusion of freedom.

NOTES AND BIBLIOGRAPHY

OF SOURCES CITED

CHAPTER ONE

1. G. Walter, *Le cerveau vivant* (*The Living Brain*), p. 53 (Éd. Delachaux Nietslé).

2. Maldiney, *Le dévoilement des concepts fondamentaux de la psychologie à travers la Dasein-Analyse de Binswanger* (*The Disclosure of the Fundamental Concepts of Psychology Through Binswanger's Dasein-Analysis*), in *Schweiz. Arch. Neurol. Neurochir. psychiatr.*, 1963, 92, No. 1, p. 215.

3. A. Martinet, *Éléments de linguistique générale* (*Elements of General Linguistics*), p. 16 (Éd. A. Colin).

4. G. Apollinaire wrote: "Memories are hunting horns the sound of which dies amid the wind."

5. P. Guillaume, *Psychologie de la Forme* (*Psychology of Form*), p. 71 (Éd. Flammarion).

6. G. Bachelard, *La Formation de l'esprit scientifique* (*The Shaping of the Scientific Mind*), p. 246 *et passim* (Éd. Vrin).

7. *Ibid.*, pp. 67-70.

8. G. G. Granger, *Objet, structures, et significations* (*Object, Structures, and Meanings*), in *Rev. Int. de Phil.* III–IV, No. 73–74, 1965, p. 257.

9. V. F. von Weizsäcker, *Reflexgesetze*, in *Handbuch der normalen und pathologischen Physiologie* (*Laws of Reflex*, in *Handbook of Normal and Pathological Physiology*), quoted by Merleau-Ponty, *La structure du comportement* (*The Structure of Behavior*), p. 11.

10. M. Merleau-Ponty, *La structure du comportement*, p. 13 (NRF).

11. Goldstein, *Aufbau des Organismus* (*Construction of the Organism*), Chap. II, p. 58.

12. Fabre, article in *Médecine et Hygiène*, 1961, 19, 528, pp. 978 ff.

13. Bush and Mosteller did in fact suggest this term in 1955 instead of the word *stimulus* in order to emphasize that the stimulus-for-the-experimenter is not necessarily the stimulus-that-the-subject-of-the-experiment-perceives.

14. Jean Delay, *Les dérèglements de l'humeur* (Mood Disorders), p. 1 (Éd. PUF).

15. Maldiney, *op. cit.*, p. 212.

16. Cf. R. Mucchielli, *Caractères et visages* (*Characters and Faces*), Bk. I (Éd. PUF).

17. R. Meili, *Les expressions caractériologiques dans les premiers mois de la vie* (*Characterological Expressions in the Early Months of Life*), in *Rev. intern. de caractérologie* (Éd. PUF), Vol. VI, 1964, pp. 25–26.

18. Cf. Jean Delay, *op. cit.*

19. E. Minkowski, *Le temps vécu* (*Time Lived*), p. 289 (Éd. Desclée, Brussels).

20. *Ibid.*, pp. 177–179.

21. P. Guillaume, *op. cit.*, p. 75.

22. Cf. K. Lewin, *Principles of Dynamic Psychology, Topological Psychology, la Psychologie dynamique* (French trans., Éd. PUF).

23. P. Guillaume, *op. cit.*, pp. 129–130.

24. Maldiney, *op. cit.*, p. 210.

25. P. Guillaume, quoting Lewin, *op. cit.*, p. 123.

26. J. Kagan, H. Moses, I. Sigel, *Psychological Significance of Styles of Conceptualization*, in *Monogr. Soc. Res. Child Development*, USA, 1963, 28, 2, pp. 73–112.

CHAPTER TWO

1. Tinbergen, *Étude de l'instinct* (*Study on Instinct*), pp. 23–24 (Éd. Payot).

2. Pavlov, *Typologie et pathologie de l'Activité nerveuse supérieure* (*Typology and Pathology of Higher Nervous Activity*), Chap. XVIII (French trans., Éd. PUF).

3. Tinbergen, *op. cit.*, p. 62 *et passim*.

4. René Spitz, *The Smiling Response* (1946) and *La première année de la vie de l'enfant* (*The First Year of the Child's Life*), pp. 20–23 (French trans., Éd. PUF).

5. Kohler, paper read to the Academy of Sciences of Berlin in 1918, *Nachweis einfacher Struktur Funktionen beim Schimpansen und beim Haushuhn* (*Report on Simple Structure Functions in the Chimpanzee and the Chicken*), quoted in Guillaume, *op. cit.*, p. 166.

6. J. F. Richard, *La généralisation du signal* (*The Generalization of the Signal*), 1966 (Éd. PUF).

7. Buytendijk, in *La psychiatrie animale* (*Animal Psychiatry*), pp. 118–120 (Éd. Desclée, Brussels).

8. Barclay, Martin, *Reward and Punishment Associated With the Same Goal Response. A Factor in the Learning of Motives*, in *Psych. Bull.*, USA, 1963, 60, 5, pp. 441–451.

9. Cf. bibliography on this subject in R. Mucchielli, *Philosophie de la médecine psychosomatique* (*Philosophy of Psychosomatic Medicine*), chapter on experimental neuroses (Aubier). Cf. also C. Cain, *Le problème des névroses expérimentales* (*The Problem of the Experimental Neuroses*), 1959, p. 74, and special chapter in *La Psychiatrie animale, op. cit.*, p. 207.

10. Jerome S. Bruner, *Contemporary Approaches to Cognition*, pp. 49–50 (Harvard University Press, 1964).

11. Munn, *Traité de psychologie* (*Treatise on Psychology*), pp. 153–157 (Éd. Payot).

12. Couffignal, *La Cybernétique* (*Cybernetics*), pp. 32–39 (Éd. PUF, *Que sais-je?*).

13. J. S. Bruner, *op. cit.*, pp. 46–47.

14. G. Walter, *Le cerveau vivant*, p. 138 (Éd. Delachaux-Nietslé).

15. Théodule Ribot, *La logique des sentiments* (*The Logic of the Emotions*), p. 6 (Éd. Alcan).

16. A. Bourcier, *Le traitement de la dyslexie* (*The Treatment of Dyslexia*), 1966 (ESF).

17. *La méthode psycho-cinétique du Dr. Le Boulch* (*The Psycho-Kinetic Method of Dr. Le Boulch*), 1966 (ESF).

18. *La méthode Ramain* (*The Ramain Method*), Public. of the Technical Schools of the CCIP, Paris.

19. Merleau-Ponty, *La structure du comportement*, pp. 20, 28 (Éd. PUF).

20. *Ibid.*, p. 9; cf. also p. 31.

21. C. L. Musatti, *Structure et expérience dans la phénoménologie de la perception* (*Structure and Experience in the Phenomenology of Perception*), in *J. Psych. Fr.*, 1960, 57, No. 2, p. 126.

22. M. D. Vernon, *The Psychology of Perception*, p. 200 (University Press of London, 1965), quoting A. C. Rosen cf. L. Mangan, A. Jones, J. S. Bruner, etc. Bibliogr., pp. 209–211.

23. L. Postman and D. R. Brown, *The Perceptual Consequence of Success and Failure*, in *J. Abn. Soc. Psychol.*, USA, 1952, 47, p. 213.

24. R. S. Lazarus and R. A. MacCleary, *Autonomic Discrimination Without Awareness*, in *Psychol. Rev.*, 1951, 58, p. 113.

25. Experiments by R. Levine and G. Murphy, *The Relation of Intensity of a Need to the Amount of Perceptual Distortion*, in *J. Psychol.*, USA, 1942, 13, p. 283; and by R. S. Lazarus, H. Yousem, and D. Arenberg, *Hunger and Perception*, in *J. Person.*, USA, 1953, 21, p. 312.

26. Experiments by Wispe, cited in Vernon, *op. cit.*, p. 208.

27. Vernon, *op. cit.*, pp. 187–188.

28. L. Postman, J. S. Bruner, and E. McGinnies, *Personal Values*

and Selective Factors in Perception, in *J. Abn. Soc. Psychol.*, 1948, 43, p. 142.

29. Cf., for example, V. Hudson, *Cultural Problems in Pictorial Perception*, in *S. Afr. J. Sci.*, 1962, 58, No. 7, pp. 189–196.

30. Experiments by C. N. Eriksen, cited in Vernon, *op. cit.*, p. 188.

31. Cf. introduction-preface by R. Mucchielli to *Manuel des techniques projectives* (*Handbook of Projective Techniques*) by Anderson and Anderson (French trans., Éd. Universitaires, Paris, 1965).

32. From this group let us mention G. Klein, B. Holt, D. Spence, and H. A. Witkin; on this point cf. U. Kragh, *Rapports entre la perception et la personnalité* (*Relationships Between Perception and Personality*), in *Scientia*, Italy, 1964, 98, No. 12, pp. 239–242.

33. Gelb and Goldstein, *Über Farbennamenamnesie* (*On Amnesia of the Names of Colors*), p. 158; cf. Merleau-Ponty, *Phénoménologie de la perception* (*Phenomenology of Perception*), Chap. VI, first part.

34. On these methods, cf. Maurice Duverger, *Techniques de Psychologie sociale* (*Techniques of Social Psychology*) (Éd. PUF), and Daval, *Traité de Psychologie sociale* (*Treatise on Social Psychology*) (Logos-PUF), bibliography in each.

35. Cf. J. S. Bruner, *op. cit.*, pp. 58–62 and bibliography.

36. Otto Koehler, *La pensée animale* (*Animal Thinking*), in *Encyclopédie des Sciences biologiques* (*Encyclopedia of the Biological Sciences*), Vol. IV, p. 93.

37. J. S. Bruner, *op. cit.*, p. 63.

38. G. Bouligand, *De l'abstraction mathématique aux Mathématiques vivantes* (*From Mathematical Abstraction to Living Mathematics*), lecture reprinted as article in *Cahiers du Centre économique et social de perfectionnement des cadres* (*Notes of the Economic and Social Center for Executive Training*), 1965.

39. R. Mucchielli, *Modèles sociométriques et formation des cadres* (*Sociometric Models and Executive Training*), Part II, Chaps. I and II (Éd. PUF, 1964).

40. Cf. G. Bachelard, *La formation de l'esprit scientifique*, *op. cit.*

41. K. Goldstein, *Human Nature in the Light of Psychopathology* (Cambridge, Harvard University Press, 1960).

CHAPTER THREE

1. Th. Ribot, *La logique des sentiments*, p. 60.

2. *Ibid.*, p. 59.

3. S. Freud, *De la technique psychanalytique* (*On the Technique of Psychoanalysis*) (French trans., Éd. PUF, 1953).

4. Collette, *Introduction à la psychologie dynamique* (*Introduction to Dynamic Psychology*), pp. 29–30 (Louvain, 1962).

5. Dugas, *La timidité, étude psychologique et morale* (*Timidity, A Psychological and Moral Study*) (Éd. Alcan, 1898).

6. Helena Deutsch, *La psychologie des femmes* (*The Psychology of Women*), Vol. II, pp. 300 ff. (French trans., Éd. PUF, 1955).

7. A. Binet, *Étude expérimentale de l'intelligence* (*Experimental Study of Intelligence*), p. 69.

8. Claude Lévi-Strauss, *Anthropologie structurale* (*Structural Anthropology*), pp. 29–31.

9. S. Freud, *Ma vie et la psychanalyse* (*My Life and Psychoanalysis*), pp. 29–30 (French trans.).

10. Lévi-Strauss, *op. cit.*, p. 28.

11. C. G. Jung, *Les types psychologiques* (*Psychological Types*), p. 349 (French trans.).

12. Goldstein, *Psychopathologie organismique* (*Psychopathology of the Organism*), Part I, Chap. VI: *Motivations and Motives of Behavior*.

13. Lévi-Strauss, *op. cit.*, p. 224.

14. Ch. Baudouin, *L'âme et l'action* (*The Soul and Action*), statement repeated in *L'oeuvre de Jung* (*The Work of Jung*), p. 56.

15. Th. Ribot, *Psychologie des sentiments* (*Psychology of the Emotions*), Part I, Chap. XIII.

16. Th. Ribot, *L'imagination créatrice* (*The Creative Imagination*), Part III, Chap. II.

17. H. Bergson, *La pensée et le mouvant* (*Thought and Actuation*), pp. 138 ff.

18. G. Bachelard, *L'eau et les rêves* (*Water and Dreams*), p. 10.

19. J. B. Pontalis, *Le petit groupe comme objet* (*The Small Group as an Object*), in *Les Temps modernes*, 1963, 19, p. 211.

20. S. Freud, *Introduction à la psychanalyse* (*Introduction to Psychoanalysis*), p. 168 (French trans., Éd. Payot, 1917).

21. Ricoeur, *De l'interprétation* (*On Interpretation*), p. 27 (Le Seuil, 1965).

22. *Ibid.*, p. 18.

23. S. Freud, *La science des rêves* (*The Interpretation of Dreams*), pp. 308, 319 (French trans.).

24. E. Minkowski, *Le temps vécu*, p. 169.

25. R. Dalbiez, *La méthode psychanalytique et la doctrine de Freud* (*The Psycho-Analytic Method and the Doctrine of Freud*), Vol. II, pp. 161 ff.

26. R. Mucchielli, *La psychothérapie décryptique* (*Psychotherapy Decoded*) (on press).

27. S. Freud, *Nouvelles conférences sur la psychanalyse* (*New Lectures on Psycho-Analysis*), pp. 17–18 (French trans., Éd. Gallimard, 1958).

28. S. Freud, *La science des rêves*, p. 595.

29. S. Freud, *Introduction à la psychanalyse*, pp. 216–217 (French trans., Éd. Payot, 1917).

30. Jolande Jacobi, *La psychologie de Jung* (*Jung's Psychology*), pp. 95–96 (Éd. Delachaux-Niestlé, 1950).

CHAPTER FOUR

1. Lévi-Strauss, *La pensée sauvage* (*Savage Thinking*), p. 21 (Éd. Plon, 1965).

2. Cf. Anna Freud, *Les mécanismes de défense du moi* (*The Defense Mechanisms of the Ego*) (French trans., Éd. PUF).

3. R. Spitz, *La première année*, etc., *op. cit.*, pp. 116–126.

4. S. Freud, *Cinq leçons sur la psychanalyse* (*Five Lessons in Psychoanalysis*), p. 159 (French trans., Éd. Payot, 1926).

5. S. Freud, *Moïse et le monothéisme* (*Moses and Monotheism*), p. 114 (French trans., Éd. Gallimard, 1948).

6. P. Guillaume, *Psychologie de la Forme*, *op. cit.*, p. 71.

7. Cf. Higgins, Mednick, and Taylor, *A Replication of Facilitation of Concept Formation Through Mediated Generalization*, in *Journ. Exper. Psychol.*, USA, 1963, 65, No. 4, pp. 421–422. Bibliography. Cf. also Mednick and Freedman, *Facilitation of Concept Formation Through Mediated Generalization*, in *J. Exp. Psych.*, 1960, 60, pp. 278–283.

8. P. Guillaume, *op. cit.*, p. 187.

9. Th. Ribot, *La logique des sentiments*, *op. cit.*, p. 94.

10. E. Minkowski, *Le temps vécu*, *op. cit.*, pp. 186–187.

11. Rosen, *L'analyse directe* (*Direct Analysis*) (French trans., Éd. PUF, 1961).

12. E. Minkowski, *op. cit.*, p. 153.

13. S. Freud, *De la technique psychanalytique* (*On the Technique of Psychoanalysis*), pp. 50–52 (French trans., Éd. PUF, 1953).

14. S. Freud, *Essais de psychanalyse* (*Essays in Psychoanalysis*), p. 30 (French trans., Éd. Payot, 1929).

15. S. Freud, "Psychologie et Médecine," in *Ma vie et la psychanalyse* ("Psychology and Medicine," in *My Life and Psychoanalysis*), p. 196 (French trans., Éd. Gallimard, 1928).

16. Quoted in Baudouin, *L'oeuvre de Jung* (*The Work of Jung*), p. 141 (Éd. Payot, 1963).

17. Cf. H. A. Witkin, H. G. Lewis, M. Hertzman, K. Machover, P. B. Meissner, and S. Wapner in *Personality Through Perception* (Harper & Row, 1954), and also the studies by Gardner (1953–1959), Holzman (1954?1960), Klein (1954). Cf. Kagan, Moses, and Sigel, *op. cit.*, and Sloane, Gorlow, and Jackson, *Cognitive Styles,* in

Rev. Percept. Motor Skills, USA, 1963, 16, No. 2, pp. 389–404 (bibliography).

18. Schilder, *Brain and Personality,* p. 61 (New York, 1931).

19. Carl Rogers, *Psychothérapie et relations humaines (Psychotherapy and Human Relations)* (Louvain, 1963) and *Le développement de la personne (The Development of the Person)* (Éd. Dunod, 1966).

20. In Anderson and Anderson, *Manual des techniques projectives, op. cit.,* Chap. XVI, *Expressive Movement and Experimental Methods in Depth Psychology,* by Werner Wolff and Joseph A. Precker, p. 488.

21. Cf. Mucchielli, *Le jeu du monde et le test du village imaginaire (The World Game and the Imaginary-Village Test)* (Ed. PUF, 1960).

22. Felix Deutsch, *Analysis of Postural Behavior,* in *Psychoanalytic Quarterly,* 1947, 16, p. 211. Quoted in Anderson and Anderson, *op. cit.,* p. 493.

23. Rapaport, *Principles Underlying Projective Techniques,* in *Char. and Pers.,* USA, 1942, 10, pp. 214–219.

24. R. Mucchielli, *L'expression de la personnalité dans le Rorschach (Personality Expression in the Rorschach Test)* (on press).

25. In Anderson and Anderson, *op. cit.,* p. 559.

26. In Anderson and Anderson, *op. cit.,* Chap. XXIV, pp. 717–731.

27. E. Minkowski, *Le temps vécu, op. cit.,* p. 30 and note.

28. A. Buorcier, *La nouvelle éducation morale (The New Moral Education),* Chap. V (Éd. ESF, 1966).

INDEX